· 新体验商务英语系列教材 ·

进出口贸易实务

Import and Export Practices

（修订本）

主编　束光辉

编者　束光辉　常　枫

清 华 大 学 出 版 社

北京交通大学出版社

· 北京 ·

内 容 简 介

本书以进出口贸易的主要业务环节为主线，系统地介绍了进出口贸易各个环节的操作规程和国际惯例，主要内容包括国际贸易概述、国际贸易理论、国际支付、信用证、交货条件、贸易合同、进出口贸易制单、商品描述及包装、国际货物运输与保险、货物检验与索赔、不可抗力及仲裁、进出口贸易流程、贸易方式等。

本书主要内容全部用英文编写，目的是让读者既熟悉进出口业务又掌握与业务有关的英文表述方式。本书每一章节的编写，力求材料翔实全面、语言难易适中、专业性强，同时紧跟国际贸易的变化和发展。对于一些贸易规则的变化，本书均做了适当调整。为了巩固对业务知识和语言的掌握，本书每章之后还附有针对性很强的练习。

本书可供英语专业学生、商务英语专业学生、国际经济与贸易专业学生及具有较好英语基础的其他经贸专业学生作为教材使用，同时也可用作从事进出口贸易工作人员的自学用书。

图书在版编目（CIP）数据

进出口贸易实务：英文／束光辉主编．—修订本．—北京：北京交通大学出版社：清华大学出版社，2016.4（2021.8 修订）

ISBN 978－7－5121－1812－6

Ⅰ．① 进…　Ⅱ．① 束…　Ⅲ．① 进出口贸易－贸易实务－英文　Ⅳ．① F740.4

中国版本图书馆 CIP 数据核字（2014）第 020379 号

进出口贸易实务
JINCHUKOU MAOYI SHIWU

责任编辑：张利军
出版发行：清 华 大 学 出 版 社　　邮编：100084　　电话：010－62776969
　　　　　北京交通大学出版社　　邮编：100044　　电话：010－51686414
印 刷 者：北京时代华都印刷有限公司
经　　销：全国新华书店
开　　本：185 mm×260 mm　　印张：16.25　　字数：406 千字
版 印 次：2021 年 8 月第 1 版第 1 次修订　　2021 年 8 月第 2 次印刷
印　　数：2 001～3 000 册　　定价：44.00 元

本书如有质量问题，请向北京交通大学出版社质监组反映。对您的意见和批评，我们表示欢迎和感谢。

投诉电话：010－51686043，51686008；传真：010－62225406；E-mail：press@ bjtu. edu. cn。

序

进入 21 世纪，随着全球经济一体化进程的加快，我国与世界的经贸联系更加紧密，贸易形式更趋多元化。与此相伴的是，中国的商务英语教学与研究也发生了巨大的变化。这至少表现在以下几个方面：第一，如今，商务英语已是一个相当大的概念，它已从最早的一门单一的"外贸英语函电"课程发展到了涉及金融、保险、国际企业管理、国际经济法、海外投资与企业合作等多领域的学科；第二，人们对商务英语学习的需求持续旺盛，不仅几乎全国所有的高校都开设了商务英语专业或课程，而且越来越多的企业在职人员也迫切需要学习商务英语；第三，外语界对商务英语的研究也提高到了一个新的层次。

为了适应新的形势，许多高校都正在对一些传统的经贸英语类课程进行调整、改革和扩充，以培养新型的国际商务专业人才。这就向教材建设提出了更高的要求。教材不仅是教学内容的表现，更体现了人才培养的规格。纵观过去的一些教材，我们便不难发现，无论从内容上还是体例上，它们都已远远落后于当今国际经贸发展的形势，例如大多围绕语法、词汇和翻译等来展开，缺乏商务英语专业的实践性和语言的真实性，难以满足工作的需要。而另一些教材则又过于突出"专业"的内容，把商务英语教材混同于国际商务专业教材。因此，编写能够适应时代要求的国际商务英语教材显得尤为重要。正是在这样的背景下，由束光辉老师主编的"新体验商务英语系列教材"面世了，它体现了"贴近时代，融合语言与专业"的编写理念，是一次积极而大胆的尝试。

该系列包括《进出口贸易实务》《现代商务英语写作》《商务英语函电与合同》《商务报刊选读》《商务英语汉英翻译教程》《跨文化商务沟通》等教材。它们在内容设计和编写形式上具有以下特点。

1. 融专业性与语言技能于一体

该系列教材在编写上突出了以培养学生的实际工作能力为目标的思路，所选材料涉及了商务环境的各个方面，均能反映出商务工作实践性的特点，同时也体现了语言技能系统化培养的理念。该系列教材通过拟定各种商务环境，将商务知识和语言技能融合在一起，使学生的语言应用能力在更接近于真实的商务实践中得以提高。

2. 选材新，贴近时代

该系列教材在材料选择上参考了国内外最近几年出版的教材和其他相关材料，充分吸收了国内外最新的教学科研成果，体现了国际商务活动不断变化的特点和商务领域专业性的特点，具有鲜明的时代特征。同时，该系列教材的许多文本、范例和研究材料均来自于近年来各类商务实践，体现了商务英语的真实性和实践性。

3. 练习形式多样，针对性强

该系列教材的练习将语言技能训练与商务环境较好地结合在一起，通过各种题型，对所涉及的商务环节和领域，有针对性地对学生进行训练。这不仅能够巩固学生所学的专业知识，而且还将提高他们的语言技能。

21 世纪的中国更加开放，更加开放的中国在诸多方面都在与世界接轨。作为国际商务沟通的一个重要工具，商务英语的教学和研究理应跟上时代的发展和社会的需求。我们要更加重视并加强对商务英语教学的研究。该系列教材的编写是一次很好的探索，希望借此能进一步提高我国高校商务英语的教学和科研水平，为培养我国新型国际商务专业人才做出贡献。

中国国际贸易学会
国际商务英语研究委员会
原副主任
2021 年 8 月

前言

中国加入 WTO 后，与世界各国的经贸联系越来越密切了，这使得中国与世界其他国家的合作也具有了更加广阔的前景。因此，培养既具有国际贸易专业知识又精通外语的复合型人才是目前商务英语教学的当务之急。正是在这样的时代大背景下，我们着手编写了《进出口贸易实务》一书，其目的就是帮助广大经贸类专业的学生在掌握专业知识的同时，学会如何用英语来表达具体的商务规程。

本书以进出口贸易的主要业务环节为主线，系统地介绍了进出口贸易各个环节的操作规程和国际惯例，主要内容包括国际贸易概述、国际贸易理论、国际支付、信用证、交货条件、贸易合同、进出口贸易制单、商品描述及包装、国际货物运输与保险、货物检验与索赔、不可抗力及仲裁、进出口贸易流程、贸易方式等。

本书所选的英文材料大多是国内外原汁原味的专业英语资料，不仅句式地道，而且表达十分专业。同时，为了让读者能够更好地掌握和理解书中的内容，我们还为一些较难理解的语言知识和专业知识配备了详细的中文注释。

本书每一章节的编写力求材料翔实全面、语言难易适中、专业性强，同时紧跟国际贸易的变化和发展；对于一些贸易规则的变化，本书均做了适当的调整和补充。

本书每一章后面所附的练习形式多样，针对性强，力求做到语言知识与专业知识相结合，克服国内教材重语言形式、轻语言运用能力之弊端，将练习的重点放在语言运用能力的培养上。这些练习包括对原文知识的理解、名词解释、英汉短文互译及补充材料的阅读理解等，目的是使学生通过各种练习来提高语言的应用技能，更好地为专业服务。

本书的主要读者对象为英语专业学生、商务英语专业学生、国际经济与贸易专业学生、具有较好英语基础的其他经贸专业学生，以及从事进出口贸易实践工作的专业人士。

本书由束光辉担任主编，负责全书大纲的编写及大部分书稿的编写工作。常枫负责编写该书第 3、4、9、10 章的注释及练习并编写了其他单元的部分练习。

　　本书的编写与出版得到了北京交通大学语言与传播学院领导的大力支持及北京交通大学出版社张利军编辑的热情帮助，在此一并表示衷心的感谢。

　　由于编者水平、经验有限，书中不足之处在所难免，欢迎广大读者批评指正。

编　者

2021 年 8 月

Contents

Chapter 1

An Introduction to International Trade

国际贸易概述

1.1 Concept of International Trade

International trade, also known as world trade, foreign trade or overseas trade, is the fair and deliberate exchange of goods and services across national boundaries. It concerns trade operations of both import and export and includes the purchase and sales of both visible and invisible goods.

The fundamental characteristic that makes international trade different from domestic trade is that international trade involves activities that take place across national borders. Special problems may arise in international trade that are not normally involved when trading at home. In particular：

- Deals might have to be transacted in foreign languages and under foreign laws, customs and regulations.
- Information on foreign countries needed by a particular firm may be difficult to obtain.
- Foreign currency transactions will be necessary. Exchange rate variations can be very wide and create many problems for international trade.
- Numerous cultural differences may have to be taken into account when trading with other nations. There are two major cultural issues that contribute to the success of international trade：（1）language, including terms of transaction,（2）customs and manners. International traders must be constantly aware that cultural problems have remained to be the major obstacles in international trade, and therefore, every effort should be made to identify and solve such problems.
- Control and communication systems are normally more complex for foreign than for domestic operations.
- Risk levels might be higher in foreign markets. The risks include political risks（of the imposition of restrictions on imports, etc.）, commercial risks（market failure, products not

appealing to foreign customers, etc.), financial risks (of adverse movements in exchange rates, high rates of inflation reducing the value level of a company's working capital, and so on), and transportation risks.

- International managers need a broader range of management skills than do managers who are only concerned with domestic problems.

- Large amount of important work might have to be left to intermediaries, consultants and advisers.

- It is more difficult to observe and monitor trends and activities (including competitor's activities) in foreign countries.

1.2 Reasons for International Trade

There are several reasons why nations trade with each other.

1. Resources Reasons

In the complex economic world, no country can be completely self-sufficient. Some countries are abundant in certain resources, while other nations may be lack of them. For example, Colombia and Brazil have the ideal climate for growing coffee beans but other countries don't. This has made them big coffee exporters. The Middle East has rich oil reserves and therefore is the main source of oil supply to the world. The developed countries are full of capital and skilled labors who are able to manufacture sophisticated equipment and machinery such as jet aircrafts and computers, etc, while developing countries which are lack of skilled workers and capital need to import technology-intensive products from these countries. In short, the uneven distribution of resources around the world is one of the most basic reasons why nations trade with each other.

2. Economic Reasons

With the development of manufacturing and technology, there arose another incentive for nations to trade, i. e. economic benefits. In addition to getting the products they need, countries also wish to gain economically by trading with each other. According to the theory of Comparative Advantage developed by David Richardo[1] (1772 −1823), it was economically advantageous for a nation to specialize in certain activities, produce those goods for which it had comparative advantages and exchange those goods for the products of other nations which had advantages in different fields.

3. Other Reasons

Some countries may not be able to produce sufficient amount of a particular product and have to import some to meet their needs. Even though a country can produce enough of an item at reasonable costs to meet its own demand, it may still import some from other countries for innovation or variety of style. Sometimes, trade may be based on different consumption preferences rather than on differences in the production capabilities of the two countries. Still, in some cases, political objectives can outweigh economic considerations between countries. One country might trade with another to support the latter's government which upholds the same political doctrine.

1.3 Benefits of International Trade

The gains from trade depend upon the basis for the trade. Where trade is based on production specialization in countries according to the Law of Comparative Advantage, the gains from trade are due to the benefits to consumers (or industrial users) of purchasing low-priced imports and the benefits to export products of a wider market for their products and favorable international prices. Where trade is based upon consumer preferences and the existence of differentiated products, the gains from trade accrue as the benefits to consumers of an increased variety of products from which to choose. An additional benefit to consumers in this latter case may also accrue if the market power of local firms is reduced and imports make pricing and other aspects of market conduct more competitive.

To sum up, the international trade can bring the following benefits.

1. Cheaper Goods or Services

Countries trade with each other because there is a cost advantage. And it is this cost advantage of the supplying country that enables an importer to buy certain goods or services of the same quality at lower prices. Furthermore, competition in the world market would tend to make prices even lower.

2. Great Variety

As no nation has all the commodities or services that it needs, undoubtedly, trade means countries can provide a wider variety of products for their consumers and thus help to improve the living standards of the people.

3. Wider Markets for the Supplying Country

International trade can greatly expand the market, which enables the suppliers to take advantage of economies of scale[2]. With the increasing number of trading partners, suppliers can also get more profits.

4. Economic Growth

International trade has become more and more important as it can lead to the full utilization of otherwise underemployed domestic resources. That is, through trade, a developing nation can move from an inefficient production point inside its production frontier, with unutilized resources because of insufficient international demand, to a point on its production frontier with trade. For such a nation, trade would represent a vent for surplus, or an outlet for its potential surplus of agricultural commodities and raw materials. In addition, by expanding the size of the market, trade makes possible division of labor and economies of scale. This is especially important and has actually taken place in the production of light manufactures in such small economic units as Taiwan, Hongkong, etc. Apart from that, international trade is the vehicle for the transmission of new ideas, new technology, and new managerial and other skills. Finally, international trade is an excellent antimonopoly weapon because it stimulates greater efficiency by domestic producers to meet foreign competition. This is particularly important to keep low the cost and price of intermediate or semifinished products used as inputs in the domestic production of other commodities.

1.4　International Trade Restrictions

1.4.1 | Reasons for Restricting Free Trade

Though free trade is encouraged in international business world, trade protectionism or restrictive measure is being adopted by a great number of countries, due to different kinds of reasons or considerations. The most popular arguments for restricting free trade among nations are usually summed up as follows:

1. To Protect Home Industries

Supporters of this argument claim that any country should protect its own industries from foreign competition; if its own industries fail, jobs will be lost. Such a law is the ultimate in protecting home industries.

2. To Protect Infant Industries[3]

This argument holds that it is important to protect new industries within the country from more mature foreign competitors, at least until the new domestic industries can grow and become effective competitors.

3. To Provide National Security Through Self-sufficiency

Clearly, a nation's security considerations may affect its policies regarding free trade. In countries where intense nationalism exists, people feel that the country should not be dependent on other nations for its standard of living or its security.

4. To Provide for a Favorable Balance of Trade

This argument supports the idea that a nation must have a favorable balance of trade each year. It views that the accumulation of foreign trade credits as the ideal goal of all foreign trade. But, as we have noted, foreign trade is a two-way street. Nations must export to be able to import. No nation can continue for long to have an unfavorable balance of trade without dire results on its own monetary system. Nations that regularly have a favorable balance of trade help to cause problems for other nations.

5. To Protect Wages and the Standard of Living

This argument is a favorite among labor groups, which see as threat to their wages when consumers are allowed to buy similar products made abroad by cheaper labor. This argument overlooks the fact that the high wages have developed because of greater productivity among the workers. Productivity is the result of labor skills, technology, and capital equipment.

1.4.2 | Methods of Restricting Free Trade

Protectionist measures often taken by governments are also barriers to trade, and typical examples are tariffs and quotas.

1. Tariffs

Tariff barriers[4] are the most common form of trade restrictions. A tariff is a tax levied on a commodity when it crosses the boundary of a customs area which usually coincides with the area of a country. A customs area extending beyond national boundaries to include two or more independent nations is called a customs union. According to the time of collection, duties can be divided into import duty and export duty. Import duty is collected when goods are imported, and export duty is collected when goods are exported in order to control the export of anything with national importance. Besides regular import duty, importers might have to pay import surtax, too. Generally speaking, import surtax is additional to import duty, is temporary in coping with international payment difficulties, maintaining balance of trade and preventing dumping, and is discriminatory against a particular country.

Import surtax has three forms.

Countervailing duty is collected against bounty or grant during production, transport and export, etc, for it is unfair for importers to get the exports subsidized by the government.

Anti-dumping duty is collected when importing country believes that there is a dumping (a not universally defined concept that can mean the selling price in a foreign country is below domestic selling price, world market price or production cost). Before the duties are imposed, the country must show that its domestic industry has suffered "material" injury by dumped imports.

Variable levy is collected at the difference between world market prices and the support prices for domestic producers to make the imported commodities.

According to the methods in which tariffs are collected, there are types of duties. Specific duty is collected per physical unit — according to weight, volume, measurement and quantity, etc. Ad valorem duty is collected according to value or price, i. e. , at a percentage of the price. Mixed or compound duty is collected according to either specific duty or ad valorem duty first, then the other. An alternative duty is collected whichever the higher between specific duty and ad valorem duty.

The duties discussed above are not independent of each other, i. e. , a duty can be an import, a protective and a compound duty at the same time.

2. Non-tariff Barriers[5]

In addition to tariffs, countries also use other methods to make import more difficult. These methods, collecting no tariffs, are called non-tariff barriers.

1) Quotas or quantitative restriction

Quotas or quantitative restriction are the most common form of non-tariff barriers. A quota limits the imports or exports of a commodity during a given period of time. The limits may be in quantity or value terms, and quotas may be on a country basis or global, without reference to countries. They may be imposed unilaterally and can also be negotiated on a so-called voluntary basis. Obviously, exporting countries do not readily agree to limit their sales. Thus, the "voluntary label" generally means that the importing country has threatened to impose even worse restrictions if voluntary cooperation is not forthcoming.

2) Import license

An import license is a permit for import, which can be independent or combined with quotas.

3) State monopoly of import and export

With this form of barrier, import and export are restricted by giving exclusive authorities of import and export to only a limited number of (state) companies.

(1) Customs Procedures. The creation of complicated and extensive custom procedures can be effective in limiting imports. It can also be used to discourage exports.

(2) Exchange Control Devices. These can take several different forms. For example, citizens and business firms may be limited in the amounts they may spend for products abroad, and even the transfer of funds may be limited. Central agencies may be created to buy and sell all foreign currencies in a country, thus controlling the amounts of foreign exchange available and its rates in accordance with government policies. The devaluation of currency is a related technique for restricting foreign trade.

4) Government procurement policy

This policy stipulates that governmental organizations must use local products unless some conditions are met. For instance, *Buy American Act 1933* says that the US government must buy American products unless the domestic price is on average 25% (from 6% to 50%) higher than foreign prices.

5) Embargoes

An embargo is a complete prohibition on imports of certain products to certain countries. The measure of embargo is adopted often for punitive purpose or for countering purposes.

6) High technical standards

Product and process standards for health, welfare, safety, quality size, and measurements can impede trade by excluding "non-standard" products. Testing and certification procedures, such as testing only in the importing country and on-site plant inspections, were cumbersome, time-consuming, and expensive. These costs must be borne by the exporter prior to any foreign sales. National governments have the right and duty to protect their citizens by setting standards to prevent the sale of hazardous or shoddy product. Standards can be used not only to ensure quality and performance, but also impede trade. For instance, some Western countries once adopted strict technical standards on tea's pesticide remnants to restrict the amount of imported teas from China.

7) Minimum price

Minimum price is the lowest price set by an importing country for imported goods. There could be a ban on imports or surtax on imports below the minimum price.

There are other forms of non-tariff barriers and countries are continuing to create more to limit both imports and exports of goods for the consideration of their own interests. For instance, importing countries can have sophisticated regulations regarding packaging and labeling in terms of sizes of letters, languages used and orders in which different languages are used. Anyway, the above-mentioned measures function as effective barriers to trade flow for the interest of the trading nations.

1.5 Invisible Trade [6]

In addition to visible trade[7], which involves the import and export of goods, there is also invisible trade, which involves the exchange of services between countries.

Transportation service across national boundaries is an important kind of invisible trade. International transportation involves different means of transport such as ocean ships, planes, trains, trucks and inland water vessels. However, the most important of them is maritime ships. When an exporter arranges shipment, he generally books space in the cargo compartment of a ship, or charters a whole vessel. Some countries such as Greece and Norway have large maritime fleets and earn a lot by way of this invisible trade.

Insurance is another important kind of invisible trade. In the course of transportation, a cargo is vulnerable to many risks such as collision, pilferage, fire, storm, explosion, and even war. Goods being transported in international trade must be insured against loss or damage. Large insurance companies provide service for international trade and earn fees for other nation's foreign trade. Lloyd's of London is a leading exporter of this service.

Tourism is yet another important form of invisible trade. Many countries may have beautiful scenery, wonderful attractions, places of historical interest, or merely a mild and sunny climate. These countries attract large numbers of tourists, who spend money for traveling, hotel accommodations, meals, taxis, and so on. Some countries depend heavily on tourism for their foreign exchange earnings, and many countries are making great efforts to develop their tourism.

The fourth type of invisible trade meriting attention is called immigrant remittance. This refers to the money sent back to home countries by people working in a foreign land. Import and export of labor service may be undertaken by individuals, or organized by companies or even by states. And this is becoming an important kind of invisible trade for some countries.

Invisible trade can be as important to some countries as visible trade is to others. In reality, the kinds of trade nations engage in are varied and complex, often a mixture of visible and invisible trade.

New Words and Expressions

deliberate	a.	故意的，有意识的
transact	v.	交易
intermediary	n.	中间商，中介
self-sufficient	a.	自给自足的
ideal	a.	理想的
technology-intensive	a.	技术密集型的
incentive	n.	刺激物，刺激
innovation	n.	创新
outweigh	v.	胜过，比……重要
doctrine	n.	教义
accrue	v.	增长
specialization	n.	专业化
differentiate	v.	区分，细分
vent	n.	发泄口，流出口
credit	v.	认为
accumulation	n.	积累
dire	a.	可怕的
tariff	n.	关税
surtax	n.	附加税
discriminatory	a.	有区别的
non-tariff	n.	非关税
quota	n.	配额
license	n.	许可证
procurement	n.	采购
devaluation	n.	贬值
embargo	n.	禁运
punitive	a.	惩罚的
cumbersome	a.	繁琐的
hazardous	a.	危险的
shoddy	a.	假冒的
charter	v.	租赁
vulnerable	a.	脆弱的

collision	*n.*	碰撞
pilferage	*n.*	盗窃
accommodations	*n.*	膳食供应，招待设备
merit	*v.*	值得
market failure		市场衰退
working capital		风险资金
consumption preferences		消费偏好
domestic industry		国内工业
favorable balance		顺差
coincide with		与······巧合
customs union		关税同盟
countervailing duty		反补贴税
anti-dumping duty		反倾销税
variable levy		差额税，差价税
specific duty		从量税
ad valorem duty		从价税
compound duties		混合税
alternative duty		可选择性关税
customs procedures		海关手续
exchange control devices		外汇手段
inland water vessels		内河船只
cargo compartment		货舱
maritime fleet		海上舰队
immigrant remittance		移民汇款

Notes

1. David Richardo：大卫·李嘉图（1772—1823），英国著名经济学家，是使经济学系统化的最早思想家，其代表作为《政治经济学及赋税原理》。他进一步发展了亚当·史密斯的《地域分工论》，提出了以"比较成本说"为核心的国际贸易理论。他的这一学说及其以后对该学说的补充、发展被称为"国际贸易纯理论"或"一般理论"。

2. economies of scale：规模经济。指企业采用大规模生产而使生产过程变得更加经济合算的行为，反映了生产要素的集中程度与经济效益之间的关系。这个概念有时也用单数来表达，即"economy of scale"。

3. infant industry：新生工业，幼稚工业。此处"infant"一词的含义是"newly begun or formed"，即"新生的"或"新近成立的"。

4. tariff barriers：关税壁垒。直接用关税手段来限制输入，通过征收高额进口税、进口附加税、差价税等来保护本国的竞争能力。关贸总协定的减税谈判削弱了关税壁垒的作用，但它仍是国家间贸易战的重要武器。

5. non-tariff barriers：非关税壁垒。指关税之外的一切直接或间接限制进口的法规和措施，例如进口限额等。随着关税壁垒在贸易保护中作用的减弱，非关税壁垒则被广泛采用。

6. invisible trade：无形贸易。与"visible trade"相对，包括运输、保险、人员交流费用、汇款、投资等，是国际收支中的重要项目。

7. visible trade：有形贸易。指商品的进出口。因商品是看得见的有形实物，故得此名。

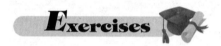

I Review questions.

1. What are the differences between international trade and domestic trade?

2. Why do nations trade with each other?

3. What benefits can international trade bring to a country?

4. What are the popular reasons for restricting free trade?

5. What are the most common form of trade restrictions and the most common form of non-tariff barriers?

6. According to the standard of methods used in imposing import duties, how are import duties classified?

7. Give an example to explain "High Technical Standards" as one of the non-tariff barriers in international trade.

8. What kinds of services does invisible trade include?

II Define the following terms briefly.

1. international trade

2. economies of scale

3. import surtax

4. anti-dumping duty

5. specific duty

6. ad valorem duty

7. quota

8. import license

9. invisible trade

Ⅲ Translate the following passages into Chinese.

The United States, stretching across a continent and rich in a variety of human and natural resources, can produce, relatively efficiently, most of the products it needs. Contrast this with small industrial nations such as Switzerland and Austria that have a few very specialized resources and produce a much smaller range of products, which they export in exchange for the many items they must import. Even large industrial nations such as Japan, Germany, France, England, Italy, and Canada rely crucially on international trade. For developing nations, exports provide employment opportunities and earnings to pay for many foreign products that cannot presently be produced domestically and the advanced technology not available at home.

Even though the United States relies to a relatively small extent on international trade, a great deal of its high standard of living depends on it. First of all, there are many commodities — coffee, bananas, cocoa, tea, scotch — that the country does not produce at all. In addition, the United States has no deposits of such minerals as tin, tungsten, and chromium, which are important to certain industrial processes, and it has only dwindling reserves of petroleum, copper, and many other minerals. Much more important quantitatively for the nation's standard of living are the many products that could be produced domestically but only at a higher cost than abroad. These account for most of the benefits or gains from trade.

Ⅳ Translate the following passage into English.

出于战略的或国内的原因, 一个国家可能继续生产不具有优势的产品. 专门化的好处也可能受到运输成本的影响, 货物和原材料不得不在全世界运来运去, 而运输成本减少了贸易利益. 如果运输大宗货物或容易腐败变质的货物, 情况就严重了. 各国政府经常采取的贸易保护主义措施也是贸易障碍, 典型的例子是关税和配额.

Ⅴ Read the following passages and answer the questions.

Forms of International Business

The international business organization in following its corporate strategy is continually adjusting to the dynamics of its changing external/internal environments. In so doing, its structure should likewise respond to these changes. Firms can either import or export goods. They can sell or buy technology or property rights through licensing and franchising agreements. They can invest in foreign firms around the globe or they can finance transactions arising from trade or international investment. As the firm progresses through its internationalizing process, its international activities may range from single export to wholly owned subsidiaries. The most common forms or ways of doing international business would include: importing and exporting, licensing and franchising, industrial cooperation and support agreements, joint ventures, or wholly owned subsidiaries.

1. Entry through Exports and Imports

Most firms enter international business through exports, for it is the simplest and least risky way. Export problems center around the marketing function. Major concerns are the design of an effective marketing mix, getting channels of distribution established, and analysis and compliance with trade/business statutes. Because of low asset exposure to political risk and stability, the firm retains the maximum flexibility to switch its geographical target areas with minimum disruption. Of course, host country "middleman" agencies are the key to exporting success, and how well they respond to market pressures and home country supervision is important. The next step is usually the establishment of a local national sales office followed by a direct investment in production facilities in selected host country sites. The major means by which a firm may engage in export activities are:

(1) Deal through an export management company (EMC). This is the simplest means because all foreign problems are handled by the export house. This is often a good way to begin exporting but consideration should be given to other potentially more profitable channels as the market grows.

(2) Deal through a foreign import house. This is also a good way to break into export. The trick is to find a reliable importer who will effectively market your product. The information services available through the regional offices of the US Department of Commerce and the international departments of major banks can be very helpful in this regard.

(3) Deal through a manufacturer's representative abroad. This is a similar situation to the import house, but one may expect more individual effort in pushing his or her own product. The nature of the product may well determine which is better.

(4) Set up a marketing subsidiary abroad (either wholly owned or a joint venture). This course is not usually undertaken unless the market potential has been established through export or careful market research. The exception is the firm with considerable multinational experience. The marketing subsidiary provides maximum sales potential, but considerable volume is required to make it profitable.

The import structure is quite similar to the export structure, and in the flow of international trade, imports move toward a balance with exports. The import structure includes import merchants, import representatives, and consumer-owned import establishments.

The import merchant today is represented by the import trading company that specializes in the products it imports and their particular distribution patterns.

Import representatives serve as international brokers, normally performing exporting as well. They are of two types: (1) commission houses that strictly serve as agents for local consumers, buying abroad and making all delivery arrangements but assuming no financial responsibility, and (2) resident representatives of foreign exporters perform the selling and distributing functions for the foreign exporters.

Consumer-owned import establishments provide more direct control over the importing process and over the establishments carrying it out. Large retailers have set up their own import units, which deal directly with the foreign exporters.

2. Licensing and Franchising

Licensing involves granting a license to a foreign firm to produce and market a product for which the foreign firm pays royalties to the parent firm. The rights that can be licensed include patents, trademarks, copyrights, production processes, and brand company names and insignia. it may be used to enter and cultivate a foreign market, which cannot otherwise be tapped by export or some other entry form or way. Sometimes licensees develop quality control problems and can possibly prevent the patent firm from entering the foreign market at a later date. The patent firm may also be creating its own competitor in the licensee's or in third country markets. The licensee can provide a low-cost, low-risk way of entering a foreign market, but in many instances its ability to provide technical knowhow for a new market is welcomed.

Franchising is primarily used in the fast food industry and allows the franchisee to exploit the franchisor's trademark and working system and to be obligated to buy certain of the franchiser's imports in the process and receive management development assistance. Normally a front-end lump sum is paid to the franchiser in addition to receiving royalty payments.

3. Industrial Cooperation and Support Agreements

Technical aid and management contracts often accompany licensing, franchising, or investment agreements. These agreement contracts are written for specific services or consulting arrangements as opposed to the all-inclusive blanket licensing agreement. Most often, they involve the use of technical or managerial personnel from the country of the parent headquarters, and these services may be requested on a continuing basis by the recipient firm until the technical "know-how" or expertise has been assimilated.

4. The Turnkey Project

The turnkey project involves a complete package where complete facilities are provided in another country to include the training and education of workers and managers. Many engineering and heavy construction projects in developing countries are accomplished with these types of agreements. When personnel and facilities are fully functional, the contracting firm turns over the key for the entire project and moves on to the next project. Some countries use this industrial policy to avoid foreign direct investment in a particular sector in their country.

Many of the turnkey contracts are in remote areas and require the importing of third country personnel and building an entire infrastructure under arduous conditions. An international engineering consultant firm head has identified five stages for economic development in developing countries: (1) expatriates do all the work, (2) local subcontractors develop, (3) small local contractors start up, (4) local contractors take over local work, (5) local contractors go abroad. Developing countries such as India, Turkey or Korea with their low labor costs are competing strongly in the more conventional, construction type, turnkey projects.

5. Joint Venture

In this form, the parent company owns only a part interest in the foreign enterprise. Some countries require that the majority ownership interest must be held by the host country firm.

Although few executives prefer this type of shared ownership, it does allow for reduced capital investment and associated risk in a foreign market area. Its major advantage is that the host country patterns may provide special assistance in marketing and dealing with governmental and political activities. Of course, cultural differences must be dealt with and sometimes foreign partners are a source of conflict. Among large multinationals, international joint ventures have been steadily increasing.

6. Wholly Owned Subsidiaries

This is the most popular form for US-based multinational organizations. Traditionally, this form of direct investment abroad has been looked at as an international movement of capital accompanied by managerial control, technology, and access to resources that might not otherwise be available. Wholly owned subsidiaries may be started from the blueprint or by acquisition of an on-going firm in the host country. Many benefits arise from latter in the marketing, distribution, and servicing areas.

Two significant trends emerged in the 1980s. First, the flow of capital in the form of economic development loans increased much more rapidly to Third World countries than direct foreign investment flow of multinationals in the form of wholly or majority owned subsidiaries. Second, different multinational forms of investment (other than wholly or majority owned subsidiaries) such as joint venture investments began to be used in increasing amounts in the less-developed countries. These trends indicate that US firms are less concerned about majority or wholly owned control than formerly.

7. General Trading Companies

The most developed of today's trading companies are those in Japan. The purpose of Japanese general trading companies (GTCs) has been to consolidate domestic trading activities and facilitate the export of domestic manufacturers into foreign markets. Basically, the GTC is a domestic company designed to generate synergy through internal cooperation and coordination of its business units, which are diversified along product, area, and on function basis. During the 1970s and 1980s, governments in several developing countries, such as Korea, Thailand, and Turkey, began to develop their own GTC capabilities to promote exports as major market countries began to expand their protectionist measures.

In 1982 the US Congress enacted the Export Trading Company Act (ETC) to facilitate the promotion of international trade and provide for the growth of ETCs. The ETCs are intended to aid small to medium-size firms that are individually too weak to identify foreign markets, generate and conduct sales in these markets, or procure foreign products and technologies.

Please answer the following questions.

1. What are the most common forms of doing international business?
2. Tell briefly the major means by which a firm may engage in export activities.

3. What is franchising? How is it different from licensing?

4. Why do firms choose franchising as a means of entering a foreign market?

5. What is an international turnkey project?

6. What is a wholly owned subsidiary? In what way is it different from joint venture?

Chapter 2

Theories of International Trade

国际贸易理论

2.1 Mercantilism

The first theory of international trade emerged in England in the mid-16th century. Referred to as mercantilism, its principle assertion was that gold and silver were the mainstays of national wealth and essential to vigorous commerce. At that time, gold and silver were the currency of trade between countries; a country could earn gold and silver by exporting goods. By the same token, importing goods from other countries would result in an outflow of gold and silver to those countries. The basic mercantilist argument was that it was in a country's best interests to maintain a trade surplus to export more than it imported. By doing so, a country would accumulate gold and silver and, consequently, increase its national wealth and prestige, as the English mercantilist writer Thomas Mun put it in 1630.

The ordinary means therefore to increase our wealth and treasure is by foreign trade, wherein we must ever observe this rule: to sell more to strangers yearly than we consume of theirs in value

Consistent with this belief, the mercantilist doctrine advocated government intervention to achieve a surplus in the balance of trade. The mercantilists saw no virtue in a large volume of trade per se. Rather, they recommended policies to maximize exports and minimize imports. In order to achieve this, imports were limited by tariffs and quotas, and exports were subsidized.

An inherent inconsistency in the mercantilist doctrine was pointed out by the classical economist David Hume in 1752. According to Hume, if England had a balance of trade surplus with France (it exported more than it imported) the resulting inflow of gold and silver would swell the domestic money supply and generate inflation in England. In France, however, the outflow of gold and silver would have the opposite effect. France's money supply would contract, and its prices would fall. This change in relative prices between France and England would encourage the French to buy more French goods (because they were becoming cheaper). The result would be a deterioration in the English balance of trade and an improvement in France's trade balance, until the English surplus was eliminated. Hence, according to Hume, in the long run no country could sustain a surplus on the balance of trade and so accumulate gold and silver as the mercantilists had envisaged.

Hume's critique apart[1], the flaw with mercantilism was that it viewed trade as a zero-sum game[2] (A zero-sum game is one in which a gain by one country results in a loss by another.). It was left to Adam Smith and David Richardo to show the shortsightedness of this approach and to demonstrate that trade is a positive-sum game in which all countries can benefit, even if some benefit more than others. We shall discuss the views of Smith next. Before doing so, however, we must note that the mercantilist doctrine is by no means dead. For example, Jarl Hagelstam, a director at the Finnish Ministry of France and a participant at the Uruguay Round of negotiations on the General Agreement on Tariffs and Trade (GATT), whose purpose is to create a more open and fair trading system, has observed that:

The approach of individual negotiating countries, both industrialized and developing, has been to press for trade liberalization in areas where their own comparative competitive advantages are the strongest, and to resist liberalization in areas where they are less competitive and fear that imports would replace domestic production.

Hagelstam attributes this strategy by negotiating countries to a neo-mercantilist belief held by the politicians of many nations. This belief equates political power with economic power, and economic power with a balance-of-trade surplus. Thus the trade strategy of many nations is designed to simultaneously boost exports and limit imports.

2.2　Absolute Advantage

In his 1776 landmark book *The Wealth of Nations*, Adam Smith attacked the mercantilist assumption that trade is a zero-sum game. Smith argued that countries differ in their ability to produce goods efficiently. In his time, for example, by virtue of their superior manufacturing processes, the English were the world's most efficient manufacturers of textiles. On the other hand, due to the combination of favorable climate, good soils, and accumulated expertise, the French had the world's most efficient wine industry. Put it another way, the English had an absolute advantage in the production of textiles, while the French had an absolute advantage in the production of a product when it is more efficient than any other country in producing it.

According to Smith, countries should specialize in the production of goods for which they have an absolute advantage, and then trade these goods for the goods produced by other countries. In Smith's time this suggested that the English should specialize in the production of textiles while the French should specialize in the production of wine. England could get all the wine it needed by selling its textiles to France and buying wine in exchange. Similarly, France could get all the textiles it needed by selling wine to England and buying textiles in exchange. Smith's basic argument, therefore, is that you should never produce goods at home that you can buy at a lower cost from other countries. Moreover, Smith demonstrates that by specializing in the production of goods in which each has an absolute advantage, both countries benefit by engaging in trade.

2.3   Comparative Advantage

David Richardo took Adam Smith's theory one step further by exploring what might happen when one country has an absolute advantage in the production of all goods. Smith's theory of absolute advantage suggests that such a country might derive no benefits from international trade. In his 1817 book *Principle of Political Economy*, Ricardo showed that this was not the case. According to Richardo, it makes sense for such a country to specialize in the production of those goods that it produces most efficiently and to buy the goods that it produces less efficiently from other countries, even if this means buying goods from other countries that it could produce more efficiently itself.

The basic message of the theory of comparative advantage is that potential world production is greater with unrestricted free trade than it is with restricted trade. Moreover, Richardo's theory suggests that consumers in all nations can consume more if there are no restrictions on trade. This occurs even in the case of countries that lack an absolute advantage in the production of any goods. In other words, to an even greater degree than the theory of absolute advantage, the theory of comparative advantage suggests that trade is a positive-sum game in which all gain. As such, this theory provides a strong rationale for encouraging free trade. Indeed, so powerful is Richardo's theory that it remains a major intellectual weapon for those who argue for free trade.

2.4   Heckscher-Ohlin Theory

Richardo's theory stresses that comparative advantage arises from differences in productivity (the efficiency with which a country utilizes its resources to produce outputs). Thus, whether Ghana is more efficient than South Korea in the production of cocoa depends upon how productivity it uses its resources. Richardo himself placed particular stress on labor productivity and argued that differences in labor productivity between nations underlie the notion of comparative advantage. Swedish economists Eli Heckscher (in 1919) and Bertil Ohlin (in 1933) put forward a different explanation of comparative advantage. They argued that comparative advantage arises from differences in national factor endowments. By factor endowments they meant the extent to which a country is endowed with such resources as land, labor, and capital. Different nations have different factor endowments, and different factor endowments explain differences in factor costs. The more abundant a factor is, the lower its cost will be. The Heckscher-Ohlin theory predicts that countries will export those goods that make intensive use of those factors that are locally abundant, while importing goods that make intensive use of those factors that are locally scarce. Thus the Hechscher-Ohlin theory attempts to explain the pattern of international trade that we observe in the world economy. Like Richardo's theory, the Heckscher-Ohlin theory argues that free trade is beneficial. Unlike Richardo's theory, however, the Heckscher-Ohlin theory argues that the pattern of international trade is determined by differences in factor endowments, rather than differences in productivity.

The Heckscher-Ohlin theory also has common-sense appeal. For example, the United States has long been a substantial exporter of agricultural goods, reflecting in part its unusual abundance of large tracts of arable land. In contrast, South Korea has excelled in the export of goods produced in labor-intensive manufacturing industries, such as textiles and footwear. This reflects South Korea's relative abundance of low-cost labor. The United States, which lacks abundant low-cost labor, has been a primary importer of these goods. Note that it is relative, not absolute, endowments that are important; a country may have larger absolute amounts of land and labor than another country, but be relatively abundant in one of them.

2.5 The Product Life-cycle Theory

Raymond Vernon initially proposed the product life-cycle theory in the mid-1960s. Vernon's theory was based on the observation that for most of the 20th century a very large proportion of the world's new products had been developed by US firms and sold first in the US market (e. g. , mass-produced automobiles, televisions, instant cameras, photocopiers, personal computers, and semiconductor chips). To explain this, Vernon argued that the wealth and size of the US, market gave US firms a strong incentive to develop new consumer products. In addition, the high cost of US labor gave US firms an incentive to develop cost saving process innovations.

Just because a new product is developed by a US firm and first sold in the US market, it does not follow that the product must be produced in the United States. It could be produced abroad at some low-cost location and then exported back into the United States. Apparently, the pioneering firms felt that it was better to keep production facilities close to the market and to the firm's center of decision making, given the uncertainty and risks inherent in new-product introduction. [3] Moreover, the demand for most new products tends to be based on non-price factors. Consequently, firms can charge relatively high prices for new products, which obviates the needs to look for low-cost production sites in other countries.

Vernon went on to argue that early in the life cycle of a typical new product, while demand is starting to grow rapidly in the United States, demand in other advanced countries is limited to high-income groups. The limited initial demand in other advanced countries does not make it worthwhile for firms in those countries to start producing the new product, but it does necessitate some exports from the United States to those countries.

Over time, however, demand for the new product starts to grow in other advanced countries (e. g. , Great Britain, France, Germany, and Japan). As it does, it becomes worthwhile for foreign producers to begin producing for their home markets. In addition, US firms might set up production facilities in those advanced countries where demand is growing. Consequently, production within other advanced countries begins to limit the potential for exports from the United States.

As the market in the United States and other advanced nations matures, the product becomes more standardized, and price becomes the main competitive weapon. As this occurs, cost considerations start to play a greater role in the competitive process. One result is that producers based in advanced countries where labor costs are lower than in the United States (e. g. , Italy, Spain) might now be able to export to the United States. If cost pressures become intense, the process might not stop there. The cycle by which the United States lost its advantage to other advanced countries might be repeated once more, as developing countries (e. g. , South Korea and Thailand) begin to acquire a production advantage over advanced countries. Thus, the locus of global production initially switches from the United States to other advanced nations, and then from those nations to developing countries.

The consequence of these trends for the pattern of world trade is that over time the United States switches from being an exporter of the product to an importer of the product as production becomes concentrated in lower-cost foreign locations.

2.6   The New Trade Theory

The new trade theory began to emerge in the 1970s. At that time a number of economists were questioning the assumption of diminishing returns[4] to specialization used in international trade theory. They argued that in many industries, because of the presence of substantial economies of scale, there are increasing returns to specialization. Put another way, as output expands with specialization, the ability to realize economies of scale increases and so the unit costs of production should decrease. Economies of scale are primarily derived by spreading fixed costs (such as the costs of developing a new product) over a larger output. As an illustration, consider the commercial jet aircraft industry. The fixed costs of developing a new commercial jet airliner are astronomical. It has been estimated that Boeing will have to spend $3 billion to develop its new 777 before it sells a single plane. The company will have to sell at least 300 777s just to recoup these development costs and break even. Thus, due to the high fixed costs of developing a new jet aircraft, the economies of scale in this industry are substantial.

The new trade theorists further argue that due to the presence of substantial scale economies, in many industries world demand will only support a few firms. This is the case in the commercial jet aircraft industry; estimates suggest that, at most, world demand can profitably support only three major manufacturers. For example, the total world demand for 300-seater commercial jet aircraft similar to Boeing's 777 model will probably be only 1500 aircrafts over the 10 years between 1995 and 2005. If we assume that firms must sell at least 500 aircrafts to get an acceptable return on their investment (which is reasonable, given the breakeven point of 300 aircraft), we can see that, at most, the world market can profitably support only three firms!

The new trade theories go on to argue that in those industries where the existence of substantial economies of scale imply that the world market will profitably support only a few firms, countries may export certain products simply because they have a firm that was an early entrant into that industry. Underpinning this argument is the notion of first mover advantages. Because they are able to gain economies of scale, the early entrants into an industry may get a lock on the world market that discourages subsequent entry. In other words, the ability of first-movers to reap economies of scale creates a barrier to entry. In the commercial aircraft industry, for example, the fact that Boeing, Airbus, and McDonnell Douglas are already in the industry and have the benefits of economies of scale effectively discourages new entry.

This theory has profound implications. The theory suggests that a country may predominate in the export of goods simply because it was lucky enough to have one or more firms among the first to produce that goods. This is at variance with the Heckscher-Ohlin theory, which suggests that a country will predominate in the export of a product when it is particularly well endowed with those factors used intensively in its manufacture. Thus, the new theorists argue that the United States leads in exports of commercial jet aircraft not because it is better endowed with the factors of production required to manufacture aircraft, but because two of the first movers in the industry, Boeing, Airbus and McDonnell Douglas, were US firms. It should be noted, however, that the new trade theory is not at variance with the theory of comparative advantage. Since economies of scale result in an increase in the efficiency of resource utilization, and hence in productivity, the new trade theory identifies an important source of comparative advantage.

How useful is this theory in explaining trade patterns? It is perhaps too early to say; the theory is so new that little supporting empirical work has been done. Consistent with the theory, however, a recent study by Harvard business historian Alfred Chandler does suggest that the existence of first-mover advantages is an important factor in explaining the dominance of firms from certain nations in certain industries. Moreover, it is true that the number of firms is very limited in many global industries. This is the case with commercial aircraft industry, the chemical industry, the heavy construction-equipment industry, the heavy truck industry, the tire industry, the consumer electronics industry, and the jet engine industry, to name but a few examples.

Perhaps the most contentious implication of the new trade theory, however, is the argument that it generates for government intervention and strategic trade policy. New trade theories stress the role of luck, entrepreneurship, and innovation in giving a firm first-mover advantages. According to this argument, the reason why Boeing was the first mover in commercial jet aircraft manufacture — rather than firms like Great Britain's DeHavilland shot itself in the foot when its Comet jet airliner, introduced two years earlier than Boeing first jet airliner, the 707, was found to be full of serious technological flaws. [5] Had DeHavilland not made some serious technological mistakes, Great Britain might now be the world's leading exporter of commercial jet aircraft! Boeing's innovativeness was demonstrated by its independent development of the technological know-how required to build a commercial jet airliner. Several new trade theorists have pointed out, however, that Boeing's R&D was largely paid for by the US government; that the 707 was in fact a spinoff from a government funded military program. Herein lies a rationale for government intervention. By the sophisticated and judicious use of subsidies, might not a government be able to increase the chances of its domestic firms becoming first movers[6] in newly emerging industries, as the US government apparently did with Boeing? If this is possible, and the new trade theory suggests it might be, then we have an economic rationale for a proactive trade policy that is at variance with the free trade prescriptions of the trade theories we have reviewed so far.

2.7　National Competitive Advantage: Porter's Diamond

In 1990 Michael Porter of Harvard School published the results of an intensive research effort that attempted to determine why some nations succeed and others fail in international competition. Porter and his team looked at 100 industries in 10 nations. The book that contains the results of this work, the Competitive Advantage of Nations, seems destined to become a modern classic. Like the work of the new trade theories, Porter's work was driven by a feeling that the existing theorists of international trade told only part of the story. For Porter, the essential task was to explain why a nation achieves international success in a particular industry. Why does Japan do so well in the automobile industry? Why does Switzerland excel in the production and export of precision instruments and pharmaceuticals? Why do Germany and the United States do so well in the chemical industry? These questions cannot be answered easily by the Heckscher-Ohlin theory, and the theory of comparative advantage offers only a partial explanation. The theory of comparative advantage would say that Switzerland excels in the production and export of precision instruments because it uses its resources very productively in these industries. Although this may be correct, this does not explain why Switzerland is more productive in this industry than Great Britain, Germany, or Spain. It is this puzzle that Porter tries to solve.

Porter's basic thesis is that four broad attributes of a nation shape the environment in which local firms compete, and that these attributes promote or impede the creation of competitive advantage. These attributes are as follows:

(1) Factor endowments. A nation's position in factors of production such as skilled labor or the infrastructure necessary to compete in a given industry.

(2) Demand conditions. The nature of home demand for the industry's product or service.

(3) Related and supporting industries. The presence or absence in a nation of supplier industries and related industries that are internationally competitive.

(4) Firm strategy, structure, and rivalry. The conditions in the nation governing how companies are created, organized, and managed and the nature of domestic rivalry.

Porter speaks of these four attributes as constituting "the diamond". He argues that firms are most likely to succeed in industries or industry segments where "the diamond is most favorable". He also argues that the diamond is a mutually reinforcing system. The effect of one attribute is contingent on the state of others. For example, Porter argues, favorable demand conditions will not result in competitive advantage unless the state of rivalry is sufficient to cause firms to respond to them.

Porter maintains that two additional variables can influence the national diamond in important ways: chance and government. Chance events, such as major innovations, create discontinuities that can unfreeze or reshape industry structure and provide the opportunity for one nation's firms to supplant another's. [7] Government, by its choice of policies, can detract from or improve national advantage. For example, regulation can alter home demand conditions, antitrust policies can influence the intensity of rivalry within an industry, and government investments in education can change factor endowments.

2.8 Implications for Business

Why does all of this matter for business? There are perhaps three main implications of the material discussed for international businesses: location implications, first mover implications, and policy implications.

2.8.1 | Location Implications

The first, and perhaps most important, way in which the material discussed in this unit matters to an international business concerns the link between the theories of international trade and a firm's decision about where to locate its various productive activities. Underlying most of the theories we have discussed is the notion that different countries have particular advantages in different productive activities. Thus, from a profit perspective, it makes sense for a firm to disperse its various productive activities to those countries where, according to the theory of international trade, they can be performed most efficiently. If design can be performed most efficiently in France, that is where design facilities should be located; if the manufacture of basic components can be performed most efficiently in Singapore, that is where they should be manufactured; and if final assembly can be performed most efficiently in China, that is where final assembly should be performed. The end result is a global web of productive activities, with different activities being performed in different location around the globe depending on considerations of comparative advantage, factor endowments, and the like. Indeed, if the firm does not do this, it may find itself at a competitive disadvantage relative to firms that do.

As an example, consider the process of producing a laptop computer, a process with four major stages: (1) basic research and development of the product design, (2) manufacturing of standard electronic components (e. g. , integrated circuits), (3) manufacture of advanced components (e. g. , flat-top color display screens), and (4) final assembly, basic R&D and design requires a pool of highly skilled and educated workers with good backgrounds in microelectronics. The two countries with a comparative advantage in basic microelectronics, R&D and design are Japan and the United States, so most producers of laptop computers locate their R&D facilities in one, or both, of these countries. (Apple, IBM, Motorola, Texas Instruments, Toshiba, and Sony all have major R&D facilities in both

Japan and the United States.)

The manufacture of standard electronic components is a capital-intensive process requiring semiskilled labor, and cost pressures are intense. The best locations for such activities today are places such as Singapore, Malaysia, etc. These places have pools of relatively skilled, low-cost labor. Thus, many producers of laptop computers have standard components produced at these locations.

The manufacture of advanced components is a capital intensive process requiring highly skilled labor, and cost pressures are less intense. Since cost pressures are not so intense at this stage of the process, these components can be — and are — manufactured in countries with high labor costs that also have pools of highly skilled labor (primarily Japan).

Finally, assembly is a relatively labor-intensive process requiring only low-skilled labor, and cost pressures are intense. As a result, final assembly may be carried out in a country such as Mexico, which has an abundance of low-cost, low-skilled labor.

The end result is that when we look at a laptop computer produced by a US manufacturer, we may find that it was designed in California, its standard components were produced in Singapore, and Taiwan area of China, its advanced components were produced in Japan, its final assembly took place in Mexico, and the finished product was then sold in the United States or elsewhere in the world. By dispersing production activities to different locations around the globe, the US manufacturer is taking advantage of the difference between countries identified by the various theories of international trade.

2.8.2 First-mover Implications

The new trade theory suggests the importance to firms of building and exploiting first-mover advantages. According to the new trade theory, firms that establish a first mover advantage with regard to the production of a particular new product may subsequently dominate global trade in that product. This is particularly true in those industries where the global market can only profitably support a handful of firms (such as the aerospace market). For the individual firm, the clear message is that it pays to invest substantial financial resources in trying to build a first-mover advantage, even if that means several years of substantial losses before a new venture becomes profitable. Although the precise details of how to achieve this are beyond the scope of this book, it should be noted that there is a vast literature on strategies for exploiting first-mover advantages. It should perhaps also be noted that in recent years, Japanese firms, rather than US firms, seem to have been prepared to undertake the vast investments and bear the years of losses required to build a first-mover advantage. This has certainly been true in the production of liquid crystal display (LCD) screens for laptop computers. While firms such as Toshiba and NEC invested heavily in this technology during the 1980s, many large US firms exited the market. As a result, today Japanese firms dominate global trade in LCD screens, even though the technology was invented in the United States.

2.8.3 | Policy Implications

The theories of international trade also matter to international businesses because business firms are major players on the international trade scene. Business firms produce exports, and business firms import the products of other countries. Because of their pivotal role in international trade, business firms can and do exert a strong influence on government trade policy. By lobbying government, business firms can help promote free trade, or they can promote trade restrictions. The message for business contained in the theories of international trade is that promoting free trade is generally in the best interests of the United States, although it may not always be in the best interest of an individual firm. Many firms do recognize this and do lobby for open markets.

For example, in 1991 when the US government announced its intention to place a tariff on Japanese imports of liquid crystal display (LCD) screens, IBM and Apple Computer protested strongly. Both IBM and Apple pointed out that (1) Japan was the lowest-cost source of LCD screens, (2) they used these screens in their own laptop computers, and (3) the proposed tariff, by increasing the cost of LCD screens, would increase the cost of laptop computers produced by IBM and Apple, thus making them less competitive in the world market. In other words, the tariff, designed to protect US firms, would be self-defeating. In response to these pressures, the US government is currently rethinking its posture on this issue.

Unlike IBM and Apple, however, businesses do not always lobby for free trade. In the United States, for example, "voluntary" restrictions[8] on imports on automobiles, machine tools, textiles, and steel are the result of direct pressures by US firms in these industries on the government. The Government has responded by getting foreign companies to agree to "voluntary" restrictions on their imports, using the implicit threat of more comprehensive formal trade barriers to get them to adhere to these agreements. As predicted by international trade theory, many of these agreements have been self-defeating. Take the voluntary restriction on machine-tool imports agreed to in 1985 as an example. Due to limited imports competition from more-efficient foreign suppliers, the prices of machine tools in the United States have risen to the highest levels than would have prevailed under a free trade scenario. Since machine tools are used throughout the manufacturing industry, the result has been to increase the costs of US manufacturing in general, and a corresponding loss in world market competitiveness. Moreover, shielded from international competition by import barriers, the US machine tool industry has had no incentive to increase its efficiency. Consequently, it has lost many of its export markets to even more efficient foreign competitor. Thus the US machine tool industry is now smaller than it was in 1985. For anyone schooled in international trade theory, none of these events are surprising.

Finally, Porter's theory of national competitive advantage also contains important policy implications. Porter's theory suggests that it is in the best interest of business for a firm to invest in upgrading advanced factors of production; for example, to invest in better training for its employees and to increase its commitment to research and development. It is also in the best interests of business to lobby the government to adopt policies that have a favorable impact on each component of the national "diamond". Thus, according to Porter, businesses should urge government to increase its investment in education, infrastructure, and basic research (since all of these enhance advanced factors) and to adopt policies that promote strong competition within domestic markets (since this makes firms stronger international competitors, according to Porter's findings).

New Words and Expressions

mainstay	n.	支柱
per se	ad.	亲自，实际上，本身
inherent	a.	固有的
deterioration	n.	恶化
envisage	v.	设想
landmark	n.	里程碑
rationale	n.	原则
obviate	v.	排除
astronomical	a.	巨大的
recoup	v.	补偿
breakeven	n.	得失相等，不亏不盈
underpin	v.	支撑，巩固
empirical	a.	以经验为基础的
spinoff	n.	派生物
judicious	a.	明智的
pharmaceutical	a.	制药的，药的
infrastructure	n.	基础设施
supplant	v.	取代
detract (from)	v.	减损
disperse	v.	使分散
pool	n.	一批，共同资金
literature	n.	文字材料
pivotal	a.	关键的，重要的
lobby	v.	游说
posture	n.	立场
corresponding	a.	相应的
shield	v.	保护
by the same token		同样的，由于同样原因
by virtue of		因为，凭借

common-sense appeal	常识性意义
semiconductor chip	半导体硅片
get a lock on	对……控制
at variance with	与……不符
precision instrument	精密仪器
contingent on	依条件而定
chance event	偶然事件
laptop computer	便携式计算机
display screen	显示器
liquid crystal display screen	液晶显示器

𝐍otes

1. Hume's critique apart . . .

   apart：*ad.* 撇开或排除。该处意为"除了休莫的评论指出的缺点外……"。

2. zero-sum game：零和博弈。在不少博弈中，一方的受益肯定是来源于其他方的损失。

   positive-sum game：常和博弈。与零和博弈不同，在有些博弈中，每种结果之下各博弈方的得益之和不等于零，但总数等于一个非零常数。

   Heckscher-Ohlin Theory：赫克歇尔-俄林理论。它是由埃利·赫克歇尔和他的学生蒂尔·俄林共同创立的理论。该理论认为生产要素禀赋的国际差异是造成国际贸易中国际竞争力不同的原因。国际贸易最重要的结果是各国能更有效地利用各种生产要素，实现合理的国际分工。

   factor endowment：要素禀赋。它指一个国家或经济体所拥有的可以利用的经济资源的总供给。在各国对外贸易竞争中，土地、劳动力、资本、技术等要素的结合起着重要的作用，它们结合后构成的价格对一国的对外贸易起着重要的影响。

3. . . . given the uncertainty and risks inherent in new-product introduction.

   "given" 意为 "considering the fact that"。该句意思为："……鉴于新产品所固有的不稳定因素和风险。"

4. diminishing returns：收益递减规律。根据这一规律，如果等额增加一种要素，而使其他要素的数量保持不变，产量的增加额一开始可能会上升，但超过了某一点后，等额增加该种要素带来的产量增加额就会下降，即该可变要素的边际产量会递减。

5. . . . shot itself in the foot when its Comet jet airliner, introduced two years earlier than Boeing's first airliner, the 707, was founded full of serious technological flaws.

   此句中的 "shot oneself in the foot" 意为 "因笨拙无能而伤害自己"；"introduce" 为 "问世" 之意。该句意为 "Comet 喷气式飞机比第一架波音 707 早两年问世，当它问世时人们发现它存在严重的技术问题……因笨拙无能而使自己受挫。"

6. By the sophisticated and judicious use of subsidies, might not a government be able to increase the chance of its domestic firms becoming first movers ...

sophisticated：富有经验的，精明的；其中"might not a government be able to ..."等于"wouldn't it be possible for a government to ..."。该句意为："靠精明审慎的使用补贴，政府难道不可能增加其国内公司成为……第一个市场启动者的机会吗？"

7. Chance events, ... create discontinuities that can unfreeze or reshape industry structure and provide the opportunities for one nation's firm to supplant another's.

chance event：偶然事件；discontinuity：中断，此处指旧的生产结构的终止；unfreeze：v. 消除对……控制，限制；reshape：v. 改组，重新制定。该句意为："偶然事件……可以造成产业结构的开放或改组，以及旧产业结构的终止，并能为一国的公司提供取代别国公司的机会。"

8. "voluntary" restriction：自动出口限制。出口国在进口国的压力下自行限制某些产品出口数量的措施，属非关税壁垒的一种。

■ Review questions.

1. What is the essence of the mercantilist doctrine and what is the inherent inconsistency in this theory?

2. Can you find out anything in common between the theory of absolute advantage and that of comparative advantage ?

3. According to Richardo, would a country purchase goods that it could produce more efficiently at home than in other countries? Why or why not?

4. In what way does the explanation of comparative advantage put forward by Heckscher and Bertil Ohlin differ from that presented by David Richardo?

5. According to product life-cycle theory, how can a country take advantage of different demand of the same product in different countries by switching from being an exporter of a product to an importer of a particular product?

6. What advantages does the first mover have in its international trade?

7. What is the most contentious implication of the new trade theory?

8. According to Porter's diamond, what are the variables that can influence the national diamond?

■ Define the following terms briefly.

1. Heckscher-Ohlin theory

2. the product life cycle theory

3. the new trade theory

4．the national competitive advantage theory

5．the comparative advantage theory

III Translate the following passages into Chinese.

Although the Law of Comparative Advantage explains many of the observed patterns of international trade, a major portion of trade is inconsistent with the "law". For instance, the United States both exports and imports significant numbers of automobiles. This aspect of international trade is often called two-way trade or intra-industry trade. Intra-industry trade appears to account for the large volume of international trade in manufactured products that exist between the developed countries.

The basis for most intra-industry trade is found in the nature of consumer preferences and the existence of differentiated products. Although local producers may satisfy most local consumers with the products offered, some consumers in each country prefer imported varieties, because of physical differences or differences in image or perception. Local producers both export to satisfy segments of foreign demand and face import competition in some parts of local market. Intra-industry trade is the result.

IV Translate the following passages into English.

1．各国为什么贸易？什么时候贸易？数百年来，这一直是经济学家感兴趣的问题。1776 年亚当·斯密论道：如一国专门出口某些产品而进口别国生产成本较低的其他产品，那么该国的实际收入将最大化；如一国生产某些产品的成本比别国低，那么该国就享有生产该产品的绝对优势。该国就应对有绝对优势的产品进行专业化生产并出口多余的产品。

2．比较优势不是一个静止的概念。一个国家可以不凭借大自然的恩赐而完全通过其自身的行动来发展某一特别的比较优势。瑞士造表业的比较优势就是一个典型的例子。同样，美国已经在使用最先进技术的许多行业发展了比较优势。
作为经济专门化的基础，绝对利益理论具有很强的直觉吸引力，但是，由英国经济学家大卫·李嘉图所提出的比较利益理论更有意义。的确，这一理论已成为现代国际贸易思想的基石。

V Read the following passages and answer the questions.

In 1970 living standards in Ghana and South Korea were roughly comparable. Ghana's 1970 gross domestic product (GDP) per head was $250, and South Korea's was $260. By 1988 the situation had changed dramatically. South Korea then had a GDP per head of $4081, while Ghana was only $369, reflecting vastly different economic growth rate. Between 1965 and 1988 the average annual growth rate in Ghana's GDP was 1.5 percent, while South Korea achieved a rate of over 9 percent per annum. What explains the difference between Ghana and South Korea? There is no simple answer, but there are reasons for believing that the attitudes of both countries towards international trade provide part of the explanation. A study by the World Bank suggests that whereas the South Korean government has had a strong pro-trade bias, the actions of the Ghanaian government discouraged domestic producers from becoming involved in international trade.

Ghana was the first of Great Britain's West African colonies to become independent, in 1957. Its first president, Kwame Nkrumah, influenced the rest of the continent with his theories of pan-African socialism. For Ghana this meant the imposition of high tariffs on many imports, an import substitution policy aimed at fostering Ghana self-sufficiency in certain manufactured goods, and the adoption of policies that discouraged Ghana's enterprises from engaging in exports. The results were an unmitigated disaster that transformed one of Africa's most prosperous nations into one of the world's poorest.

As an illustration of how Ghana's antitrade policies destroyed the Ghanaian economy, consider the Ghanaian government's involvement in the cocoa trade. A combination of favorable climate, good soils, and ready access to world shipping routes has given Ghana an absolute advantage in cocoa production. Quite simply, it is one of the best places in the world to grow cocoa. As a consequence, Ghana was the world's largest producer and exporter of cocoa in 1957. Then the government of the newly independent nation created a state-controlled cocoa marketing board. The board was given the authority to fix prices for cocoa and was designated the sole buyer of all cocoa grown in Ghana. The board held down the prices that it paid farmers for cocoa, while selling the cocoa that it bought from them on the world market at world prices. Thus it might buy cocoa from farmers at 25 cents a pound and sell it on the world market for the world price of 50 cents a pound. In effect, the board was taxing exports by paying farmers considerably less for their cocoa than it was worth on the world market and putting the difference into government coffers. This money was used to fund the government policy of nationalization and industrialization.

One result of the cocoa policy was that between 1963 and 1979 the price paid by the cocoa marketing board to Ghana's farmers increased by a factor of 6, while the price of consumer goods in Ghana increased by a factor of 22, and while the price of cocoa in neighboring countries increased by a factor of 36! In real terms, the Ghanaian farmers were paid less every year for their cocoa by the cocoa marketing board, while the world price increased significantly. Ghana's farmers responded by switching to the production of subsistence foodstuffs that could be sold within Ghana, and the country's production and exports of cocoa plummeted by more than one third in seven years. At the same time, the Ghanaian government's attempt to build an industrial base through state-run enterprises was a complete failure. The resulting drop in Ghana's export earnings plunged the country into recession, led to a decline in its foreign currency reserves, and severely limited its ability to pay for necessary imports.

In essence, what happened in Ghana is that the inward-oriented trade policy of the Ghanaian government resulted in a shift of that country's resources away from the profitable activity of growing cocoa-where it had an absolute advantage in the world economy towards growing subsistence foods and manufacturing, where it had no advantage. This inefficient use of the country's resources severely damaged the Ghanaian economy and held back the country's economic development.

In contrast, consider the trade policy adopted by the South Korean government. The World

Bank has characterized the trade policy of South Korea as "strongly outward-oriented". Unlike in Ghana, the policies of the South Koreas government emphasized low import barriers on manufactured goods (but not on agricultural goods) and the creation of incentives to encourage South Korean firms to export. Beginning in the late 1950s, the South Korean government progressively reduced import tariffs from an average of 60 percent of the price of one imported goods to less than 20 percent in the mid-1980s. Moreover, on most nonagricultural goods, import tariffs were reduced to zero. In addition, the number of imported goods subjected to quotas was reduced from more than 90 percent in the late 1950s to zero by the early 1980s. Over the same period South Korea progressively reduced the subsidies given to South Korean exporters from an average of 80 percent of their sales price in the late 1950s to an average of less than 20 percent of their sales prices in 1965, and down to zero in 1984. Put another way, with the exception of the agricultural sector (where a strong farm lobby maintained import controls), South Korea moved progressively towards a free trade stance.

South Korea's outward-looking orientation has been rewarded by a dramatic transformation of its economy. Initially, South Korea's resources shifted from agriculture to the manufacture of labor-intensive goods, especially textiles, clothing, and footwear. An abundant supply of cheap but well-educated labor helped form the basis of South Korea's comparative advantage in labor-intensive manufacturing. More recently, as labor costs have risen, the growth areas in the economy have been in the more capital-intensive manufacturing sectors, especially motor vehicles, aerospace, consumer electronics, and advanced materials. As a result of these developments, South Korea has gone through some dramatic changes. In the late 1950s 77 percent of the country's employment was in the agricultural sector; today the figure is less than 25 percent. Over the same period the percentage of its GDP accounted for by manufacturing increased from less than 10 percent to more than 30 percent, while the overall GDP grew at an annual rate of more than 9 percent.

Please answer the following questions.

1. How does Ghana differ from South Korea in attitudes towards international trade?
2. Use its cocoa trade as an example to explain how Ghana's antitrade policies destroyed the Ghanaian economy.
3. Account for the differences between the inward-oriented trade policy and the outward oriented one.
4. What can we learn from the two nations' experience?

Chapter 3

International Payment

国际支付

Generally speaking, it is not very difficult for buyers and sellers in domestic trade to get to know each other's financial status and other information, and payment is likely to be made in a straightforward manner, say by remittance or by debiting the debtor's account. In international trade, however, things are far more complicated. Purchase and sale of goods and services are carried out beyond national boundaries, which makes it rather difficult for the parties concerned in the transaction to get adequate information about each other's financial standing and creditworthiness. Therefore, mutual trust is hard to build. Both the exporter and the importer face risks as there is always the possibility that the other party may not fulfill the contract.

3.1 Payment Instruments of International Trade

In international trade, payment can be made by various means: drafts, promissory note, checks, money orders, credit cards[1], and cash, etc. Cash is rarely used except for some small transactions. Credit cards are not widely used either, especially for large transaction, because verification with and approval from the credit card company can be inconvenient and time-consuming when a credit limit is exceeded. So far drafts[2] have been used as the most common instrument of payment in international trade, although promissory notes and checks are also sometimes used.

3.1.1 | Draft or Bill of Exchange

A draft or bill of exchange is an unconditional order in writing signed by one party(drawer) requesting a second party (drawee/payer) to make payment in lawful money immediately or at a determined future time to a third party (payee).

In the context of international trade, the drawer and payee is usually the seller and the drawee and payer is usually the buyer.

1. Basic Contents of a Draft

The forms of draft might be different, but the contents are basically the same as listed below.

(1) Date and place of issue.

(2) Time of payment.

(3) Name of payee.

(4) Currency and amount.

(5) Credit reference.

(6) Name of drawee/payer.

(7) Drawer's name and signature.

2. Types of Draft

(1) Commercial draft. A commercial draft is one that is drawn by a firm or an exporter. The drawee can be a firm, an exporter or a bank. A commercial draft is commonly used in international trade in settlement of payment.

(2) Banker's draft[3]. A banker's draft is drawn by one bank on another bank. It is used in settling payment obligations between banks.

(3) Sight draft. A sight draft is one that is payable on presentation, i. e. , the drawee should immediately pay the amount on the draft drawn on him.

(4) Time/usance draft. A time or usance draft is one that is payable in a special number of days after ① its date of issuance; ② its date of acceptance; ③ the date of B/L or at a fixed future date. The specified number of days is called the "usance period".

(5) Clean draft. A clean draft is one that is paid without the presentation of any other documents attached. A banker's draft is usually clean.

(6) Documentary draft. A documentary draft is one that should be paid only when certain documents have been attached to and presented together with the draft.

Commercial drafts are usually documentary. The most important document is bill of lading that represents the title to the goods. These types of draft are not mutually exclusive. For instance, one draft can be documentary, commercial, and usance at the same time.

3. Use of Drafts

1) Issuance

This is the process in which a drawer completes the items in a draft, for example, drawee, amount, payee, date and place of payment, etc.

A payee can be restricted to a specified party only (e. g. , "pay ABC company only"), and such a draft will not be negotiable.

A payee can also be made a "to order" instrument[4]. For example, under payee, the phrase "pay to the order of ABC Company" can be used. Such a draft will be transferable with the endorsement of the payee.

If the payee is made "to bearer", no endorsement is needed for transfer.

2) Presentation

Presentation means the holder of the draft lets the drawee sight the draft for payment or acceptance, depending on whether a sight draft or a time draft[5] is presented.

3) Acceptance

If a usance draft is presented, the drawee takes up the obligation of payment when the draft becomes due by putting the word "accepted", his signature and the date of acceptance on the face of the draft. The accepted draft will be returned to the holder who will represent it for payment when it is due.

4) Payment

For a sight draft, the drawee will pay the amount on the draft immediately when it is presented. For a usance draft, the drawee will pay when it is due.

5) Dishonored[6] bills and protests

Sometimes the drawee refuses or is unable to pay or accept a draft, then this draft is called a "dishonored bill".

If a draft is dishonored, the holder of the draft can exercise his right of recourse[7] and ask the drawer or the endorser[8] to pay the draft amount. However, the holder must obtain a "certificate of protest[9]" from a notary public, a law court or other institutions that have been authorized by law to issue such a certificate to certify the dishonor of the draft. The certificate includes the date and place of the first presentation, and the statement that the drawee refuses to pay or accept. This is a legal procedure to register officially that the draft presented for payment or acceptance has been dishonored by the drawee.

After he has obtained the certificate of protest, the holder can present the draft the second time. If the drawee still refuses to pay, the certificate can be published in trade journals in some countries. The possibility of publishing the certificate of protest gives the drawee some pressure to pay; otherwise, his commercial creditability will be damaged in the business community.

However, the exporter should remember that protest does not ensure payment and further legal action might affect an ongoing relationship with an importer.

3.1.2 | Promissory Note[10]

A promissory note is an unconditional promise in writing made by one person (the maker) to another (the payee/the holder) signed by the maker engaging to pay on demand or at a fixed or determinable future time a sum of money to or to the order of a specified person or to bearer.

A promissory note can be issued by a person, a firm, or a bank. But promissory notes issued by individuals and firms are not widely used in trade today.

3.1.3 | Check[11]

A check is an unconditional order in writing addressed by the customer (drawee) to a bank (drawee) signed by the customer authorizing the bank to pay on demanding a specified sum of money to or to the order of a named person or to bearer(payee).

A check is a special kind of draft in that the drawee is always a bank with which the drawer has an account. Besides, a check is always paid upon presentation. If the drawer wants to write a check now but does not want the payee to collect the money immediately, the drawer can postdate the check.

A check can be made to order, to bearer, crossed with two parallel lines for account deposit only, or certified by a bank that is going to pay. If a check is issued by a bank, it is called a banker's demand draft.

3.2   Five Basic Methods of Payment

There are five basic terms of payment used in international trade. The payment process basically involves multiple relationships between the exporter and the importer, their respective banks, national regulations, and international agreements. These five are described briefly below, and in greater detail in the pages that immediately follow. They are cash in advance, open account[12], consignment[13], documentary collection, and letter of credit.

3.2.1 | Cash in Advance

The buyer simply prepares the seller prior to shipment of the goods. This term of payment requires that the buyer have a high level of confidence in the ability and willingness of the seller to deliver the goods as ordered. It requires that the buyer pay the seller prior to shipment of the goods ordered. Cash in advance provides the seller with the most security but leaves the buyer at great risk that the seller will not comply with all the terms of the contract. The cash payment is received before, and independently of, shipment of the goods. If the goods are delayed or are of inferior quality, the buyer's last resort is to take legal action on the basis of the sales contract, unless the seller makes a satisfactory adjustment. Due to the high degree of risk, the buyer should always consider whether any alternatives are available before agreeing to cash in advance terms.

Cash in advance payments are made either by bank draft or check or through a wire payment to the bank account specified by the seller/exporter. If receiving payment by check, the seller should verify that it has been cleared by the buyer's bank before proceeding with shipment.

Generally, only two categories of sellers can require cash in advance terms: those fortunate to have unique or high-demand products, and sellers receiving orders from unknown buyers in unstable countries.

Cash terms can sometimes be asked when shipping a small sample order to a buyer. Also, in some cases involving a large buyer, a small seller, and a large order, the buyer may be willing to make an advance payment to help the smaller company carry out the manufacturing process. In addition, in some situations, such as when the relationship is new, the transaction is small, and the buyer is unwilling to pay the costs of documentary payments, cash in advance terms may be preferred.

Overall, cash in advance payment terms cannot be required from buyers and this type of payment constitutes a small proportion of payments made in international transactions.

3.2.2 | Open Account

Open account is an arrangement in which the credit is extended to an individual, firm, corporation or other legal entity based on an estimate of the general ability to pay, as distinguished from the credit that is extended and supported by a note, mortgage or other formal written evidence of indebtedness. Purchase on open account means that the buyer agrees to pay for goods ordered within a designated time after their shipment. Common terms are 30, 60, or 90 days although longer terms of 180 days are not unheard of.

1. Procedure of Using Open Account

Open account is quite simple to use. First, the seller dispatches the goods. Then he sends the invoice to the buyer and waits for payment from the buyer. When the goods are dispatched, the title to the goods transfers to the buyer from seller.

Normally, the seller will stipulate a time period in which payment is to be made. For instance, 2/10 means that the buyer can take two percent off the invoice amount if he pays within 10 days, and n/30 means that full invoice value must be paid within a month.

2. Advantages of Using Open Account

(1) There is a great flexibility and convenience in using open account since the arrangement is simple. Sales can be increased because of this.

(2) Since remittance is mostly used in settling payment under open account and the use of banks is reduced to minimum, there is less cost and bank charges. This helps reduce the cost of transactions.

3. Disadvantages of Using Open Account

(1) There is a risk of total loss for the seller due to lack of real evidence of indebtedness which makes legal action very difficult. There are two types of risks, buyer credit risk and country risk. The former refers to the buyer's insolvency or willful default on payment and the later refers to the importing country's exchange controls due to political or financial reasons. To avoid the buyer credit risk, the seller should obtain credit report on the buyer from companies specialized in collecting, analyzing and reporting data of a great number of businesses, or the seller should take out insurance against non-payment.

(2) The delay in payment can be indefinite and, if the payment is ever made, it is difficult to determine the interest charges since there can be at least two different interest rates to use, domestic rate and foreign rate.

4. Prime Consideration for a Sale on Open Account

Since there is a very high risk of loss of goods and payment, sellers should take special care in using open account. They should consider:

(1) the credit standing of the buyer;

(2) the relationship between the buyer and the seller;

(3) prior collection experience with a buyer;

(4) the payment record and rules of the importing country such as the types of foreign exchange controls.

Although open account terms are common in domestic trade, where the legal system provides ready recourse against defaulting buyers, these terms are much less common in international trade. Winning a judgment abroad is at least several times more difficult than the same procedure domestically.

Generally, open account terms are utilized only when goods are shipped to a foreign branch or subsidiary of a multinational company or when there is a high degree of trust between seller and buyer, and the seller has significant faith in the buyer's ability and willingness to pay. If the transaction is with an unknown buyer, the seller is advised to find a different payment method.

Overall, open account payment terms cannot be expected from sellers early in the relationship.

3.2.3 | Consignment

Under a consignment contract, the exporter ships the goods to the importer, but the exporter still retains the title of the goods until the importer has sold them to a third party and has paid the exporter (consignor). Under this arrangement, the exporter runs considerable risk, since he cannot get paid until the merchandise is sold. He takes this route of payment normally under the circumstances that the importer is his branch or affiliate or the marketability of the goods (say, a new product) cannot be limited by time. If the consignee defaults, laws in foreign countries make it difficult to enforce payment.

Therefore, this arrangement should only be made with full understanding of the risks involved and is preferably to be limited to stable countries where the exporter has a trusted agent to look after his interest.

3.2.4 | Documentary Collection

1. Definition

A documentary collection is an order by the seller to his bank to collect payment from the buyer in exchange for the transfer of documents that enable the holder to take possession of the goods.

Under a documentary collection, the seller ships goods to the buyer but forwards shipping documents (including title document) to the forwarding bank for transmission to the buyer's bank.

The buyer's bank is instructed not to transfer the documents to the buyer until payment is made.

Like letters of credit, documentary collections focus on the transfer of title documents to goods rather than on immediate transfer of the goods themselves. However, unlike letters of credit, banks involved in transaction do not guarantee payment but act only as collectors of payment.

Documentary collections are excellent for buyers who wish to purchase goods without risking prepayment and without having to go through the more cumbersome letter of credit procedures. Documentary collections are easier to use than letters of credit, and bank charges are usually lower.

Documentary collection procedures, however, entail some risks for both sellers and buyers. For sellers, risk is incurred because payment is not made until after the goods are shipped; also, the seller assumes risk while the goods are in transit or in storage until payment or acceptance takes place. Also, banks involved in the transaction do not guarantee payments. For buyers, risk is incurred when the goods shipped by the seller don't have the quality or quantity ordered. Therefore, from the seller's standpoint, documentary collection falls somewhere in between a letter of credit and open account in its desirability. This term of payment is generally utilized when the buyer and seller have an established and ongoing business relationship, and when the transaction does not require the additional protection and expense of a documentary credit.

2. The Parties to a Documentary Collection

There are four main parties to a documentary collection transaction. Note below that each party has several names. This is because businesspeople and banks each have their own way of thinking about and naming each party to the transaction. For example, as far as businesspeople are concerned there are just buyers and sellers and the buyer's bank and the seller's bank. Banks, however, are not concerned with buying and selling. They are concerned with remitting (sending) documents from the principal (seller) and presenting drafts (orders to pay) to the drawee (buyer) for payment. The four main parties are as follows:

1) The principal (seller/exporter/drawer)

The principal is generally the seller/exporter as well as the party that prepares documentation (collection document) and submits (remits) them to his bank (remitting bank) with a collection order for payment from the buyer (drawee). The principal is also sometimes called the remitter.

2) The remitting (principal's /seller's/exporter's) bank

The remitting bank receives documentation(collection documents) from the seller (principal) for forwarding (remitting) to the buyer's bank (collecting/presenting bank) along with instructions for payment.

3) The collecting or presenting (buyer's) bank

This is the bank that presents the documents to the buyer and collects cash payment (payment of a bank draft) or a promise to pay in the future (a bill of exchange) from the buyer (drawee of the draft) in exchange for the documents.

4) The drawee (buyer/importer)

The drawee (Buyer/Importer) is the party that makes cash payment or signs a draft according to the terms of the collection order in exchange for the documents from the presenting/collecting bank and takes possession of the goods. The drawee is the one on whom a draft is drawn and who owes the indicated amount.

3. Basic Documentary Collection Procedures

The documentary collection procedure involves the step-by-step exchange documents giving title to goods for either cash or a contracted promise to pay at a later time.

1) Buyer and seller

The buyer and the seller agree on the terms of sale of goods: (1) specifying a documentary collection as the means of payment, (2) naming a collecting/presenting bank (usually the buyer's bank), and (3) listing required document.

2) Principal (Seller)

The seller (principal) ships the goods to the buyer(drawee) and obtains a negotiable transport document(bill of lading) from the shipping firm/agent.

The seller (principal) prepares and presents (remits) a document package to his bank (the remitting bank) consisting of (1) a collection order specifying the terms and conditions under which the bank is to hand over documents to the buyer and receive payment, (2) the negotiable transport document (bill of lading), and (3) other documents (e. g., insurance document, certificate of origin, inspection certificate, etc.) as required by the buyer.

3) Remitting bank

The remitting bank sends the documentation package by mail or by courier to the designated collecting/presenting bank in the buyer's country with instructions to present them to the drawee (buyer) and collect payment.

4) Collecting bank

The presenting (collecting) bank (1) reviews the documents making certain they are in conformity with the collection order, (2) notifies the buyer (drawee) about the terms and conditions of the collection order, and (3) releases the documents once the payment conditions have been met.

5) Buyer/Drawee

The buyer (drawee) (1) makes a cash payment (signing the draft), or if the collection order allows, signs an acceptance (promise to pay at a future date) and (2) receives the documents and takes possession of the shipment.

6) Collecting bank

The collecting bank pays the remitting bank either with an immediate payment or, at the maturity date of the accepted bill of exchange.

7) Remitting bank

The remitting bank then pays the seller(principal).

The remitting bank may find it necessary or desirable to use an intermediary bank (called a correspondent bank) rather than sending the collection order and documents directly to the collecting bank. For example, the collecting bank may be very small or may not have an established relationship with the remitting bank.

4. Three Types of Collections

There are three types of documentary collections and each relates to a buyer option for payment for the documents at presentation. The second and third, however, are dependent upon the seller's willingness to accept the option and his specific instructions in the collection order. The three types are as follows:

1) Documents against payments (D/P) [14]

In D/P terms, the collecting bank releases the documents to the buyer only upon full and immediate cash payment. D/P terms most closely resemble a traditional cash-on-delivery transaction. Therefore, the buyer must pay the presenting/collecting bank the full payment in freely available funds in order to take possession of the documents. This type of collection offers the greatest security to the seller.

2) Documents against acceptance (D/A) [15]

In D/A terms the collecting bank is permitted to release the documents to the buyer against acceptance (signing) of a bill of exchange or signing of a time draft at the bank promising to pay at a later date (usually 30, 60 or 90 days).

The completed draft is held by the collecting bank and presented to the buyer for payment at maturity, after which the collecting bank sends the funds to the remitting bank, which in turn sends them to the principal/seller. The seller should be aware that he gives up title to the shipment in exchange for the signed bill of exchange that now represents his only security in the transaction.

3) Acceptance documents against payment

An acceptance documents against payment has features from both D/P and D/A types. It works like this: (1) the collecting bank presents a bill of exchange to the buyer for acceptance, (2) the accepted bill of exchange remains at the collecting bank together with the documents up to maturity, (3) the buyer pays the bill of exchange at maturity, (4) the collecting bank releases the documents to the buyer who takes possession of the shipment, and (5) the collecting bank sends the funds to the remitting bank, which then in turn sends them to the seller.

This gives the buyer time to pay for the shipment but gives the seller security that title to the shipment will not the handed over until payment has been made. If the buyer refuses acceptance of the bill of exchange or does not honor payment at maturity, the seller makes other arrangements to sell his goods. This type of collection is seldom used in actual practice.

5. General Notes and Cautions

Listed below are notes and cautions that are fundamental to the process and of importance to all parties to the transaction.

(1) The banks involved in a documentary collection do not guarantee payment or assume any

credit risk, as they do in documentary credit transactions. The banks act merely as intermediaries to facilitate payment for a shipment.

(2) If the shipper/seller sends goods directly to the buyer's address, the shipment will be handed over without the buyer first making payment. The seller, therefore, will usually address the shipment to his agent in the buyer's country or to the collecting bank if it is known to him and prior agreement has been obtained to do so.

(3) Goods are transported, stored, and insured at the expense and risk of the seller until payment or acceptance occurs. Generally, banks are under no obligation to protect the goods. Banks are also not responsible if the shipment is seized by customs or confiscated to cover any accrued storage costs.

(4) Documentary collections have one additional safeguard over transactions conducted on an open-account basis. The existence of the draft itself, which has been duly presented and accepted through a bank in the buyer's country, is an acknowledged evidence of debt. However, this may not be of great value against a purchaser who is determined not to pay.

(5) In D/P terms the buyer may refuse to pay, in which case the seller maintains title to the shipment. The seller may decide to negotiate new terms with the buyer, locate another buyer, or have the goods returned, incurring the cost of shipping, insurance, and bank fees. If the goods are perishable, the seller may be in a difficult position to find a new buyer quickly.

(6) In D/A terms the buyer may refuse to accept the draft, in which case the seller is in the same position as in D/P terms where the buyer refuses to pay the draft.

(7) In D/A terms the buyer may accept (sign) the draft, take possession of the goods, but then refuse to pay the draft at maturity. In this case the seller had neither payment nor the goods. The seller's options are effectively reduced to trying to enforce the buyer's obligation to pay the draft through banking channels or legal action, both of which involve additional costs.

(8) Since the banks are under no obligation to authenticate documents, it is possible that the seller will send a short shipment, the incorrect goods, or inferior goods. The only recourse available to the buyer is through direct contact with the seller or legal action.

To sum up, in actual trade, payment by collection should be accepted with discretion. It is usually used when the financial standing of the importers is sound, or when the exporter wishes to push the sale of his goods, or when the transaction involves only a small quantity of his goods; otherwise, the letter of credit is generally preferred. The letter of credit will be dealt with in the next chapters, for it involves lots of procedures and parties.

3.2.5 | Documentary Letter of Credit

A letter of credit is a bank's commitment to pay the seller a specified sum on behalf of the buyer under precisely defined conditions. The buyer specifies certain documents (including a title document) from the seller before the bank is to make payment, and seller is assured that payment will be received after the goods are shipped so long as the specified documents are provided. Since documentary letter of credit involves lots of parties and rather more complicated procedures, which can not be accounted for within this unit, the next two units will be committed to the letter of credit.

New Words and Expressions

creditworthiness	n.	信誉
verification	n.	验证，鉴定
drawer	n.	出票人
drawee	n.	受票人
bearer	n.	持票人
issuance	n.	出票
presentation	n.	提示
acceptance	n.	承兑
recourse	n.	追索
endorser	n.	背书人
certify	v.	证明
protest	n.	拒付证书
postdate	v.	迟签日期
consignment	n.	寄售
mortgage	n.	抵押
indebtedness	n.	债务
invoice	n.	发票
insolvency	n.	无偿债能力
default	n./v.	不履约，违约
affiliate	n.	附属机构
principal	n.	委托人
negotiable	a.	可流通的
maturity	n.	到期
honor	v.	兑付
confiscate	v.	没收
perishable	a.	易腐的
authenticate	v.	确定真实性
discretion	n.	谨慎
financial standing		财务状况
payment instruments		支付工具
money order		汇款单

credit limit	信贷额度
sight draft	即期汇票
time/usance draft	远期汇票
clean draft	光票
documentary draft	跟单汇票
bill of lading	提单
dishonored bill	拒付票据
open account	记账交易
documentary collection	跟单托收
legal entity	法人
credit risk	信用风险
credit standing	资信状况
remitting bank	托收行
collecting bank	代收行
presenting bank	提示行
collection order	托收委托书
cash-on-delivery	货到付现

Notes

1. credit card：信用卡。指商业银行向个人提供的一种赊购商品的凭证，持卡人可以在本地或外地指定的商店、公司、旅馆等凭卡签字购买商品、车票及就餐等，并可向发卡银行的分支行或代理行透支小额现金。信用卡通常每月结算一次。

2. draft：亦称"bill of exchange"，汇票。汇票是一种债权凭证，是一方（出票人）向另一方（受票人）签发的，要求对方立即或在可以确定的未来日期支付一定金额予收款人的无条件的书面支付命令。

3. banker's draft：银行汇票。指主要用于国内汇款或向国外汇款的由一银行签发以另一银行为付款人的汇票。由汇款人向当地银行购买银行汇票，寄交收款人，在付款地银行取款。银行汇票多为光票，不附单据，而且要求即付。银行本身进行资金调拨也用这种汇票。

4. order instrument：指示票据。指受款人抬头写的是"pay to the order of"（凭指示付给）字样的支票、汇票或期票。例如，一张支票的抬头写的是"pay to the order of A. D. Smith"或"pay to A. D. Smith or order"，则史密斯可以收取该支票的票款，也可以由史密斯加以背书转让给另一人，由受让人收取票款。

5. time/usance draft：远期汇票。指在一定的未来日期付款的汇票，付款期限一般为30天、60天、90天等。收款人取得远期汇票后，须向付款人提示，要求承兑。

6. dishonor：拒付。指付款人拒绝支付汇票或其他商业票据的票款，或承兑人拒绝承兑汇票。如汇票在合理时间内遭拒付，对持票人立即产生追索权。

7. recourse：追索权。指票据持有人在付款人拒付时，向票据的背书人或出票人索回票款的权利。

8. endorser：背书人；endorsement：背书。在票据或其他单证的背面签字，有时还写一些字句，称为背书。在票据背面签上姓名是转让票据所赋予的权利的一种手续。

9. protest：拒付证书。指当支票、汇票被付款人拒绝承兑或拒绝付款时，由付款地的公证人出具的证明。持票人须凭拒付证书进行票款的追索。

10. promissory note：本票。指出票人同意在未来某固定日期或可确定的日期无条件支付收款人一定金额的书面保证。

11. check：亦可为"cheque"，支票。它是出票人委托付款人（银行）对收款人或持票人支付一定金额的支付命令。支票的出票人必须是银行的存户。

12. open account：记账交易。指国际贸易中交货后付款的一种付款方式。依此条件交易，卖方将货物装运出口后，即将货运单据直接寄交买方提货，有关货款则记入买方账户借方，到约定期限届满时，进行结算。这种付款方式通常见于国内贸易，一般仅在一些大公司对其海外分公司或附属子公司销售产品时采用此方式交易。

13. consignment：寄售。寄售是国际贸易的一种方式。其做法是寄售人（即出口人）把货物运交事先约定的代销人保管，由代销人根据寄售协议规定的条件和办法，代寄售人在当地出售，所得货款由代销人扣除佣金和费用后，通过银行交给寄售人。

14. documents against payment（D/P）：付款交单。指国际贸易中采用托收货款的支付方式时，卖方委托代收银行于买方付清货款时将货运单据交与买方，使其提货的办法。

15. documents against acceptance（D/A）：承兑交单。指国际贸易中采用托收货款的支付方式下，出口方委托代收银行向进口方以承兑为条件交付货运单据的一种办法。

1. Review questions.

1. What are the four basic terms of payment used in international trade?

2. Under what circumstances payment by cash in advance is applicable in international trade?

3. Under what circumstances payment by open account is applicable in international trade?

4. "To order" type and "to bearer" type of draft are both transferable, what do they require respectively for transfer?

5. What is the difference between a sight draft and a usance draft?

6. What is the meaning of acceptance of a bill of exchange?

7. How can the holder of a time draft get cash before the draft matures?

8. Explain the similarities and differences between a draft and a check in nature.

9. How many parties are mainly involved in a documentary collection transaction? Who are they?

10. Who is responsible for making the presentation of documents?

11. What is the meaning of D/A and how does it work?

12. Which is much safer to the exporter, payment by D/P or by D/A? Why?

13. What are the points to which the exporter should pay attention when using collection as the means of payment?

Ⅱ Define the following terms briefly.

1. cash in advance

2. open account

3. consignment

4. draft

5. promissory note

6. documentary collection

Ⅲ Decide whether the following statements are True or False. Then put T for True or F for False in the brackets at the end of each statement.

1. The writer of a draft is the drawer. (   )

2. The draft is accepted by the exporter. (   )

3. The drawee gets credit by accepting the draft. (   )

4. The documentary bill is a bill accompanied by the contract between the drawer and the drawee. (   )

5. Protest is a document made by the payee testifying that the drawee has dishonored the bill. (   )

6. If the payment is to be made "30 days'sight", it means that the payment will have to be made 30 days after the issuing of this draft. (   )

7. Exporters always insist on payment by cash in advance when they are trading with old customers. (   )

8. Unlike the bill of exchange, the promissory note has two parties: the maker and the payee. (   )

9. A crossed check can only be paid to individuals instead of banks. (   )

10. To the seller, payment by D/P is much safer than by D/A. (   )

Ⅳ Translate the following passages into Chinese.

Both the exporter and the importer face risks in an export transaction because there is always the possibility that the other party may not fulfill the contract.

For exporters there is the risk that buyer defaults; the customers might not pay in full for the goods. There are several reasons for this: the importers might go bankrupt; a war might start or the importers' government might ban trade with the exporting country; or they might ban imports of certain commodities. Another possibility is that the importers might run into difficulties getting the foreign exchange to pay for the goods. It is even possible that the importers are not reliable and simply refuse to pay the agreed amount of money.

For importers there is the risk that the goods will be delayed and they might only receive them a long time after paying for them. This may be caused by port congestion or strikes. Delays in fulfillment of orders by exporters and difficult customs clearance in the importing country can cause loss of business. There is also a risk that the wrong goods might be sent.

It is to guard against such possibilities that different methods of payment have been developed.

V Translate the following passages into English.

汇票是一种有用的结算手段，因为：（1）提供可以在法庭使用的债务书面证据；（2）如果是即期汇票，一经出示，即能使出口商马上获得货款；如果是远期汇票，通过转让，也能使出口商马上获得货款；（3）使得进口商能够延迟到汇票到期再付款。

托收对于进口人来说具有以下的优点：（1）有利于资金融通，如能争取到远期付款，还可以不占用或少占用资金；（2）费用低，进口商可以免去申请开立信用证的手续费用。在市场竞争激烈的情况下，托收常被出口商用来作为一种争夺客户、扩大销售的竞争手段。

VI Read the following passages and answer the questions.

Every commercial transaction specifies the price of the merchandise and how and when it will be paid for. Pricing merchandise in an international transaction is more complicated than in a purely domestic setting because more than one currency is involved. Determining the precise method that will be used to make the payment is also more difficult because traditional methods like cheques and drafts pose legal technical problems in processing, clearing and enforcement. As a result, the financing terms of an international transaction are often restricted.

One of the most important elements in international commercial transaction is the currency used for invoicing. Choosing an invoicing currency involves comparing the amount of the invoice billed directly in domestic currency with the domestic currency equivalent of the amount of the invoice billed in foreign currency. Making the comparison is not a straightforward operation. Since payment will be made some time in the future, the spot rate cannot be used in making the comparison because the spot rate can, and probably will, change in the meantime. The forward rate is the obvious solution. In practice, however, the forward rate is not always directly applicable. Take the case where deliveries and invoices will occur several times over the year. Applying the appropriate forward rate to each separate invoice implies a different price for each delivery. In this case, an average forward price would probably be better.

The problem is the same for both the buyer and the seller. If the buyer agrees to be billed in foreign currency, the amount he owes will be exposed to foreign exchange risk. If the seller agrees to bill in foreign currency, the amount he receives will be exposed to foreign exchange risk. One or the other is going to have to cover his foreign exchange risk and they will both have recourse to the same financial intermediaries offering the same products. If markets were completely efficient, the choice of the invoicing currency would be completely neutral. In fact, it is not neutral at all. In the first place, not all companies have access to the same financial products at the same prices. Smaller companies are limited in the products they can use and often pay higher prices for the ones that are available to them. Furthermore, rules and regulations imposed by the monetary and tax authorities can create barriers and supplementary costs. Finally, all companies are not equally endowed with the knowledge and expertise to deal with problems associated with foreign exchange transactions. Thus, companies with the required know-how can offer the financial service of billing in their clients' domestic currency along with the merchandise they are selling and make a profit on both ends.

There can also be a speculative element involved in pricing and billing in foreign currency. A professional that follows the foreign exchange market closely is going to form opinions on how different currencies will do. He may feel that some currencies are strong and are likely to appreciate. Others, he may feel, are weak and likely to depreciate. If he has any confidence in his opinions, he will try to take advantage of them by selling in strong currencies and purchasing in weak ones. A word of caution is in order. Most corporate treasurers agree that multicurrency invoicing should exclude exotic currencies with narrow markets where financial services are costly or non-existent.

For international payments, the traditional means of settling debts in a domestic economy such as cash, credit cards and traveller's cheques, are only relevant to tourism. Bank transfers are probably the fastest and most efficient means of settling international debts. In a bank transfer, the importer instructs his bank to debit his account and credit the exporter's account at the exporter's bank. The transfer is made by telex, or SWIFT, which guarantees its speedy execution. The disadvantage of a bank transfer is that it is generated at the initiative of the importer and the exporter has no guarantee in the case of non-payment. Consequently, except for cash payment in advance, bank transfers are appropriate only for the most trustworthy relationships.

Cheques are another instrument generated at the initiative of the importer. Unlike the bank transfer, however, they are not rapid. First of all, they have to be sent, which takes time, and could get lost in the mail. Furthermore, banks credit foreign cheques only after a long delay due to difficulties in processing and clearing them.

A draft or bill of exchange is the most common means of payment in international trade. A draft is an unconditional order in writing, initiated and signed by the exporter, ordering the importer to pay on demand or at a given future date a given sum of money. It can be payable to a particular beneficiary or a bearer.

Please answer the following questions.

1. What should be noted in specifying the price of the merchandise if foreign currency is used for invoicing in an international transaction?

2. Will spot rate be always applied to the comparison between the amount of the invoice billed in domestic currency and that billed in foreign currency? Why or why not?

3. Why cannot the seller and the buyer make a neutral choice of the invoicing currency in overseas trade when both of them have equal access to the same financial intermediaries offering the same products to cover their own foreign exchange risk?

4. What are the advantages and disadvantages of bank transfers in settling international debts?

Chapter 4

The Letter of Credit (I)
信用证 (一)

In the international trade it is almost impossible to match payment with physical delivery of the goods[1], which constitutes conflicting problems for trade, since the exporter prefers to get paid before releasing the goods and the importer prefers to gain control over the goods before paying the money. The letter of credit[2] is an effective means to solve these problems. Its objective is to facilitate international payment by means of the creditworthiness of the bank. This method of payment offers security to both the seller and the buyer. The former has the security to get paid provided he presents impeccable documents while the latter has the security to get the goods required through the documents he stipulates in the credit. This bilateral security is the unique and characteristic feature of the letter of credit.

"Letter of credit" is often shortened as L/C or L. C. and is sometimes referred to as "banker's commercial letter of credit" or "documentary credit", which means that documentation is very important in international transaction. Modern credits were introduced in the second half of the 19th century and had substantial development after the First World War. A documentary credit is the written promise of a bank, undertaken on behalf of a buyer, to pay a seller the amount specified in the credit provided the seller complies with the terms and conditions set forth in the credit. The terms and conditions of a documentary credit revolve around two issues (1) the presentation of documents that evidence title to goods shipped by the seller, and (2) payment. In simple terms, banks act as intermediaries to collect payment from the buyer in exchange for the transfer of documents that enable the holder to make possession of the goods. Therefore, documentary credits provide a high level of protection and security to both buyers and sellers engaged in international trade.

4.1 The Major Contents of L/C

Letters of credit are varied in form, length, language, and stipulations. Generally speaking, however, they include the following contents.

(1) The number of the credit and the place and time of its establishment.

(2) The type of the credit.

(3) The contract on which it is based.

(4) The major parties relevant to the credit, such as the applicant, opening bank, beneficiary, advising bank, etc.

(5) The amount or value of the credit.

(6) The place and date on which the credit expires.

(7) The description of the goods including name of commodity, quantity, specifications, packing, unit price, price terms, etc.

(8) Transportation clause including the port of shipment, the port of destination, the time of shipment, whether allowing partial shipment or transshipment.

(9) Stipulations relating to the draft.

(10) Stipulations concerning the shipping documents required.

(11) Certain special clauses if any, e. g. restrictions on the carrying vessel and the route.

(12) Instructions to the negotiating bank[3].

(13) The seal or signature of the opening bank.

(14) Whether the credit follows "the uniform customs and practice for documentary credits".

4.2　Parties to the Transaction

There are four main parties to a bank documentary letter of credit transaction. They will be introduced below. Note that each party has multiple names. The name used for each party to the transaction depends upon who is speaking. Businesspeople like to use the names buyer, seller, buyer's bank and seller's bank. The banks prefer to use the names applicant, beneficiary, issuing bank, and advising bank. The four parties are as follows:

1. The Buyer (Applicant/Importer)

The buyer initiates the documentary credit process by applying to his bank to open a documentary credit naming the seller as the beneficiary. The buyer, therefore, may be called the buyer in commercial terms, the importer in economic terms, and the applicant in banking terms. They are all one and the same.

2. The Issuing (Buyer) Bank[4]

Upon instructions from the buyer, the issuing bank (typically the buyer's regular business bank) issues a documentary credit naming the seller as the beneficiary and sends it to the advising bank (typically the seller's bank).

3. The Advising (Seller's) Bank[5]

Upon instructions from the issuing bank and the buyer, the advising bank (typically the seller's bank) advising the seller of the credit. The advising bank is typically the seller's regular business bank and is in the seller's country.

4. The Seller (Beneficiary[6]/Exporter)

The seller receives notification (advice) of the credit from the advising bank, complies with the terms and conditions of the credit, and gets paid. The seller is the beneficiary of the documentary credit. The seller, therefore, may be called the seller in commercial terms, the exporter in economic terms, and the beneficiary in banking terms. They are all one and the same.

4.3   Details on Procedures

4.3.1 | The Buyer (Importer Applicant[7])

Since a documentary credit is a pledge by the bank to make payment to the seller, the bank will evaluate the creditworthiness of the buyer. If the buyer's credit and relationship with the bank is excellent, the bank will issue a credit for the full value. If the buyer's relationship is good, but perhaps not excellent, the bank will require that the buyer pledge[8] a percentage of the value of the documentary credit in cash funds. If the buyer's relationship with the bank is less established, the bank will require that the buyer pledge 100 percentage of the value of the documentary credit in cash funds in advance.

It is essential that the application for the documentary credit be in conformity with the underlying sales contract between the buyer and the seller. The buyer's instructions to the issuing bank must be clear with respect to the type of credit, the amount, duration, required documents, shipping date, expiration date, and beneficiary.

To be more specific, the wording in a documentary credit should be simple but specific. The more detailed the documentary credit is, the more likely the seller will reject it as too difficult to fulfill. It is also more likely that the banks will find a discrepancy in the details, thus voiding the credit, even though simpler terms might have been found to be in compliance with credit. The buyer should, however, completely and precisely set forth the details of the agreement as it relates to credit terms and conditions and the presentation of documents.

In addition, the documentary credit should not require documents that the seller cannot obtain; nor should it call for details in a document that are beyond the knowledge of the issuer of the document. The documents specified should be limited to those required to smoothly and completely conclude an international sale of goods.

4.3.2 | The Issuing (Buyer's) Bank

Upon receiving the buyer's application, the opening bank checks the credit of the applicant, determines whether cash security is necessary, and scrutinizes the contents of the application to see whether they generally are consistent with national and international banking and legal requirements.

If the application is satisfactory to the bank, the buyer and the opening bank will sign an agreement to open a documentary credit. The credit must be written and signed by an authorized person of the issuing bank. The issuing bank usually sends the original documentary credit to the seller (called the beneficiary) through an advising bank. The seller may request that a particular bank be the advising bank, or the buyer's bank may select one of its correspondent banks[9] in the seller's country.

4.3.3 | The Advising (Seller's) Bank

Upon receipt of the credit from the issuing bank, the advising bank informs the seller that the credit has been issued.

The advising bank will examine the credit upon receipt. The advising bank, however, examines the terms of the credit itself; it does not determine whether the terms of the credit are consistent with those of the contract between the buyer and seller, or whether the description of goods is correctly stated in accordance with the contract. The advising bank then forwards the credit to the seller.

If the advising bank is simply "advising the credit", it is under no obligation or commitment to make payment, and it will so advise the seller. In some cases the advising bank confirms (adds its guarantee to pay) the seller. In this case it becomes the confirming bank. The confirming bank can also be undertaken by another prime bank, and a fee will be charged to the buyer for this service. The advising bank can also pay or accept or negotiate the bill of exchange. The advising bank then becomes the paying bank[10], which acts as the agent of the opening bank and gets reimbursed by the opening bank after paying the beneficiary. If a bank, either nominated by the opening bank or at its own choice, buys the exporter's draft submitted to it under a credit, it is called the negotiating bank. The draft and the document will be sent to the opening bank for reimbursement.

4.3.4 | The Seller Exporter Beneficiary

In addition to assessing the reputation of the buyer prior to signing a sales contract, the seller should also assess the reputation of the buyer's (issuing) bank before agreeing to rely upon that bank for payment in a documentary credit. It is not unknown for sellers to receive fictitious documentary credits from non-existent banks and to realize their mistake after shipment.

The seller must carefully review all conditions the buyer has stipulated in the documentary credit. If the seller cannot comply with one or more of the provisions, or if the terms of the credit are not in accordance with those of the contract, the buyer should be notified immediately and asked to make an amendment to the credit.

The seller should also scrutinize the credit to make certain that it does not contain provisions that specify documents such as acceptance reports, progress reports, etc. that have to be signed or approved by the buyer. By refusing to sign such documents, the buyer can block payment. If when seller receives the L/C and is satisfied with the stipulations he will be in a position to load the goods.

After shipment of the goods, the seller will send the draft accompanied by all the necessary documents to the negotiating bank for negotiation within the validity of the L/C.

4.3.5 | The Advising Bank and the Issuing Bank

If the documents are full and correct, the bank will pay, or accept the draft and then send the documents to the paying bank (issuing bank). After careful checking of the documents, and no problems are found, the paying bank will reimburse the money to the negotiating bank in accordance with the terms of the credit. The issuing bank (paying bank) then presents the documents to the buyer for payment of the amount due or acceptance of the draft. With the documents, the buyer can take delivery of the goods.

4.4　Conformity with the Documentary Credit

The letter of credit provides security to both the exporter and the importer. However, it only assures payment to the beneficiary provided the terms and conditions of the credit are fulfilled. It does not guarantee that the goods purchased will be those invoiced or shipped. It is stipulated in Article 4 of the Uniform Customs and Practice for Documentary Credit that "in credit operations all parties concerned deal in documents, and not in goods, service and/or other performance to which the documents may relate." That is to say the banks are only concerned with the documents representing the goods instead of the underlying contracts. They have no legal obligation whether the goods comply with the contract. They will be considered as having fulfilled their responsibility so long as all the documents comply with the stipulations of the credit. The quality and quantity of goods shipped, although specified in the documents, ultimately depends on the seller who has manufactured, packaged, and arranged shipment for the goods. If the importer finds any problems with the goods, e. g. inferior quality or insufficient quantity, he has to contact or even take legal action against the exporter instead of the bank so long as the documents are "proper" on their face.

4.5　How to Handle Documentary Discrepancies

Despite the carefulness on the part of exporters, about half of the documents presented to banks have discrepancies that cause banks to reject payments. In such a case, an exporter can try the following methods to get paid.

(1) Correct the discrepancies and resubmit the documents and drafts within the validity of the L/C. The exporter should not wait until the last day to present documents, otherwise they might not have the time at all to correct the discrepancies and resubmit the documents.

(2) Request the importer to waive discrepancies if they do not materially affect the shipment.

The importer can give the issuing bank the authority to pay, accept, or negotiate even if there are discrepancies, but the importer may request a price reduction or otherwise waive from the exporter.

(3) Provide a documentary discrepancy guarantee if, unwilling to wait for the waiver, the exporter is confident that the importer will accept the discrepancy.

The exporter can ask a party that is acceptable to the paying bank to issue a guarantee in favor of the paying bank. The exporter himself can also issue an indemnity if that is acceptable. With such arrangements, the paying bank pays under reserve. If the importer refuses to take up the documents due to the discrepancy, payment must be refunded to the paying bank.

(4) Submit the documents on collection basis.

When the exporter is unable to do the above, he will not be able to get paid under the documentary credit. Then he can use collection in which the importer should be the drawee. Since the original draft is drawn on a bank under a documentary credit, a new draft on the importer should be issued to replace the original one.

4.6 Regarding the Role of Banks

It is important to note that documentary credit procedures are not infallible. Things can and do go wrong. Since banks act as intermediaries between the buyer and seller, both look to the banks as protectors of their interests. However, while banks have clear-cut responsibilities, they are also shielded from certain problems deemed to be out of their control or responsibility. Several instances are as follows:

(1) Banks act upon specific instructions given by the applicant (buyer) in the documentary credit. Buyer's instructions left out of the credit by mistakes or omitted because "we've always done it that way". The buyer, therefore, should take great care in preparing the application so that it gives complete and clear instructions.

(2) Banks are required to act in good faith and exercise reasonable care to verify that the documents submitted appear to be as listed in the credit. They are, however, under no obligation to confirm the authenticity of the documents submitted.

(3) Banks are not liable nor can they be held accountable for the acts of third parties. Third parties include freight forwarders, forwarding agents, customs authorities, insurance companies, and other banks. Specifically, they are not responsible for delays, wars, civil commotions, strikes, lockouts, or other causes beyond their control.

(4) Banks also assume no liability or responsibility for loss arising out of delays or loss in transit of messages, letters, documents, etc.

(5) Because banks deal in documents and not goods, they assume no responsibility regarding the quantity or quality of goods shipped. They are only concerned that documents presented appear on their face to be consistent with the terms and conditions of the documentary credit. Any dispute

as to quality or quantity of goods delivered must be settled between the buyer and the seller.

(6) So long as the documents presented to the banks appear on their face to comply with the terms and conditions of the credit, banks may accept them and initiate the payment process as stipulated in the documentary credit.

If there are any conclusions to be made from the above, they are: first, that the buyer and seller should know each other and have at least some basis of trust to be doing business in the first place, and second, that all parties to the transaction should take responsibility to follow through on their part carefully.

4.7   Limitations with Documentary Credits

It has already been mentioned that the letter of credit has greatly facilitated and promoted international trade. However, like any other methods of payment, it is not perfect. It cannot provide absolute security for the contracting parties. The seller may sustain losses because of the buyer's delay or even failure in the establishment of credit. The buyer may suffer losses as a result of the documents presented by the seller which do not truly represent the goods shipped. And it is not absolutely avoidable that the bank may become insolvent or bankrupt. Besides, it is more expensive to use the letter of credit than remittance or collection as the bank will charge its client for all the services it provides. So the letter of credit may not be the most ideal method of payment for a particular transaction, and the contracting parties should make their best choice according to the specific conditions.

New Words and Expressions

impeccable	a.	无缺点的
stipulation	n.	规定；条件
expire	v.	到期
transshipment	n.	转运
applicant	n.	（开证）申请人
beneficiary	n.	受益人
pledge	n./v.	抵押；以……为担保
underlying	a.	作为基础的
discrepancy	n.	不符点，差异
void	v./a.	使……无效；无效的
reimburse	v.	偿付

fictitious	*a.*	假的
scrutinize	*v.*	仔细地审查
waive	*v.*	放弃
waiver	*n.*	放弃
indemnity	*n.*	赔偿保证
infallible	*a.*	绝对无误的，绝对可靠的
authenticity	*n.*	真实性
accountable	*a.*	应负责的
lockout	*n.*	闭厂，停工
partial shipment		分批装运
issuing bank		开证行
advising bank		通知行
cash security		现金抵押
acceptance report		验收报告
progress report		进度报告
under reserve		有保留的，有条件的
freight forwarder		货物运输行

1. to match payment with physical delivery of the goods：这里指付款和实际交货同时进行。"match" 是 "使一致，使互相配合" 的意思，"physical" 是 "实际上的" 的意思。

2. letter of credit：信用证，缩写为 L/C。信用证是银行根据进口商的请求开立的，由该银行承诺，只要出口商履行信用证条款，提交符合信用证规定的单据，就向出口商付款的书面保证。

3. negotiating bank：议付行。是指愿意买入受益人交来的跟单汇票的银行。单证相符，可以议付；单证不符，有权拒付。议付行有权向开证行索偿。

4. issuing bank：开证行。指在国际贸易中采用信用证付款方式时开立信用证的银行。

5. advising bank：通知行。指受信用证开证行的委托，将信用证转交给出口商的银行。它只证明信用证的真实性，并不承担其他的义务。通知行一般是开证银行在出口人所在地的分行、往来行或代理行。

6. beneficiary：受益人。在国际贸易中使用的信用证内，所列获得开证银行授予开具汇票收取货款权利的人即为受益人，通常是出口商。

7. applicant：信用证申请人。在国际贸易中采用信用证支付方式，由进口商向银行申请开立信用证，即为信用证申请人。

8. pledge：抵押。债务人把自己的财产抵押给债权人，作为清偿债务的保证。

9. correspondent bank：代理银行，往来银行。本国银行经营外汇业务可在国外设立分支行，但一家银行不可能在世界各地遍设分支机构，在未设分支机构的地方就觅当地的银行与其签订代理协定，即成为往来行或代理行。

10. paying bank：付款行。是指信用证上指定的付款银行。信用证以进口地货币开出时，开证行为付款行；信用证以第三国货币开出时，付款行为第三国银行，负责付款给汇票持有人。

Ⅰ Review questions.

1. Why can the documentary credit solve the possible problems arising from the distrust between the exporter and the importer?

2. What are the procedures of the L/C transaction?

3. What measures does the issuing bank take to prevent the importer's dishonor when the issuing bank approves his application for a letter of credit?

4. When and by whom should the documents be carefully checked to see whether they are full and correct in the course of L/C transaction?

5. What are the major contents of the L/C?

6. What is the meaning of "banks deal in documents and not goods in the L/C procedures"?

7. What methods can the exporter adopt to get paid when discrepancies are found in the documents presented to the bank?

8. What are the limitations of L/C payment?

Ⅱ Define the following terms briefly.

1. letter of credit

2. issuing bank

3. negotiating bank

4. confirming bank

Ⅲ Decide whether the following statements are True or False. Then put T for True or F for False in the brackets at the end of each statement.

1. The opening bank bears the prime liability for payment. (   )

2. In terms of documentary discrepancies, any discrepancies, however minor, should be asked to

amend. (　　　)

3. Banks deal in documents and not goods, therefore, they are only concerned that documents presented appear on their face to comply with the terms and conditions of the documentary credits. (　　　)

4. So far, documentary credits are the most ideal method of payment to provide security for both buyers and sellers. Therefore, in whatever conditions, L/C should be the first consideration in the method of payment for transactions. (　　　)

5. The credit is legally independent of the underlying transaction. (　　　)

6. A letter of credit is a conditional undertaking to make payment in the case of conformity. (　　　)

7. An issuing bank must always reimburse the advising bank if the latter pays the credit. (　　　)

8. After issuance of the letter of credit, the issuing bank may refuse payment if the applicant becomes bankrupt. (　　　)

9. In any disputes over the terms and conditions of a credit, international law will be referred to for interpretation. (　　　)

10. Confirmation to credit may be given by an advising bank at the request of the issuing bank. (　　　)

Ⅳ Translate the following passages into Chinese.

The issuance of a letter of credit acts to facilitate international trade in that a bank pledges its credit on behalf of its customer. After signing a contract, the importer requests his bank to issue a letter of credit in favour of the exporter. Assuming that the credit risk is acceptable, the bank opens its letter of credit, which, in essence, says to the exporter: "We, the bank, promise that we will pay you when you submit certain documents evidencing that you have made the agreed-upon shipment." The bank is in effect putting itself in the place of the importer. It is lending its name and its good offices to the importer so that the exporter can be assured that he will receive payment.

An acceptance credit is a credit available by acceptance, under which a nominated bank is authorized to accept. It must be a usance credit and the draft thereunder must be a time bill drawn on the issuing bank, the advising bank, or any other drawee bank. By accepting the draft under the credit, the accepting bank signifies its commitment to pay the face value of the credit at maturity. The beneficiary will discount the accepted draft with his own bank or in local money market if he wishes to get paid immediately.

Ⅴ Translate the following passage into English.

国际贸易中最常见的是议付信用证，议付信用证指允许受益人向某一指定银行或任何银行交单议付的信用证。通常在单证相符的条件下，银行扣取垫付利息和手续费后，即将货款垫付给受益人。议付信用证可分为公开议付信用证和限制议付信用证，前者受益人可选择一家银行作为议付行，后者则由开证行在信用证中指定一家银行为议付行。开证行对议付行承担付款责任。

VI **Read the following passages and answer the questions.**

Banker's Letter of Guarantee

In international trade, each party of the contract wants to be ensured that the other party is in a position to honor its commitment as contracted. Such security may be obtained through banks in the form of letter of guarantee. A banker's letter of guarantee (L/G) or bond is a contract by which a bank (the guarantor) agrees to pay another's debt or to perform another's obligation only if other individual or legal entity fails to pay or perform. A banker's letter of guarantee is usually a separate contract from the principal agreement, and therefore the letter of guarantee is secondarily liable to the third person.

1. Parties to a Letter of Guarantee

1) Principal

The principal is the person who applies for the issuance of L/G. For instance, in loan guarantee, the principal is the borrower.

2) Guarantor

The guarantor is a bank or a financial institution, which issues a letter of guarantee undertaking to make payments to the beneficiary in the event of non-performance of a contract by the principal.

3) Beneficiary

The beneficiary is the person in whose favor the guarantee is issued. For example, in import guarantee, the beneficiary is the exporter. He will obtain a certain sum of money if the principal fails to fulfill its obligations.

2. Types of Letter of Guarantee

The main types of the bank guarantee are tender guarantee and performance guarantee.

1) Tender guarantee, tender bond, or bid bond

A tender guarantee is a guarantee issued by a bank or a financial institution at the request of a tenderer (the principal) in favor of a party inviting tenders abroad (the beneficiary), whereby the guarantor undertakes, in the event of default by the principal in the obligations resulting from the submission of tender, to make payment to the beneficiary within the limits of a stated sum of money. As a rule, the guaranteed amount is 1% −5% of the amount offered. The period of validity is usually between three and six months until the signing of the contract or issuing of a performance bond.

2) Performance guarantee or performance bond

A performance guarantee is a letter of guarantee issued by a bank or financial institution (the guarantor) at the request of one party of a contract (the principal) to another party of a contract (the beneficiary), whereby the guarantor guarantees, in the event of the principal's failure to perform the contract in compliance with its terms, or make payment to the beneficiary within the limits of a stated sum of money. The guaranteed amount is usually 10% of the contract amount. The bond remains valid for the full amount until complete performance of the contract.

The following are abstracts of two performance letters of guarantee in international sales of goods.

(1) Abstracts of an import L/G to Chinese exporter by foreign bank at the request of foreign importer.

"... We, upon receipt of your statement, certifying that buyer failed to fulfill any of the said contract terms and specifying the fixed amount to be claimed, accompanied by the certificate issued by the Bank of China, Shanghai, stating that sellers' statement is true and genuine, shall immediately remit the amount to your account with Bank of China, Shanghai."

(2) Abstracts of an export L/G to foreign buyer by the Bank of China at the request of Chinese exporter.

"At the request of xxx (hereinafter referred to as the Seller) and in consideration of your agreeing to pay to the Seller, in accordance with the contract signed by you (hereinafter referred to as the Buyer) and the Seller, the price for the ship in instalments before delivery of the ship, we, the Bank of China, hereby guarantee to repay you upon your demand all or part of the aforesaid instalments with interest if and when the aforesaid instalments become repayable to you and the Seller fails to effect the repayment as required by the contract stipulation."

3. Differences Between a Letter of Guarantee and a Letter of Credit

(1) In terms of the issuing bank's liability, the issuing bank of a letter of credit is primarily liable to the beneficiary, no matter whether the applicant is in default or not; whereas under a letter of guarantee, the issuing bank is liable only if the principal fails to fulfill his obligations. (Note: In practice, some letters of guarantee state that the beneficiary asks the guarantor to make payment first. In this case, the issuing bank undertakes the primary liability. Thus whether the guarantor is primarily liable to the beneficiary depends on the terms.)

(2) The letter of credit is used in the condition that the international sales contracts of goods are smoothly performed. The seller (beneficiary) is assured to get payment if his documents are in conformity with the credit. The letter of guarantee, however, is used only in the event of non-performance of a contract by the principal.

(3) As far as the basis of payment is concerned, the documentary letter of credit calls for documents, which are in conformity with the credit and has no relevance with the sales contract. But under a letter of guarantee, when the beneficiary may claim for payment with the guarantor, the latter usually needs to verify that its principal actually breaches the contract and refuses to make reimbursement. Thus the guarantor is usually involved in the disputes of parties to the contract.

Please answer the following questions.

1. What is a letter of guarantee?
2. Under what circumstances is the L/G adopted?
3. How many parties are usually involved in L/G?
4. Can you describe the two types of L/G?
5. What differences are there between L/C and L/G?
6. Does L/G have more advantages over the L/C? Why?

Chapter 5

The Letter of Credit (II)
信用证（二）

Letters of credit fall under several categories depending on their function, form and mechanism. Here are the major types of credits.

5.1 Clean Credit and Documentary Credit

Credits that only require clean draft, i. e. draft not accompanied with shipping documents, for payment are clean credit. They are generally used in non-trade settlement or in payment in advance by means of the L/C. Most of the credits used in international trade are documentary credits, i. e. credits used in international trade are documentary credits that require shipping documents to be presented together with the draft.

5.2 Revocable Credit and Irrevocable Credit

Documentary credit may be issued by the buyer and issuing bank as revocable or irrevocable. The buyer must indicate either revocable or irrevocable on the application form to the issuing bank. Each has a distinct advantage for buyers and sellers.

Revocable credits are, conversely, of great importance to the seller as the credit may be canceled at any time, even while the goods are in transit, giving the seller no security whatsoever. Although revocable credits are sometimes used between affiliated firms, sellers are advised never to accept a revocable credit as a payment method.

An irrevocable credit constitutes a firm contractual obligation on the part of the issuing bank[1] to honour the terms of payment of the credit as issued. The buyer and issuing bank cannot amend or cancel the credit without the express approval of the seller. Irrevocable credits are of advantage to the seller. As long as the seller complies with the terms of the credit, payment will be made by the issuing bank. Virtually all documentary credits issued today are irrevocable and so state on their face (on the face of the documentary credit itself). Sellers are advised to insist upon an irrevocable credit from the buyer.

According to UCP 400 Article 7-c, if an L/C does not say it is irrevocable, it is then revocable. However, UCP 500 Article 6-c stipulates that in the absence of indication, the credit shall be deemed to be irrevocable, and UCP 600 Article 3 simply says that a credit is irrevocable even if there is no indication to that effect. Then if he receives an L/C that does not clearly indicate whether it is revocable or irrevocable, the beneficiary should find out first whether the L/C is subject to the interpretation of UCP 400, UCP 500 or that of UCP 600. [2]

5.3 Confirmed Credit and Unconfirmed Credit

Confirmed letters of credit carry the commitment to pay for both the issuing and the advising bank. The advising bank adds its undertaking to pay to that of the issuing bank, and its commitment is independent of that of the issuing bank. Therefore, when documents conforming to the requirements of the confirmed documentary credit are presented in a timely manner, the payment from the advising bank to the seller is final in all respects as far as the seller is concerned.

Confirmed irrevocable letters of credit give the seller the greatest protection, since sellers can rely on the commitment of two banks to make payment. The confirming bank will pay even if the issuing bank cannot or will not honor the draft for any reason whatever. In accordance with the additional risk assumed by the banks, however, confirmed, irrevocable letters of credit are more expensive than unconfirmed letters of credit, and confirmed, irrevocable letters of credit are used most frequently in transactions involving buyers in developing countries.

Under an unconfirmed documentary credit only the issuing bank assumes the undertaking to pay, thus payment is the sole responsibility of the issuing bank. An unconfirmed documentary credit will be communicated (advised) to the seller through a bank most likely located in the seller's country, and the related shipping and other documents will usually be presented to that bank for eventual payment. However, the final responsibility for payment rests with the issuing bank alone. The advising bank may or may not negotiate the seller's draft depending on the degree of political and financial risk anticipated in the issuing bank's country, as well as the credit standing of the issuing bank.

In dealing with a readily identifiable issuing bank in a developed country, an unconfirmed documentary credit is very probably an acceptable, safe instrument for most sellers. If you have any doubt about the issuing bank and its standing, you can check the name through a local bank with an international department.

5.4 Sight Credit and Usance Credit

A sight credit is one where payment can be made upon presentation of the draft and impeccable documents by the beneficiary to the bank. It gives the beneficiary better security and helps him speed up his capital turnover. Most of China's export contracts stipulate for sight credit in payment terms. Obviously, a sight credit calls for a sight draft. A usance credit, also referred to as term credit or time credit, is one by which payment cannot be made until a specific date or a specific time after the date or after sight. The usance varies from 30, 60, 90 days to as long as 180 days or even longer. It is also clear that this type of credit requires a usance draft. If the beneficiary wishes to get payment before the maturity of the draft, he can ask the bank to discount the acceptance[3], and then immediately pay him the net proceeds, i. e. the face value of the draft minus the discount charges.

5.5   Non-draft Credit

There is a modern tendency for payment to be made by presentation of the documents without the formality of drawing and presenting a draft. Such credits are non-draft credit. They mainly include payment credit and deferred payment credit which are respectively similar to sigh credit and usance credit with the difference that no draft is drawn and presented in the case of non-draft credit.

5.6   Transferable Credit and Non-transferable Credit

Transferable documentary credit is one where the beneficiary may request that part of the proceeds (payment) of the credit be transferred to one or more other parties who become second beneficiaries. A transferable credit is used by a "middleman" who acts as an intermediary between a buyer and a seller to earn a profit for structuring the transaction.

The buyer opens a documentary credit naming the intermediary as the beneficiary. The intermediary then transfers both the obligation to supply the goods and part of the proceeds of the credit to the actual supplier.

In the process, the intermediary commits little or no funds to the transaction. This form of payment is often used in situations where the intermediary does not wish the buyer and the actual supplier to know each other's identity. At the time of opening the credit the buyer must request that it should be made transferable, and the credit itself, as issued, must be clearly marked as "transferable". Terms such as "divisible", "fractionally", "assignable", or "transmissible" do not make the credit transferable.

Transferable credits can be transferred once. A second beneficiary cannot transfer to a third beneficiary, and transferable credits can be transferred in whole or in part. If a credit does not specify whether it is transferable, it should be regarded as a non-transferable documents according to the credit stipulations. In addition, when the L/C is transferred, the first beneficiary is still responsible for fulfilling the contract between him and the importer.

5.7　Deferred Payment Credit

A documentary credit available by deferred payment will specifically nominate a paying bank and indicate a fixed or determinable date on which payment is to be effected.

By nominating a bank in the credit as the paying bank, the issuing bank authorizes such bank to effect payment under the credit at the fixed or determinable date indicated in the credit and undertakes to reimburse that bank on the due date. In such cases the beneficiary will present documents to the paying bank and such bank will settle at the stipulated date. The documents will, however, be passed by the paying bank to the issuing bank immediately.

If the credit is confirmed by the advising bank, the beneficiary will receive an undertaking from that bank that will effect settlement at the agreed future date. If on the other hand the credit has not been confirmed by the advising bank, the beneficiary will merely receive an acknowledgement for documents which conform to the credit terms and conditions, and an indication to the effect that the advising bank has been authorized to settle at the future date. This will not however be a commitment on the part of the advising bank to make such settlement. In both cases the beneficiary will have rights against the issuing bank.

A deferred payment credit is used to extend the normal 180-day payment terms of a trade L/C when banker's acceptances over 180 days cannot be discounted in the market. Under such an arrangement, the seller ships the goods, presents shipping documents promptly after shipment and gives permission to release the documents to the buyer. He will be paid in a specified period of time counted from the date of issue or presentation of shipping documents. A draft would not normally be called for although a sight draft could be drawn and presented.

The seller has to wait for funds under a deferred payment credit since discounting is not available; nevertheless, he can use the credit as collateral to borrow.

5.8　Revolving Credit

A revolving documentary credit is an obligation on the part of an issuing bank to restore a credit to the original amount after it has been utilized, without the need for amendment. A revolving documentary credit can be revocable or irrevocable, cumulative or non-cumulative, and can "revolve "in number, time, or value. A revolving credit is designed to facilitate ongoing relationships between buyers and sellers where buyers wish to purchase either (1) a set maximum value of product per period of time, (2) a certain maximum value of product, or (3) as much product as the seller can produce or supply.

(1) Number/time. In this form, the credit may be available for a set value for a set number of times — for example, US$10,000 per month for twelve months. Each month the seller may draw up to US$10,000 and the issuing bank will automatically reinstate it for another US$10,000 for twelve

months. This form of credit may be cumulative or non-cumulative.

(2) Cumulative. In a cumulative revolving credit any sum not utilized by the beneficiary during an installment period may be carried over and added to a subsequent installment period. Using the above example, if the beneficiary only utilizes US$8,000 the first month, the value of the credit the following month increases to US$12,000. With a total value of US$120,000, this cumulative revolving credit can be utilized for a cumulative total of up to US$10,000 the first month, US$20,000 the second month, etc.

(3) Non-cumulative. In this credit any value not utilized during an installment period may not be carried over and added to a subsequent installment period.

Revolving documentary credits are used in situations where a buyer and seller agree that goods will be shipped on a continuing basis and where the parties to the credit wish to establish one credit to handle all the shipments rather than to establish individual letters of credit for each shipment.

5.9 Standby Credit

A standby documentary credit is an obligation on the part of an issuing bank to pay a beneficiary in the case of the non-performance of the applicant[4].

In a standard commercial documentary credit the issuing bank has an obligation to pay the beneficiary based on the performance of the beneficiary (the beneficiary's fulfillment of the terms and conditions of the credit). In a standby documentary credit the issuing bank is obligated to pay the beneficiary based on the nonperformance of the applicant.

Standby documentary credits are, therefore, also called "non-performing letters of credit", because they are only used as a backup payment method if the collection on a primary payment method is past due. A standby documentary credit is generally obtained and held in reserve or paid out only as a result of non-compliance with some underlying contract between the parties involved.[5] Exporters may be asked to provide a standby documentary credit as a requirement of working on complicated infrastructure projects abroad or as an assurance under a contractual obligation that they will perform as agreed. If the goods are provided, or the service performed, as agreed, the standby documentary credit will expire unused. The exporter must also be certain that the documents submitted are exactly as required in the documentary credit.

Since the beneficiary (typically the seller) of a standby documentary credit can draw from it on demand, the buyer assumes added risk.

5.10 Red Clause Credit

A red clause documentary credit is an obligation on the part of an issuing bank to guarantee advance payments made by a confirming or any other nominated bank to the beneficiary prior to presentation of documents.

A red clause documentary credit is a mechanism for providing funding to the seller prior to the shipment of goods. It is often used to assist manufacturers in paying for labor and materials used in manufacturing or to middlemen who need financing to conclude a transaction. Ultimately, it is a form of financing provided by the buyer to the seller.

A red clause credit is so named because the clause authorizing advance payment is traditionally written in red ink. The clause states the amount(s) of the authorized advances and any terms and conditions of the advance(s). The authorized advance may be for up to the full amount of the credit.

A red clause credit is useful to the buyer in situations where the supplier is trusted and the difficulty of obtaining the raw materials/goods directly is high. The disadvantage to the buyer is that the seller may not perform and the buyer may totally lose the paid advances. The advantage to the seller is that another party is providing financing for the transaction. The disadvantage to the seller is that he still maintains responsibility for ultimate delivery of goods, and he is liable for repayment of the full amount of the credit, plus costs, if unable to perform.

5.11　Back to Back Credit

A back to back L/C is opened at the request of an exporter who is the beneficiary of an export L/C, which is offered as the security for the back-to-back L/C. The concept involves the issue of a second credit applied by the exporter in favor of his supplier. As applicant for this second credit, the exporter is responsible for reimbursing the bank for payments made under it, regardless of whether or not he himself is paid under the first credit. There is, however, not compulsion for the bank to issue the second credit, and, in fact, many banks will not do so.

The second credit must be so worded as to produce the documents (apart from the commercial invoice) required by the first credit — and to produce them within the time limits set by the first credit — in order that exporter, as the beneficiary under the first credit, may be entitled to be paid within those limits.

There is risk to banks that makes them unwilling to open a back-to-back L/C. For example, if the exporter cannot perform its duty well when the issuing bank of the back to-back L/C has fulfilled its obligation to pay for the documents, then the issuing bank will face a loss because, on one hand, it cannot get paid from the exporter and, on the other hand, it cannot get paid from the issuing bank of the first L/C as it is unable to provide the documents required by the first L/C.

Therefore, banks often insist that the back-to-back L/C be fully secured by the exporter or the first L/C to be opened in favor of the issuing bank of the back-to-back L/C so it can provide its own documents to be paid. In all cases, banks will want to make sure that there is a good coordination between the terms of the original L/C and those of the back-to-back L/C in order to eliminate the risks they might otherwise face.

New Words and Expressions

category	n.	种类
honour	v.	履行
commitment	n.	承担的责任
negotiate	v.	议付
maturity	n.	到期，期满
proceeds	n.	货款
discount	v.	贴现
middleman	n.	中间人
intermediary	n.	中间商
authorize	v.	授权
collateral	a.	附带的
cumulative	a.	累积的
reinstate	v.	恢复到
installment	n.	分期付款
non-performance		未履行
reimburse	v.	偿付
compulsion	n.	强制
secure	v.	获得，保障

fall under		归为……类
clean credit		光票信用证
non-trade settlement		非贸易结算
revocable credit		可撤销信用证
irrevocable credit		不可撤销信用证
confirmed credit		保兑信用证
credit standing		资信状况
sight credit		即期信用证
usance credit		远期信用证
capital turnover		资金周转
face value		面值
transferable credit		可转让信用证
non-draft credit		无汇票信用证
deferred payment nominate		延期信用证

revolving credit	循环信用证
standby credit	备用信用证
red clause credit	红色条款信用证
back-to-back credit	背对背信用证

1. on the part of the issuing bank：在开证行方面。"on the part of"经常用来表示"proceeding from"或"done by"。

2. ... whether the L/C is subject to interpretation of UCP 400, UCP 500 or that of UCP 600.
……信用证是否应该根据 UCP 400、UCP 500 或 UCP 600 来进行解释。
UCP（Uniform Customs and Practice for Documentary Credits）：跟单信用证统一惯例。指巴黎国际商会于 1930 年制订的银行处理信用证业务方面的国际贸易惯例。目前被世界上160 多个国家和地区银行采用的《跟单信用证统一惯例》是于 2007 年修订，并于 2007年 7 月 1 日起实施的国际商会第 600 号出版物。

3. ask the bank to discount the acceptance：要求银行对汇票贴现。具备转让条件的远期汇票等票据未到期，持票人要求取得票款而将票据卖给银行或贴现商并支付利息的行为称为贴现。

4. in the case of the non-performance of the applicant
"in the case of"意为"在……的情况下"，它不同于"in case of"。后者的含义为"万一，以防"。此句的意义为"在信用证申请人不履行付款义务时"。

5. A standby documentary credit is generally obtained or held in reserve or paid out only as a result of noncompliance with some underlying contract between the parties involved.　只有当当事人双方出现未履行合同的有关条例，通常才获得此类信用证或作为备用或对此信用证进行支付。

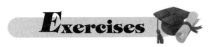

■ Review questions.

1. What is the difference between revocable L/C and irrevocable L/C?

2. Why is the confirmed irrevocable L/C more secure to the seller than others?

3. What is the main reason for the fact that deferred payment L/C cannot be discounted at the discounting house?

4. How many times can a transferable L/C be transferred?

5. When is a revolving L/C used?

6. Please illustrate how a cumulative revolving credit works?

7. Under what type of L/C, can the issuing bank authorize the paying bank to make the payment in advance to the exporter?

8. What is the difference between a back to back credit and a transferable credit?

Ⅱ Define the following terms briefly.

1. sight credit

2. usance credit

3. standby credit

4. confirmed L/C

5. transferable L/C

6. back-to back L/C

7. red clause L/C

Ⅲ Decide whether the following statements are True or False. Then put T for True or F for False in the brackets at the end of each statement.

1. In the case of a deferred payment credit, there is no need to draw a draft. (   )

2. The beneficiary must do the following to be paid, he must present documents which conform to the credit, and must present them on or before the expiry date. (   )

3. Only the beneficiary must approve any amendments to a confirmed irrevocable letter of credit. (   )

4. In a documentary credit, terms such as "divisible", "assignable", and "transmissible" carry the same meaning and have the same effect as the term "transferable" and are interchangeably used with such a term. (   )

5. When a letter of credit is confirmed, all of the risks are then borne by the confirming bank free of charge. (   )

6. A transferable credit can be transferred by the original beneficiary to several other (second) beneficiaries for more than once. (   )

7. As a back-to-back L/C is used, it is the responsibility of the second applicant (i. e. the exporter) to reimburse the bank for payments made under it, regardless of whether or not he himself is paid under the first credit. (   )

8. According to UCP 600, the credit should clearly indicate whether it is revocable or irrevocable. In the absence of such indication, the credit shall be deemed to be revocable. (   )

9. In a red clause credit, the advising bank itself gives a packing loan to the beneficiary. (   )

10. The sum of the transferred credit may not be the same as in the credit before transfer. (   )

Ⅳ Translate the following passages into Chinese.

The use of the letters of credit for financing export shipments has long been popular with exporters. They have found that this means of arranging payment affords a high degree of protection against the risk inevitably arising in export business. This is particularly true when the letter of credit is issued in irrevocable form and is further confirmed by a bank of unquestioned standing in the exporter's country. A letter of credit is only as good as the bank which issues it and, if confirmed, the bank which confirms it.

Except in their general form and phraseology, letters of credit vary greatly because each one is drawn to cover the requirements of an individual transaction. Such credits, however, have certain characteristics in common. All contain authorizations for the seller of goods to draw upon a bank that promise to honor the drafts, although in the case of revocable credits this promise is contingent upon the letter of credit not having been cancelled. The bank thus places the security of its name behind the buyer; and in the case of irrevocable credits this security cannot be taken away except with the consent of the beneficiary. Here lies the main point of attractiveness of letters of credit from the seller's point of view. The exporter is assured of obtaining payment for his or her goods, provided the terms specified in the letter of credit are met.

Ⅴ Translate the following passage into English.

在国际贸易中，通常有买方从卖方定期连续购买的情况出现。为了便于相同的买卖双方间的这种反复交易，可采用循环信用证。开证行只需开出一张而不是多张一段时间内有效的固定金额的信用证。一批货装运及单证被出示和兑付后，信用证自动恢复原样以便于另一批货的装运。这就免去了每发一批货都要开一张新的信用证的麻烦。这种信用证可以是撤销的，也可以是不撤销的，但受时间期限的约束。

Ⅵ Read the following passages and answer the questions.

International Payments

In international economic intercourses, the residents of one country engage in a variety of transactions with residents of other countries. These transactions such as exports and imports of goods, services rendered, cash payments and receipts, gifts, loans and investments, and other transactions, are interrelated in many ways, and together they comprise the international payments of a country.

International transactions shown in the balance of international payments (commonly known as balance of payment) statements of most countries may be grouped in several ways. Three distinctions have a major analytical significance: (1) the distinction between real or current transactions such as goods or services and financial or capital transactions, (2) the distinction between long-term (non-liquid) and short-term (liquid) financial transactions, and (3) the distinction between transactions of national monetary authorities (central banks and Treasury) on the one hand and all other transactions on the other hand. A balance of payments should make these distinctions in one way or another.

Balance of Payments Statements are compiled on a double-entry system of accounting. All receipts (increases in liabilities or decreases in assets) are recorded as credit items (plus items), while all payments (increases in assets and decreases in liabilities) are recorded as debit items (minus items). As every transaction relating to international payments involves records both on the debit side and credit side with the same amount, the total amount of debit items in the statement should, on principle, equal that of the credit items, thus bringing the statement into equilibrium.

Statements of balance of international payments usually present three kinds of transactions: (1) Current Account, (2) Capital Account, and (3) Balancing Account.

1. Current Account

The current amount includes three sub-accounts: (1) imports and exports of merchandise, (2) services, and (3) unilateral transfer.

For most countries, the values of the merchandise entries are by far the biggest in the current account that cover imports and exports of goods. The net balance on merchandise transactions is called the trade balance. Exports are entered in the credit side while imports the debit side.

Services include all receipts and payments between the residents and foreigners on transportation, insurance, travel, communication, investment returns such as interest, dividends, and profits generated from loans and investments, technology (royalties and any other services). Receipts of services are entered in the credit side while payments the debit side.

Unilateral transfers are transactions that are only one-sided since there is no offsetting payment. Private transfer consists of institutional expenditures for missionary, charitable, educational and others of like purposes, and personal remittances. Government transfers include pension, tax receipt from non-residents, non-military grants and others. A net debit in transfer payments increases the country's international payments in the same way as its imports of goods and services. Similarly, a net credit in transfers adds to the country's international receipts.

2. Capital Account

The capital account records the changes in a country's international financial assets and liabilities, but excludes changes in official reserves over the balance of payment's period. Capital transactions, whether long-term or short-term, are customarily designated as capital inflows or outflows. Capital inflows are credit items (or plus items) while outflows debit items (or minus items).

Capital account usually consists of the following three sub-accounts.

(1) Direct investment: It is usually defined as investment in enterprises located in the country bur effectively controlled by residents in another country.

(2) Portfolio investment: The term designated all long-term capital flows that do not give investors effective control over their investments. It covers all international transactions in assets and liabilities (other than direct investment) with an original maturity of more than one year to which domestic residents are creditors or debtors. These transactions involve mainly loans and securities.

(3) Short-term capital: It records the net changes in international assets and liabilities with an

original maturity of one year or less in which domestic residents (excluding official monetary institutions) are creditors or debtors. Short-term capital flows include the normal, everyday receipts and payments arising out of international trade and finance that occur mainly through shift in the ownership of demand deposits and other liquid deposits in banks at home and abroad. Estimates of private short-term capital movement are the least reliable of the balance of payments items because of their variety, intangibility and private character.

3. Balancing Account

Balancing account consists of (1) errors and omissions and (2) official reserve assets.

As the balance of payments uses a double-entry system of accounting, total credits and debits must always equal each other. However, two offsetting entries may not be made explicitly and simultaneously for each transaction; instead, different items are recorded separately on the basis of statistical or aggregate data drawn from a variety of sources. Since at least some of these sources are incomplete and inaccurate, an item called "errors and omission"is needed to bring the total debits and credits into an arithmetic equilibrium.

Official reserve assets comprise: (1) foreign exchange in convertible currencies, (2) reserve position in the International Monetary Fund, (3) allocation of Special Drawing Rights, and (4) Gold Stock.

The net official reserve account shows the net foreign transactions of, the central bank, the central government Treasury, and possibly an exchange stabilization agency that collectively constitutes the country's monetary authorities. These authorities hold the country's official reserve assets. The foreign transactions of these authorities provide the residual compensation required to finance any net balance on the other items in the balance payments.

Ballance of payment can be analyzed as follows:

The debit and credit items in a balance of payments seldom balance. As a result, the balance of payments is either in surplus or in deficit. For the purpose of analysis, items of the balance of payments are classified into at least four different types of balance, namely (1) net goods and services balance, (2) net current account balance, (3) basic balance, and (4) official reserve transaction balance.

1) Net goods and services balance

In the very long run, a country must pay for its imports of goods and services through its exports of goods and services. It cannot depend on international credit, whether short-term or long-term, to finance a net import balance or a net goods and service surplus. Long-run equilibrium demands that the net balance on goods and services become zero over the secular time period.

2) Net current account balance

The net current account balance measures the net international lending or borrowing of a country over the balance of payments period. A deficit on current account would mean that the country was a net international borrower, while a surplus would mean a net international lender.

3) Basic balance

The basic balance is the sum of the current account balance and the net movement of long-term capital (direct and portfolio investment) . It is intended to be an indicator of the long-term trends in a country's balance of payments. Its deficit would indicate that long-term trends were worsening a country's payment position, while its surplus would indicate that long-term trends were strengthening the country's balance of payments.

4) Official reserve transaction balance

It is intended to measure that net exchange market pressure on a country's currency. The official reserve transactions balance is most useful when the monetary authorities are charged with the maintenance of stable exchange rate. Thus, the size of these transactions is the best measure of the degree of intervention by monetary authorities in the exchange market and hence of payment disequilibrium.

The description of the concepts of surplus and deficit in the balance of payments has its greatest analytical use in an international monetary system of stable exchange rates. Conversely, they are of least use in an international regime of purely floating rate. Monetary authorities do not intervene in foreign exchange market. In balance of payments analysis today, the different concepts of surplus and deficit should be used with caution and supplemented with analysis of exchange behavior.

Please answer the following questions.

1. What is "the balance of international payment"?
2. In balance of payments how many ways are international transactions grouped into?
3. What are the two sides on double-entry? What is the difference between the two sides?
4. How many kinds of transactions are recorded in statements of balance of international payments?
5. What does balancing account consist of?
6. Why is "Error and Omissions" necessary in a double-entry system?
7. What are the four types of balance necessary?

Chapter 6

Terms of Delivery

交货条件

6.1 Vital Aspects of Transaction

International trade has, even in a single transaction, numerous procedures encompassing packing, insurance, license, customs entry[1], shipping, loading or unloading, transshipment, and import or export duties. Each procedure must be completed by either the seller or the buyer. There must be a clear specification regarding the following issue.

1. Responsibilities and Associated Costs

There must be no ambiguity in the interpretation by either party of the terms of delivery quoted, particularly in the area of costs and expenses. Problems would often mean loss of good relations and loss of repeat orders. It is therefore essential for both the buyer and the seller to agree on the terms of delivery and their interpretations.

2. Time and Place of Delivery

Time and place of delivery are crucial factors in defining the point where the responsibilities and the risks pass from the seller to the buyer. Sellers and buyers can choose the place of delivery according to the responsibilities and risks that each party wants to take.

3. Documents and Expense

International trade transactions require more documents than domestic sales and purchases. Almost for each procedure there is a document and nearly each of the documents entails a cost, either hidden or apparent.

It needs to be clear what documents the exporter should prepare and who should pay the expense so that a transaction can be processed smoothly.

4. Title to Goods[2]

Different terms of delivery mean different responsibilities of the seller and the buyer. Accordingly, title to the goods will pass over from the seller to the buyer at different time and places.

Sellers and buyers need to know when and how they will lose or acquire the title to the goods.

It is therefore of vital importance to establish a clearly defined cut-off point to show where the exporter's responsibilities and risks end and where the importers begin so that the exporter can price his goods accurately and the importer can calculate the full cost of import.

6.2　The Purpose of Terms of Delivery and Incoterms

The problem in international trade is that different countries might have different ways of interpreting the same contract wording. Such a problem can be solved only by creating a set of internationally agreed terms.

The Incoterms aim to provide such a set of standardized terms which mean exactly the same to both parties to a contract and which will be interpreted in exactly the same way by courts in every country. Incoterms are not part of national or international law, but they can be binding upon buyers or sellers provided the sales contract specifies that a particular Incoterms will apply. [3]

If it is necessary to refer to the customs of a particular trade place or to the practices which the parties themselves may have established in their previous dealings, it is desirable that sellers and buyers clarify their legal positions by appropriate clauses in their contract of sale. Such special provisions would supersede or vary anything that is set forth as a rule for interpreting the various Incoterms.

Besides Incoterms, there are also Warsaw-Oxford Rules 1932 and Revised American Foreign Trade Definition 1941 that respectively provide standard interpretation for CIF and delivery terms which are widely used in America. However, it is Incoterms that have been most widely used in international trade. In 1936, the International Chamber of Commerce first published in 1936 a set of international rules for the interpretation of trade terms. These rules were known as INCOTERMS 1936. Amendments and addition were later made in 1953, 1967, 1976, 1980, 1990 and presently 2000 in order to bring the rules in line with the current international trade practices.

6.3　A brief Introduction to Incoterms 2010

The global economy has given business broader access than ever before to markets all over the world. Goods are sold in more countries, in large quantities, and in greater variety. But as the volume and complexity of global sales increase, so do possibilities for misunderstandings and costly disputes when sale contracts are not adequately drafted.

The Incoterms rules, the ICC rules on the use of domestic and international trade terms, facilitate the conduct of global trade. Reference to an Incoterms 2010 rule in a sale contract clearly defines the parties' respective obligations and reduces the risk of legal complications.

Since the creation of the Incoterms rules by ICC in 1936, this globally accepted contractual standard has been regularly updated to keep pace with the development of international trade. The

Incoterms 2010 rules take account of the continued spread of customs-free zones, the increased use of electronic communications in business transactions, heightened concern about security in the movement of goods in transport practices. Incoterms 2010 updates and consolidates the "delivered" rules, reducing the total number of rules from 13 to 11, and offers a simpler and clearer presentation of all the rules. Incoterms 2010 is also the first version of the Incoterms rules to make all references to buyers and sellers gender-neutral.

The broad expertise of ICC's Commission on Commercial Law and Practice, whose membership is drawn from all parts of the world and all trade sectors, ensures that the Incoterms 2010 rules respond to business needs everywhere.

Main features of the Incoterms 2010 rules are as follows:

(1) Two new Incoterms rules — DAT and DAP— have replaced the Incoterms 2000 rules DAF, DES, DEQ and DDU.

The number of Incoterms rules has been reduced from 13 to 11. This has been achieved by substituting two rules that may be used irrespective of the agreed mode of transport — DAT, Delivered at Terminal, and DAP, Delivered at Place — for the Incoterms 2000 rules DAF, DES, DEQ and DDU.

(2) Incoterms rules, however, say nothing about the price to be paid or the method of its payment. Neither do they deal with the transfer of ownership of the goods, or the consequences of a breach of contract. These matters are normally dealt with through express terms in the contract of sale or in the law governing that contract. The parties should be aware that mandatory local law may override any aspect of the sale contract, including the chosen Incoterms rules

(3) Under both new rules, delivery occurs at a named destination: in DAT, at the buyer's disposal unloaded from the arriving vehicle (as under the former DEQ rule); in DAP, likewise at the buyer's disposal, but ready for unloading (as under the former DAF, DES and DDU rules).

(4) The new rules make the Incoterms 2000 rules DES and DEQ superfluous. The named terminal in DAT may well be in a port, and DAT can therefore safely be used in cases where the Incoterms 2000 rule DEQ once was. Likewise, the arriving "vehicle" under DAP may well be a ship and the named place of destination may well be a port: consequently, DAP can safely be used in cases where the Incoterms 2000 rule DES once was. These new rules, like their predecessors, are "delivered", with the seller bearing all the costs (other than those related to import clearance, where applicable) and risks involved in bringing the goods to the named place of destination.

6.3.1 | Rules for Any Mode or Modes of Transport

EX Works

EXW(insert named place of delivery)

GUIDANCE NOTE

This rule may be used irrespective of the mode of transport selected and may also be used where more than one mode of transport is employed.

It is suitable for domestic trade, while FCA is usually more appropriate for international trade.

"Ex Works" means that the seller delivers when it places the goods at the disposal of the buyer at the seller's premises or at another named place (i. e., works, factory, warehouse, etc.). The seller does not need to load the goods on any collecting vehicle, nor does it need to clear the goods for export, where such clearance is applicable.

The parties are well advised to specify as clearly as possible the point within the named place of delivery, as the costs and risks to that point are for the account of the seller. [4] The buyer bears all costs and risks involved in taking the goods from the agreed point, if any, at the named place of delivery.

EXW represents the minimum obligation for the seller. The rule should be used with care as:

a) The seller has no obligation to the buyer to load the goods, even though in practice the seller may be in a better position to do so. If the seller does load the goods, it does so at the buyer's risk and expense. In cases where the seller is in a better position to load the goods, FCA, which obliges the seller to do so at its own risk and expense, is usually more appropriate.

b) A buyer who buys from a seller on an EXW basis for export needs to be aware that the seller has an obligation to provide only such assistance as the buyer may require to effect that export: the seller is not bound to organize the export clearance. Buyers are therefore well advised not to use EXW if they cannot directly or indirectly obtain export clearance.

c) The buyer has limited obligations to provide to the seller any information regarding the export of the goods. However, the seller may need this information for, e. g., taxation or reporting purposes.

A THE SELLER'S OBLIGATIONS

A1 General obligations of the seller

The seller must provide the goods and the commercial invoice in conformity with the contract of sale and any other evidence of conformity that may be required by the contract. Any document referred to in A1 − A10 may be an equivalent electronic record or procedure if agreed between the parties or customary.

A2 Licences, authorizations, security clearances and other formalities

Where applicable, the seller must provide the buyer, at the buyer's request, risk and expense, assistance in obtaining any export license, or other official authorization necessary for the export of the goods. [5]

Where applicable, the seller must provide, at the buyer's request, risk and expense, any information in the possession of the seller that is required for the security clearance of the goods.

A3 Contracts of carriage and insurance

a) Contract of carriage

The seller has no obligation to the buyer to make a contract of carriage.

b) Contract of insurance

The seller has no obligation to the buyer to make a contract of insurance. However, the seller must provide the buyer, at the buyer's request, risk and expense (if any), with information that the buyer needs for obtaining insurance.

A4　Delivery

The seller must deliver the goods by placing them at the disposal of the buyer at the agreed point, if any, at the named place of delivery, not loaded on any collecting vehicle. If no specific point has been agreed within the named place of delivery, and if there are several points available, the seller may select the point that best suits its purpose. The seller must deliver the goods on the agreed date or within the agreed period.

A5　Transfer of risks

The seller bears all risks of loss of or damage to the goods until they have been delivered in accordance with A4 with the exception of loss or damage in the circumstances described in B5.

A6　Allocation of costs

The seller must pay all costs relating to the goods until they have been delivered in accordance with A4, other than those payable by the buyer as envisaged in B6.

A7　Notices to the buyer

The seller must give the buyer any notice needed to enable the buyer to take delivery of the goods.

A8　Delivery document

The seller has no obligation to the buyer.

A9　Checking-packaging-marking

The seller must pay the costs of those checking operations (such as checking quality, measuring, weighing, counting) that are necessary for the purpose of delivering the goods in accordance with A4.

The seller must, at its own expense, package the goods, unless it is usual for the particular trade to transport the type of goods sold unpackaged. The seller may package the goods in the manner appropriate for their transport, unless the buyer has notified the seller of specific packaging requirements before the contract of sale is concluded. Packaging is to be marked appropriately.

A10　Assistance with information and related costs

The seller must, where applicable, in a timely manner, provide to or render assistance in obtaining for the buyer, at the buyer's request, risk and expense, any documents and information, including security-related information, that the buyer needs for the export and/or import of the goods and/or for their transport to the final destination.

B　THE BUYER'S OBLIGATIONS

B1　General obligations of the buyer

The buyer must pay the price of the goods as provided in the contract of sale.

Any document referred to in B1 −B10 may be an equivalent electronic record or procedure if agreed between the parties or customary.

B2 Licences, authorizations, security clearances and other formalities

Where applicable, it is up to the buyer to obtain, at its own risk and expense, any export and import licences or other official authorization and carry out all customs formalities for the export of the goods.

B3 Contracts of carriage and insurance

a) Contract of carriage

The buyer has no obligation to the seller to make a contract of carriage.

b) Contract of insurance

The buyer has no obligation to the seller to make a contract of insurance.

B4 Taking delivery

The buyer must take delivery of the goods when A4 and A7 have been complied with.

B5 Transfer of risks

The buyer bears all risks of loss of or damage to the goods from the time they have been delivered as envisaged in A4. If the buyer fails to give notice in accordance with B7, then the buyer bears all risks of loss of or damage to the goods from the agreed date or the expiry date of the agreed period for delivery, provided that the goods have been clearly identified as the contract goods.

B6 Allocation of costs

The buyer must:

a) pay all costs relating to the goods from the time they have been delivered as envisaged in A4;

b) pay any additional costs incurred by failing either to take delivery of the goods when they have been placed at its disposal[6] or to give appropriate notice in accordance with B7, provided that the goods have been clearly identified as the contract goods;

c) pay, where applicable, all duties, taxes and other charges, as well as the costs of carrying out customs formalities payable upon export; and

d) reimburse all costs and charges incurred by the seller in providing assistance as envisaged in A2.

B7 Notices to the seller

The buyer must, whenever it is entitled to determine the time within an agreed period and/or the point of taking delivery within the named place, give the seller sufficient notice thereof.

B8 Proof of delivery

The buyer must provide the seller with appropriate evidence of having taken delivery.

B9 Inspection of goods

The buyer must pay the costs of any mandatory pre-shipment inspection, including inspection mandated by the authorities of the country of export.

B10 Assistance with information and related costs

The buyer must, in a timely manner, advise the seller of any security information requirements so that the seller may comply with A10.

The buyer must reimburse the seller for all costs and charges incurred by the seller in providing or rendering assistance in obtaining documents and information as envisaged in A10.

Free Carrier
FCA (insert named place of delivery)

GUIDANCE NOTE

This rule may be used irrespective of the mode of transport selected and may also be used where more than one mode of transport is employed.

"Free Carrier" means that the seller delivers the goods to the carrier or another person nominated by the buyer at the seller's premises or another named place. The parties are well advised to specify as clearly as possible the point within the named place of delivery, as the risk passes to the buyer at that point.

If the parties intend to deliver the goods at the seller's premises, they should identify the address of those premises as the named place of delivery. If, on the other hand, the parties intend the goods to be delivered at another place, they must identify a different specific place of delivery.

FCA requires the seller to clear the goods for export, where applicable. However, the seller has no obligation to clear the goods for import, pay any import duty or carry out any import customs formalities.

A THE SELLER'S OBLIGATIONS

A1 General obligations of the seller

The seller must provide the goods and the commercial invoice in conformity with the contract of sale and any other evidence of conformity that may be required by the contract.

Any document referred to in A1 − A10 may be an equivalent electronic record or procedure if agreed between the parties or customary.

A2 Licences, authorizations, security clearances and other formalities

Where applicable, the seller must obtain, at its own risk and expense, any export licence or other official authorization and carry out all customs formalities necessary for the export of the goods.

A3 Contracts of carriage and insurance

a) Contract of carriage

The seller has no obligation to the buyer to make a contract of carriage. However, if requested by the buyer or if it is commercial practice and the buyer does not give an instruction to the contrary in due time, the seller may contract for carriage on usual terms at the buyer's risk and expense. In either case, the seller may decline to make the contract of carriage and, if it does, shall promptly notify the buyer.

b) Contract of insurance

The seller has no obligation to the buyer to make a contract of insurance. However, the seller must provide the buyer, at the buyer's request, risk, and expense (if any), with information that the buyer needs for obtaining insurance.

A4 Delivery

The seller must deliver the goods to the carrier or another person nominated by the buyer at the agreed point, if any, at the named place on the agreed date or within the agreed period.

Delivery is completed:

a) if the named place is the seller's premises, when the goods have been loaded on the means of transport provided by the buyer.

b) in any other case, when the goods are placed at the disposal of the carrier or another person nominated by the buyer on the seller's means of transport ready for unloading.

If no specific point has been notified by the buyer under B7 d) within the named place of delivery, and if there are several points available, the seller may select the point that best suits its purpose.

Unless the buyer notifies the seller otherwise, the seller may deliver the goods for carriage in such a manner as the quantity and/or nature of the goods may require.

A5   Transfer of risks

The seller bears all risks of loss of or damage to the goods until they have been delivered in accordance with A4, with the exception of loss or damage in the circumstances described in B5.

A6   Allocation of costs

The seller must pay

a) all costs relating to the goods until they have been delivered in accordance with A4, other than those payable by the buyer as envisaged in B6; and

b) where applicable, the costs of customs formalities necessary for export, as well as all duties, taxes, and other charges payable upon export.

A7   Notices to the buyer

The seller must, at the buyer's risk and expense, give the buyer sufficient notice either that the goods have been delivered in accordance with A4 or that the carrier or another person nominated by the buyer has failed to take the goods within the time agreed.

A8   Delivery document

The seller must provide the buyer, at the seller's expense, with the usual proof that the goods have been delivered in accordance with A4.

The seller must provide assistance to the buyer, at the buyer's request, risk and expense, in obtaining a transport document.

A9   Checking-packaging-marking

The seller must pay the costs of those checking operations (such as checking quality, measuring, weighing, counting) that are necessary for the purpose of delivering the goods in accordance with A4, as well as the costs of any pre-shipment inspection mandated by the authority of the country of export.

The seller must, at its own expense, package the goods, unless it is usual for the particular trade to transport the type of goods sold unpackaged. The seller may package the goods in the manner appropriate for their transport, unless the buyer has notified the seller of specific packaging requirements before the contract of sale is concluded. Packaging is to be marked appropriately.

A10   Assistance with information and related costs

The seller must, where applicable, in a timely manner, provide to or render assistance in obtaining for the buyer, at the buyer's request, risk and expense, any documents and information, including security-related information, that the buyer needs for the import of the goods and/or for their transport to the final destination.

B   THE BUYER'S OBLIGATIONS

B1   General obligations of the buyer

The buyer must pay the price of the goods as provided in the contract of sale.

Any document referred to in B1 $-$ B10 may be an equivalent electronic record or procedure if agreed between the parties or customary.

B2   Licences, authorizations, security clearances and other formalities

Where applicable, it is up to the buyer to obtain, at its own risk and expense, any import licence or other official authorization and carry out all customs formalities for the import of the goods and for their transport through any country.

B3   Contracts of carriage and insurance

a) Contract of carriage

The buyer must contract at its own expense for the carriage of the goods from the named place of delivery, except when the contract of carriage is made by the seller as provided for in A3 a) .

b) Contract of insurance

The buyer has no obligation to the seller to make a contract of insurance.

B4   Taking delivery

The buyer must take delivery of the goods when they have been delivered as envisaged in A4.

B5   Transfer of risks

The buyer bears all risks of loss of or damage to the goods from the time they have been delivered as envisaged in A4.

If

a) the buyer fails in accordance with B7 to notify the nomination of a carrier or another person as envisaged in A4 or to give notice; or

b) the carrier or person nominated by the buyer as envisaged in A4 fails to take the goods into its charge, then, the buyer bears all risks of loss of or damage to the goods:

(i) from the agreed date, or in the absence of an agreed date,

(ii) from the date notified by the seller under A7 within the agreed period; or, if no such date has been notified,

(iii) from the expiry date of any agreed period for delivery,

provided that the goods have been clearly identified as the contract goods.

B6   Allocation of costs

The buyer must pay

a) all costs relating to the goods from the time they have been delivered as envisaged in A4, except, where applicable, the costs of customs formalities necessary for export, as well as all duties, taxes, and other charges payable upon export as referred to in A6 b);

b) any additional costs incurred, either because:

(i) the buyer fails to nominate a carrier or another person as envisaged in A4, or

(ii) the carrier or person nominated by the buyer as envisaged in A4 fails to take the goods into its charge, or

(iii) the buyer has failed to give appropriate notice in accordance with B7, provided that the goods have been clearly identified as the contract goods; and

c) where applicable, all duties, taxes and other charges as well as the costs of carrying out customs formalities payable upon import of the goods and the costs for their transport through any country.

B7　Notices to the seller

The buyer must notify the seller of

a) the name of the carrier or another person nominated as envisaged in A4 within sufficient time as to enable the seller to deliver the goods in accordance with that article;

b) where necessary, the selected time within the period agreed for delivery when the carrier or person nominated will take the goods;

c) the mode of transport to be used by the person nominated; and

d) the point of taking delivery within the named place.

B8　Proof of delivery

The buyer must accept the proof of delivery provided as envisaged in A8.

B9　Inspection of goods

The buyer must pay the costs of any mandatory pre-shipment inspection, except when such inspection is mandated by the authorities of the country of export.

B10　Assistance with information and related costs

The buyer must, in a timely manner, advise the seller of any security information requirements so that the seller may comply with A10.

The buyer must reimburse the seller for all costs and charges incurred by the seller in providing or rendering assistance in obtaining documents and information as envisaged in A10.

The buyer must, where applicable, in a timely manner, provide to or render assistance in obtaining for the seller, at the seller's request, risk and expense, any documents and information, including security-related information, that the seller needs for the transport and export of the goods and for their transport through any country.

Carriage Paid to
CPT (insert named place of destination)

GUIDANCE NOTE

This rule may be used irrespective of the mode of transport selected and may also be used where more than one mode of transport is employed.

"Carriage Paid to" means that the seller delivers the goods to the carrier or another person nominated by the seller at an agreed place (if any such place is agreed between the parties) and that the seller must contract for and pay the costs of carriage necessary to bring the goods to the named place of destination.

When CPT, CIP, CFR or CIF are used, the seller fulfils its obligation to deliver when it hands the goods over to the carrier and not when the goods reach the place of destination.

This rule has two critical points, because risk passes and costs are transferred at different places. The parties are well advised to identify as precisely as possible in the contract both the place of delivery, where the risk passes to the buyer, and the named place of destination to which the seller must contract for the carriage. If several carriers are used for the carriage to the agreed destination and the parties do not agree on a specific point of delivery, the default position is that risk passes when the goods have been delivered to the first carrier at a point entirely of the seller's choosing and over which the buyer has no control. Should the parties wish the risk to pass at a later stage (e. g., at an ocean port or airport), they need to specify this in their contract of sale.

The parties are also well advised to identify as precisely as possible the point within the agreed place of destination, as the costs to that point are for the account of the seller. The seller is advised to procure contracts of carriage that match this choice precisely. If the seller incurs costs under its contract of carriage related to unloading at the named place of destination, the seller is not entitled to recover such costs from the buyer unless otherwise agreed between the parties.

CPT requires the seller to clear the goods for export, where applicable. However, the seller has no obligation to clear the goods for import, pay any import duty or carry out any import customs formalities.

A THE SELLER'S OBLIGATIONS

A1 General obligations of the seller

The seller must provide the goods and the commercial invoice in conformity with the contract of sale and any other evidence of conformity that may be required by the contract. Any document referred to in A1 −A10 may be an equivalent electronic record or procedure if agreed between the parties or customary.

A2 Licences, authorizations, security clearances and other formalities

Where applicable, the seller must obtain, at its own risk and expense, any export licence or other official authorization and carry out all customs formalities necessary for the export of the goods, and for their transport through any country prior to delivery.

A3 Contracts of carriage and insurance

a) Contract of carriage

The seller must contract or procure a contract for the carriage of the goods from the agreed point of delivery, if any, at the place of delivery to the named place of destination or, if agreed, any point at that place. The contract of carriage must be made on usual terms at the seller's expense and provide for carriage by the usual route and in a customary manner. If a specific point is not agreed or is not determined by practice, the seller may select the point of delivery and the point at the named place of destination that best suit its purpose.

b) Contract of insurance

The seller has no obligation to the buyer to make a contract of insurance. However, the seller must provide the buyer, at the buyer's request, risk, and expense (if any), with information that the buyer needs for obtaining insurance.

A4　Delivery

The seller must deliver the goods by handing them over to the carrier contracted in accordance with A3 on the agreed date or within the agreed period.

A5　Transfer of risks

The seller bears all risks of loss of or damage to the goods until they have been delivered in accordance with A4, with the exception of loss or damage in the circumstances described in B5.

A6　Allocation of costs

The seller must pay

a) all costs relating to the goods until they have been delivered in accordance with A4, other than those payable by the buyer as envisaged in B6;

b) the freight and all other costs resulting from A3 a), including the costs of loading the goods and any charges for unloading at the place of destination that were for the seller's account under the contract of carriage; and

c) where applicable, the costs of customs formalities necessary for export, as well as all duties, taxes and other charges payable upon export, and the costs for their transport through any country that were for the seller's account under the contract of carriage.

A7　Notices to the buyer

The seller must notify the buyer that the goods have been delivered in accordance with A4.

The seller must give the buyer any notice needed in order to allow the buyer to take measures that are normally necessary to enable the buyer to take the goods.

A8　Delivery document

If customary or at the buyer's request, the seller must provide the buyer, at the seller's expense, with the usual transport document(s) for the transport contracted in accordance with A3.

This transport document must cover the contract goods and be dated within the period agreed for shipment. If agreed or customary, the document must also enable the buyer to claim the goods from the carrier at the named place of destination and enable the buyer to sell the goods in transit by the transfer of the document to a subsequent buyer or by notification to the carrier.

When such a transport document is issued in negotiable form and in several originals, a full set of originals must be presented to the buyer.

A9　Checking-packaging-marking

The seller must pay the costs of those checking operations (such as checking quality, measuring, weighing, counting) that are necessary for the purpose of delivering the goods in accordance with A4, as well as the costs of any pre-shipment inspection mandated by the authority of the country of export.

The seller must, at its own expense, package the goods, unless it is usual for the particular trade to transport the type of goods sold unpackaged. The seller may package the goods in the manner appropriate for their transport, unless the buyer has notified the seller of specific packaging requirements before the contract of sale is concluded. Packaging is to be marked appropriately.

A10   Assistance with information and related costs

The seller must, where applicable, in a timely manner, provide to or render assistance in obtaining for the buyer, at the buyer's request, risk and expense, any documents and information, including security-related information, that the buyer needs for the import of the goods and/or for their transport to the final destination.

The seller must reimburse the buyer for all costs and charges incurred by the buyer in providing or rendering assistance in obtaining documents and information as envisaged in B10.

B   THE BUYER'S OBLIGATIONS

B1   General obligations of the buyer

The buyer must pay the price of the goods as provided in the contract of sale.

Any document referred to in B1 − B10 may be an equivalent electronic record or procedure if agreed between the parties or customary.

B2   Licences, authorizations, security clearances and other formalities

Where applicable, it is up to the buyer to obtain, at its own risk and expense, any import licence or other official authorization and carry out all customs formalities for the import of the goods and for their transport through any country.

B3   Contracts of carriage and insurance

a) Contract of carriage

The buyer has no obligation to the seller to make a contract of carriage.

b) Contract of insurance

The buyer has no obligation to the seller to make a contract of insurance. However, the buyer must provide the seller, upon request, with the necessary information for obtaining insurance.

B4   Taking delivery

The buyer must take delivery of the goods when they have been delivered as envisaged in A4 and receive them from the carrier at the named place of destination.

B5   Transfer of risks

The buyer bears all risks of loss of or damage to the goods from the time they have been delivered as envisaged in A4.

If the buyer fails to give notice in accordance with B7, it must bear all risks of loss of or damage to the goods from the agreed date or the expiry date of the agreed period for delivery, provided that the goods have been clearly identified as the contract goods.

B6   Allocation of costs

The buyer must, subject to the provisions of A3 a), pay

a) all costs relating to the goods from the time they have been delivered as envisaged in A4, except, where applicable, the costs of customs formalities necessary for export, as well as all duties, taxes, and other charges payable upon export as referred to in A6 c);

b) all costs and charges relating to the goods while in transit until their arrival at the agreed place of destination, unless such costs and charges were for the seller's account under the contract of carriage;

c) unloading costs, unless such costs were for the seller's account under the contract of carriage;

d) any additional costs incurred if the buyer fails to give notice in accordance with B7, from the agreed date or the expiry date of the agreed period for dispatch, provided that the goods have been clearly identified as the contract goods; and

e) where applicable, all duties, taxes and other charges, as well as the costs of carrying out customs formalities payable upon import of the goods and the costs for their transport through any country, unless included within the cost of the contract of carriage.

B7　Notices to the seller

The buyer must, whenever it is entitled to determine the time for dispatching the goods and/or the named place of destination or the point of receiving the goods within that place, give the seller sufficient notice thereof.

B8　Proof of delivery

The buyer must accept the transport document provided as envisaged in A8 if it is in conformity with the contract.

B9　Inspection of goods

The buyer must pay the costs of any mandatory pre-shipment inspection, except when such inspection is mandated by the authorities of the country of export.

B10　Assistance with information and related costs

The buyer must, in a timely manner, advise the seller of any security information requirements so that the seller may comply with A10.

The buyer must reimburse the seller for all costs and charges incurred by the seller in providing or rendering assistance in obtaining documents and information as envisaged in A10.

The buyer must, where applicable, in a timely manner, provide to or render assistance in obtaining for the seller, at the seller's request, risk and expense, any documents and information, including security-related information, that the seller needs for the transport and export of the goods and for their transport through any country.

Carriage and Insurance Paid to
CIP (insert named place of destination)

GUIDANCE NOTE

This rule may be used irrespective of the mode of transport selected and may also be used where more than one mode of transport is employed.

"Carriage and Insurance Paid to" means that the seller delivers the goods to the carrier or another person nominated by the seller at an agreed place (if any such place is agreed between the parties) and that the seller must contract for and pay the costs of carriage necessary to bring the goods to the named place of destination.

The seller also contracts for insurance cover against the buyer's risk of loss of or damage to the goods during the carriage. The buyer should note that under CIP the seller is required to obtain insurance only on minimum cover. Should the buyer wish to have more insurance protection, it will need either to agree as much expressly with the seller or to make its own extra insurance arrangements.

When CPT, CIP, CFR or CIF are used, the seller fulfills its obligation to deliver when it hands the goods over to the carrier and not when the goods reach the place of destination.

This rule has two critical points, because risk passes and costs are transferred at different places. The parties are well advised to identify as precisely as possible in the contract both the place of delivery, where the risk passes to the buyer, and the named place of destination to which the seller must contract for carriage. If several carriers are used for the carriage to the agreed destination and the parties do not agree on a specific point of delivery, the default position is that risk passes when the goods have been delivered to the first carrier at a point entirely of the Seller's choosing and over which the buyer has no control. Should the parties wish the risk to pass at a later stage (e. g. , at an ocean port or an airport) , they need to specify this in their contract of sale.

The parties are also well advised to identify as precisely as possible the point within the agreed place of destination, as the costs to that point are for the account of the seller. The seller is advised to procure contracts of carriage that match this choice precisely. If the seller incurs costs under its contract of carriage related to unloading at the named place of destination, the seller is not entitled to recover such costs from the buyer unless otherwise agreed between the parties.

CIP requires the seller to clear the goods for export, where applicable. However, the seller has no obligation to clear the goods for import, pay any import duty or carry out any import customs formalities.

A　THE SELLER'S OBLIGATIONS

A1　General obligations of the seller

The seller must provide the goods and the commercial invoice in conformity with the contract of sale and any other evidence of conformity that may be required by the contract.

Any document referred to in A1 −A10 may be an equivalent electronic record or procedure if agreed between the parties or customary.

A2　Licences, authorizations, security clearances and other formalities

Where applicable, the seller must obtain, at its own risk and expense, any export licence or other official authorization and carry out all customs formalities necessary for the export of the goods and for their transport through any country prior to delivery.

A3　Contracts of carriage and insurance

a) Contract of carriage

The seller must contract or procure a contract for the carriage of the goods from the agreed point of delivery, if any, at the place of delivery to the named place of destination or, if agreed, any point at that place. The contract of carriage must be made on usual terms at the seller's expense and provide for carriage by the usual route and in a customary manner. If a specific point is not agreed or is not determined by practice, the seller may select the point of delivery and the point at the named place of destination that best suit its purpose.

b) Contract of insurance

The seller must obtain at its own expense cargo insurance complying at least with the minimum cover as provided by Clauses (C) of the Institute Cargo Clauses (LMA/IUA) or any similar clauses. The insurance shall be contracted with underwriters or an insurance company of good reputation and entitle the buyer, or any other person having an insurable interest in the goods, to claim directly from the insurer.

When required by the buyer, the seller shall, subject to the buyer providing any necessary information requested by the seller, provide at the buyer's expense any additional cover, if procurable, such as cover as provided by Clauses (A) or (B) of the Institute Cargo Clauses (LMA/IUA) or any similar clauses, and/or cover complying with the Institute War Clauses and/or Institute Strikes Clauses (LMA/IUA) or any similar clauses.

The insurance shall cover, at a minimum, the price provided in the contract plus 10% (i. e., 110%) and shall be in the currency of the contract.

The insurance shall cover the goods from the point of delivery set out in A and A5 to at least the named place of destination.

The seller must provide the buyer with the insurance policy or other evidence of insurance cover.

Moreover, the seller must provide the buyer, at the buyer's request, risk, and expense (if any), with information that the buyer needs to procure any additional insurance.

A4 Delivery

The seller must deliver the goods by handing them over to the carrier contracted in accordance with A3 on the agreed date or within the agreed period.

A5 Transfer of risks

The seller bears all risks of loss of or damage to the goods until they have been delivered in accordance with A4, with the exception of loss or damage in the circumstances described in B5.

A6 Allocation of costs

The seller must pay

a) all costs relating to the goods until they have been delivered in accordance with A4, other than those payable by the buyer as envisaged in B6;

b) the freight and all other costs resulting from A3 a), including the costs of loading the goods and any charges for unloading at the place of destination that were for the seller's account under the contract of carriage;

c) the costs of insurance resulting from A3 b); and

d) where applicable, the costs of customs formalities necessary for export, as well as all duties, taxes and other charges payable upon export, and the costs for their transport through any country that were for the seller's account under the contract of carriage.

A7 Notices to the buyer

The seller must notify the buyer that the goods have been delivered in accordance with A4.

The seller must give the buyer any notice needed in order to allow the buyer to take measures that are normally necessary to enable the buyer to take the goods.

A8 Delivery document

If customary or at the buyer's request, the seller must provide the buyer, at the seller's expense, with the usual transport document(s) for the transport contracted in accordance with A3.

This transport document must cover the contract goods and be dated within the period agreed for shipment. If agreed or customary, the document must also enable the buyer to claim the goods from the carrier at the named place of destination and enable the buyer to sell the goods in transit by the transfer of the document to a subsequent buyer or by notification to the carrier.

When such a transport document is issued in negotiable form and in several originals, a full set of originals must be presented to the buyer.

A9 Checking-packaging-marking

The seller must pay the costs of those checking operations (such as checking quality, measuring, weighing, counting) that are necessary for the purpose of delivering the goods in accordance with A4 as well as the costs of any pre-shipment inspection mandated by the authority of the country of export.

The seller must, at its own expense, package the goods, unless it is usual for the particular trade to transport the type of goods sold unpackaged. The seller may package the goods in the manner appropriate for their transport, unless the buyer has notified the seller of specific packaging requirements before the contract of sale is concluded. Packaging is to be marked appropriately.

A10 Assistance with information and related costs

The seller must, where applicable, in a timely manner, provide to or render assistance in obtaining for the buyer, at the buyer's request, risk and expense, any documents and information, including security-related information, that the buyer needs for the import of the goods and/or for their transport to the final destination.

The seller must reimburse the buyer for all costs and charges incurred by the buyer in providing or rendering assistance in obtaining documents and information as envisaged in B10.

B THE BUYER'S OBLIGATIONS

B1 General obligations of the buyer

The buyer must pay the price of the goods as provided in the contract of sale.

Any document referred to in B1 − B10 may be an equivalent electronic record or procedure if agreed between the parties or customary.

B2 Licences, authorizations, security clearances and other formalities

Where applicable, it is up to the buyer to obtain, at its own risk and expense, any import licence or other official authorization and carry out all customs formalities for the import of the goods and for their transport through any country.

B3　Contracts of carriage and insurance

a) Contract of carriage

The buyer has no obligation to the seller to make a contract of carriage.

b) Contract of insurance

The buyer has no obligation to the seller to make a contract of insurance. However, the buyer must provide the seller, upon request, with any information necessary for the seller to procure any additional insurance requested by the buyer as envisaged in A3 b).

B4　Taking delivery

The buyer must take delivery of the goods when they have been delivered as envisaged in A4 and receive them from the carrier at the named place of destination.

B5　Transfer of risks

The buyer bears all risks of loss of or damage to the goods from the time they have been delivered as envisaged in A4.

If the buyer fails to give notice in accordance with B7, it must bear all risks of loss of or damage to the goods from the agreed date or the expiry date of the agreed period for delivery, provided that the goods have been clearly identified as the contract goods.

B6　Allocation of costs

The buyer must, subject to the provisions of A3 a), pay

a) all costs relating to the goods from the time they have been delivered as envisaged in A4, except, where applicable, the costs of customs formalities necessary for export, as well as all duties, taxes and other charges payable upon export as referred to in A6 d);

b) all costs and charges relating to the goods while in transit until their arrival at the agreed place of destination, unless such costs and charges were for the seller's account under the contract of carriage;

c) unloading costs, unless such costs were for the seller's account under the contract of carriage;

d) any additional costs incurred if it fails to give notice in accordance with B7, from the agreed date or the expiry date of the agreed period for dispatch, provided that the goods have been clearly identified as the contract goods;

e) where applicable, all duties, taxes and other charges as well as the costs of carrying out customs formalities payable upon import of the goods and the costs for their transport through any country, unless included within the cost of the contract of carriage; and

f) the costs of any additional insurance procured at the buyer's request under A3 and B3.

B7　Notices to the seller

The buyer must, whenever it is entitled to determine the time for dispatching the goods and/or the named place of destination or the point of receiving the goods within that place, give the seller sufficient notice thereof.

B8　Proof of delivery

The buyer must accept the transport document provided as envisaged in A8 if it is in conformity with the contract.

B9 Inspection of goods

The buyer must pay the costs of any mandatory pre-shipment inspection, except when such inspection is mandated by the authorities of the country of export.

B10 Assistance with information and related costs

The buyer must, in a timely manner, advise the seller of any security information requirements so that the seller may comply with A10. The buyer must reimburse the seller for all costs and charges incurred by the seller in providing or rendering assistance in obtaining documents and information as envisaged in A10.

The buyer must, where applicable, in a timely manner, provide to or render assistance in obtaining for the seller, at the seller's request, risk and expense, any documents and information, including security-related information, that the seller needs for the transport and export of the goods and for their transport through any country.

Ddelivered at Terminal
DAT (insert named terminal at port or place of destination)

GUIDANCE NOTE

This rule may be used irrespective of the mode of transport selected and may also be used where more than one mode of transport is employed.

"Delivered at Terminal" means that the seller delivers when the goods, once unloaded from the arriving means of transport, are placed at the disposal of the buyer at a named terminal at the named port or place of destination. "Terminal" includes any place, whether covered or not, such as a quay, warehouse, container yard or road, rail or air cargo terminal. The seller bears all risks involved in bringing the goods to and unloading them at the terminal at the named port or place of destination.

The parties are well advised to specify as clearly as possible the terminal and, if possible, a specific point within the terminal at the agreed port or place of destination, as the risks to that point are for the account of the seller. The seller is advised to procure a contract of carriage that matches this choice precisely.

Moreover, if the parties intend the seller to bear the risks and costs involved in transporting and handling the goods from the terminal to another place, then the DAP or DDP rules should be used.

DAT requires the seller to clear the goods for export, where applicable.

However, the seller has no obligation to clear the goods for import, pay any import duty or carry out any import customs formalities.

A THE SELLER'S OBLIGATIONS

A1 General obligations of the seller

The seller must provide the goods and the commercial invoice in conformity with the contract of sale and any other evidence of conformity that may be required by the contract.

Any document referred to in A1 −A10 may be an equivalent electronic record or procedure if agreed between the parties or customary.

A2　Licences, authorizations, security clearances and other formalities

Where applicable, the seller must obtain, at its own risk and expense, any export licence and other official authorization and carry out all customs formalities necessary for the export of the goods and for their transport through any country prior to delivery.

A3　Contracts of carriage and insurance

a) Contract of carriage

The seller must contract at its own expense for the carriage of the goods to the named terminal at the agreed port or place of destination. If a specific terminal is not agreed or is not determined by practice, the seller may select the terminal at the agreed port or place of destination that best suits its purpose.

b) Contract of insurance

The seller has no obligation to the buyer to make a contract of insurance. However, the seller must provide the buyer, at the buyer's request, risk, and expense (if any), with information that the buyer needs for obtaining insurance.

A4　Delivery

The seller must unload the goods from the arriving means of transport and must then deliver them by placing them at the disposal of the buyer at the named terminal referred to in A3 a) at the port or place of destination on the agreed date or within the agreed period.

A5　Transfer of risks

The seller bears all risks of loss of or damage to the goods until they have been delivered in accordance with A4 with the exception of loss or damage in the circumstances described in B5.

A6　Allocation of costs

The seller must pay

a) in addition to costs resulting from A3 a), all costs relating to the goods until they have been delivered in accordance with A4, other than those payable by the buyer as envisaged in B6; and

b) where applicable, the costs of customs formalities necessary for export as well as all duties, taxes and other charges payable upon export and the costs for their transport through any country, prior to delivery in accordance with A4.

A7　Notices to the buyer

The seller must give the buyer any notice needed in order to allow the buyer to take measures that are normally necessary to enable the buyer to take delivery of the goods.

A8　Delivery document

The seller must provide the buyer, at the seller's expense, with a document enabling the buyer to take delivery of the goods as envisaged in A4/B4.

A9　Checking-packaging-marking

The seller must pay the costs of those checking operations (such as checking quality, measuring, weighing, counting) that are necessary for the purpose of delivering the goods in accordance with A4, as well as the costs of any pre-shipment inspection mandated by the authority of the country of export.

The seller must, at its own expense, package the goods, unless it is usual for the particular trade to transport the type of goods sold unpackaged. The seller may package the goods in the manner appropriate for their transport, unless the buyer has notified the seller of specific packaging requirements before the contract of sale is concluded. Packaging is to be marked appropriately.

A10 Assistance with information and related costs

The seller must, where applicable, in a timely manner, provide to or render assistance in obtaining for the buyer, at the buyer's request, risk and expense, any documents and information, including security-related information, that the buyer needs for the import of the goods and/or for their transport to the final destination.

The seller must reimburse the buyer for all costs and charges incurred by the buyer in providing or rendering assistance in obtaining documents and information as envisaged in B10.

B THE BUYER'S OBLIGATIONS

B1 General obligations of the buyer

The buyer must pay the price of the goods as provided in the contract of sale.

Any document referred to in B1 −B10 may be an equivalent electronic record or procedure if agreed between the parties or customary.

B2 Licences, authorizations, security clearances and other formalities

Where applicable, the buyer must obtain, at its own risk and expense, any import licence or other official authorization and carry out all customs formalities for the import of the goods.

B3 Contracts of carriage and insurance

a) Contract of carriage

The buyer has no obligation to the seller to make a contract of carriage.

b) Contract of insurance

The buyer has no obligation to the seller to make a contract of insurance. However, the buyer must provide the seller, upon request, with the necessary information for obtaining insurance.

B4 Taking delivery

The buyer must take delivery of the goods when they have been delivered as envisaged in A4.

B5 Transfer of risks

The buyer bears all risks of loss of or damage to the goods from the time they have been delivered as envisaged in A4.

If

a) the buyer fails to fulfill its obligations in accordance with B2, then it bears all resulting risks of loss of or damage to the goods, or

b) the buyer fails to give notice in accordance with B7, then it bears all risks of loss of or damage to the goods from the agreed date or the expiry date of the agreed period for delivery,

provided that the goods have been clearly identified as the contract goods.

B6 Allocation of costs

The buyer must pay

a) all costs relating to the goods from the time they have been delivered as envisaged in A4;

b) any additional costs incurred by the seller if the buyer fails to fulfill its obligations in accordance with B2, or to give notice in accordance with B7, provided that the goods have been clearly identified as the contract goods; and

c) where applicable, the costs of customs formalities as well as all duties, taxes and other charges payable upon import of the goods.

B7　Notices to the seller

The buyer must, whenever it is entitled to determine the time within an agreed period and/or the point of taking delivery at the named terminal, give the seller sufficient notice thereof.

B8　Proof of delivery

The buyer must accept the delivery document provided as envisaged in A8.

B9　Inspection of goods

The buyer must pay the costs of any mandatory pre-shipment inspection, except when such inspection is mandated by the authorities of the country of export.

B10　Assistance with information and related costs

The buyer must, in a timely manner, advise the seller of any security information requirements so that the seller may comply with A10.

The buyer must reimburse the seller for all costs and charges incurred by the seller in providing or rendering assistance in obtaining documents and information as envisaged in A10.

The buyer must, where applicable, in a timely manner, provide to or render assistance in obtaining for the seller, at the seller's request, risk and expense, any documents and information, including security-related information, that the seller needs for the transport and export of the goods and for their transport through any country.

Delivered at Place
DAP (insert named place of destination)

GUIDANCE NOTE

This rule may be used irrespective of the mode of transport selected and may also be used where more than one mode of transport is employed.

"Delivered at Place" means that the seller delivers when the goods are placed at the disposal of the buyer on the arriving means of transport ready for unloading at the named place of destination. The seller bears all risks involved in bringing the goods to the named place.

The parties are well advised to specify as clearly as possible the point within the agreed place of destination, as the risks to that point are for the account of the seller. The seller is advised to procure contracts of carriage that match this choice precisely. If the seller incurs costs under its contract of carriage related to unloading at the place of destination, the seller is not entitled to recover such costs from the buyer unless otherwise agreed between the parties.

DAP requires the seller to clear the goods for export, where applicable.

However, the seller has no obligation to clear the goods for import, pay any import duty or carry out any import customs formalities. If the parties wish the seller to clear the goods for import, pay any import duty and carry out any import customs formalities, the DDP term should be used.

A　THE SELLER'S OBLIGATIONS

A1　General obligations of the seller

The seller must provide the goods and the commercial invoice in conformity with the contract of sale and any other evidence of conformity that may be required by the contract.

Any document referred to in A1 − A10 may be an equivalent electronic record or procedure if agreed between the parties or customary.

A2　Licences, authorizations, security clearances and other formalities

Where applicable, the seller must obtain, at its own risk and expense, any export licence and other official authorization and carry out all customs formalities necessary for the export of the goods and for their transport through any country prior to delivery.

A3　Contracts of carriage and insurance

a) Contract of carriage

The seller must contract at its own expense for the carriage of the goods to the named place of destination or to the agreed point, if any, at the named place of destination. If a specific point is not agreed or is not determined by practice, the seller may select the point at the named place of destination that best suits its purpose.

b) Contract of insurance

The seller has no obligation to the buyer to make a contract of insurance. However, the seller must provide the buyer, at the buyer's request, risk, and expense (if any), with information that the buyer needs for obtaining insurance.

A4　Delivery

The seller must deliver the goods by placing them at the disposal of the buyer on the arriving means of transport ready for unloading at the agreed point, if any, at the named place of destination on the agreed date or within the agreed period.

A5　Transfer of risks

The seller bears all risks of loss of or damage to the goods until they have been delivered in accordance with A4, with the exception of loss or damage in the circumstances described in B5.

A6　Allocation of costs

The seller must pay

a) in addition to costs resulting from A3 a), all costs relating to the goods until they have been delivered in accordance with A4, other than those payable by the buyer as envisaged in B6;

b) any charges for unloading at the place of destination that were for the seller's account under the contract of carriage; and

c) where applicable, the costs of customs formalities necessary for export as well as all duties, taxes and other charges payable upon export and the costs for their transport through any country, prior to delivery in accordance with A4.

A7　Notices to the buyer

The seller must give the buyer any notice needed in order to allow the buyer to take measures that are normally necessary to enable the buyer to take delivery of the goods.

A8　Delivery document

The seller must provide the buyer, at the seller's expense, with a document enabling the buyer to take delivery of the goods as envisaged in A4/B4.

A9　Checking-packaging-marking

The seller must pay the costs of those checking operations (such as checking quality, measuring, weighing, counting) that are necessary for the purpose of delivering the goods in accordance with A4, as well as the costs of any pre-shipment inspection mandated by the authority of the country of export.

The seller must, at its own expense, package the goods, unless it is usual for the particular trade to transport the type of goods sold unpackaged. The seller may package the goods in the manner appropriate for their transport, unless the buyer has notified the seller of specific packaging requirements before the contract of sale is concluded. Packaging is to be marked appropriately.

A10　Assistance with information and related costs

The seller must, where applicable, in a timely manner, provide to or render assistance in obtaining for the buyer, at the buyer's request, risk and expense, any documents and information, including security-related information, that the buyer needs for the import of the goods and/or for their transport to the final destination.

The seller must reimburse the buyer for all costs and charges incurred by the buyer in providing or rendering assistance in obtaining documents and information as envisaged in B10.

B　THE BUYER'S OBLIGATIONS

B1　General obligations of the buyer

The buyer must pay the price of the goods as provided in the contract of sale.

Any document referred to in B1 −B10 may be an equivalent electronic record or procedure if agreed between the parties or customary.

B2　Licences, authorizations, security clearances and other formalities

Where applicable, the buyer must obtain, at its own risk and expense, any import licence or other official authorization and carry out all customs formalities for the import of the goods.

B3　Contracts of carriage and insurance

a) Contract of carriage

The buyer has no obligation to the seller to make a contract of carriage.

b) Contract of insurance

The buyer has no obligation to the seller to make a contract of insurance. However, the buyer must provide the seller, upon request, with the necessary information for obtaining insurance.

B4　Taking delivery

The buyer must take delivery of the goods when they have been delivered as envisaged in A4.

B5   Transfer of risks

The buyer bears all risks of loss of or damage to the goods from the time they have been delivered as envisaged in A4.

If

a) the buyer fails to fulfill its obligations in accordance with B2, then it bears all resulting risks of loss of or damage to the goods, or

b) the buyer fails to give notice in accordance with B7, then it bears all risks of loss of or damage to the goods from the agreed date or the expiry date of the agreed period for delivery,

provided that the goods have been clearly identified as the contract goods.

B6   Allocation of costs

The buyer must pay

a) all costs relating to the goods from the time they have been delivered as envisaged in A4;

b) all costs of unloading necessary to take delivery of the goods from the arriving means of transport at the named place of destination, unless such costs were for the seller's account under the contract of carriage;

c) any additional costs incurred by the seller if the buyer fails to fulfill its obligations in accordance with B2 or to give notice in accordance with B7, provided that the goods have been clearly identified as the contract goods; and

d) where applicable, the costs of customs formalities, as well as all duties, taxes and other charges payable upon import of the goods.

B7   Notices to the seller

The buyer must, whenever it is entitled to determine the time within an agreed period and/or the point of taking delivery within the named place of destination, give the seller sufficient notice thereof.

B8   Proof of delivery

The buyer must accept the delivery document provided as envisaged in A8.

B9   Inspection of goods

The buyer must pay the costs of any mandatory pre-shipment inspection, except when such inspection is mandated by the authorities of the country of export.

B10   Assistance with information and related costs

The buyer must, in a timely manner, advise the seller of any security information requirements so that the seller may comply with A10.

The buyer must reimburse the seller for all costs and charges incurred by the seller in providing or rendering assistance in obtaining documents and information as envisaged in A10.

The buyer must, where applicable, in a timely manner, provide to or render assistance in obtaining for the seller, at the seller's request, risk and expense, any documents and information, including security-related information, that the seller needs for the transport and export of the goods and for their transport through any country.

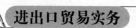
Delivered Duty Paid
DDP (insert named place of destination)

GUIDANCE NOTE

This rule may be used irrespective of the mode of transport selected and may also be used where more than one mode of transport is employed.

"Delivered Duty Paid" means that the seller delivers the goods when the goods are placed at the disposal of the buyer, cleared for import on the arriving means of transport ready for unloading at the named place of destination. The seller bears all the costs and risks involved in bringing the goods to the place of destination and has an obligation to clear the goods not only for export but also for import, to pay any duty for both export and import and to carry out all customs formalities.

DDP represents the maximum obligation for the seller.

The parties are well advised to specify as clearly as possible the point within the agreed place of destination, as the costs and risks to that point are for the account of the seller. The seller is advised to procure contracts of carriage that match this choice precisely. If the seller incurs costs under its contract of carriage related to unloading at the place of destination, the seller is not entitled to recover such costs from the buyer unless otherwise agreed between the parties.

The parties are well advised not to use DDP if the seller is unable directly or indirectly to obtain import clearance.

If the parties wish the buyer to bear all risks and costs of import clearance, the DAP rule should be used.

Any VAT or other taxes payable upon import are for the seller's account unless expressly agreed otherwise in the sales contract.

A THE SELLER'S OBLIGATIONS

A1 General obligations of the seller

The seller must provide the goods and the commercial invoice in conformity with the contract of sale and any other evidence of conformity that may be required by the contract.

Any document referred to in A1 −A10 may be an equivalent electronic record or procedure if agreed between the parties or customary.

A2 Licences, authorizations, security clearances and other formalities

Where applicable, the seller must obtain, at its own risk and expense, any export and import licence and other official authorization and carry out all customs formalities necessary for the export of the goods, for their transport through any country and for their import.

A3 Contracts of carriage and insurance

a) Contract of carriage

The seller must contract at its own expense for the carriage of the goods to the named place of destination or to the agreed point, if any, at the named place of destination. If a specific point is not agreed or is not determined by practice, the seller may select the point at the named place of destination that best suits its purpose.

b) Contract of insurance

The seller has no obligation to the buyer to make a contract of insurance. However, the seller must provide the buyer, at the buyer's request, risk, and expense (if any), with information that the buyer needs for obtaining insurance.

A4　Delivery

The seller must deliver the goods by placing them at the disposal of the buyer on the arriving means of transport ready for unloading at the agreed point, if any, at the named place of destination on the agreed date or within the agreed period.

A5　Transfer of risks

The seller bears all risks of loss of or damage to the goods until they have been delivered in accordance with A4, with the exception of loss or damage in the circumstances described in B5.

A6　Allocation of costs

The seller must pay

a) in addition to costs resulting from A3 a), all costs relating to the goods until they have been delivered in accordance with A4, other than those payable by the buyer as envisaged in B6;

b) any charges for unloading at the place of destination that were for the seller's account under the contract of carriage; and

c) where applicable, the costs of customs formalities necessary for export and import as well as all duties, taxes and other charges payable upon export and import of the goods, and the costs for their transport through any country prior to delivery in accordance with A4.

A7　Notices to the buyer

The seller must give the buyer any notice needed in order to allow the buyer to take measures that are normally necessary to enable the buyer to take delivery of the goods.

A8　Delivery document

The seller must provide the buyer, at the seller's expense, with a document enabling the buyer to take delivery of the goods as envisaged in A4/B4.

A9　Checking-packaging-marking

The seller must pay the costs of those checking operations (such as checking quality, measuring, weighing, counting) that are necessary for the purpose of delivering the goods in accordance with A4, as well as the costs of any pre-shipment inspection mandated by the authority of the country of export or of import.

The seller must, at its own expense, package the goods, unless it is usual for the particular trade to transport the type of goods sold unpackaged. The seller may package the goods in the manner appropriate for their transport, unless the buyer has notified the seller of specific packaging requirements before the contract of sale is concluded. Packaging is to be marked appropriately.

A10　Assistance with information and related costs

The seller must, where applicable, in a timely manner, provide to or render assistance in obtaining for the buyer, at the buyer's request, risk and expense, any documents and information, including security-related information, that the buyer needs for the transport of the goods to the final destination, where applicable, from the named place of destination.

The seller must reimburse the buyer for all costs and charges incurred by the buyer in providing or rendering assistance in obtaining documents and information as envisaged in B10.

B THE BUYER'S OBLIGATIONS

B1 General obligations of the buyer

The buyer must pay the price of the goods as provided in the contract of sale.

Any document referred to in B1 −B10 may be an equivalent electronic record or procedure if agreed between the parties or customary.

B2 Licences, authorizations, security clearances and other formalities

Where applicable, the buyer must provide assistance to the seller, at the seller's request, risk and expense, in obtaining any import licence or other official authorization for the import of the goods.

B3 Contracts of carriage and insurance

a) Contract of carriage

The buyer has no obligation to the seller to make a contract of carriage.

b) Contract of insurance

The buyer has no obligation to the seller to make a contract of insurance. However, the buyer must provide the seller, upon request, with the necessary information for obtaining insurance.

B4 Taking delivery

The buyer must take delivery of the goods when they have been delivered as envisaged in A4.

B5 Transfer of risks

The buyer bears all risks of loss of or damage to the goods from the time they have been delivered as envisaged in A4.

If

a) the buyer fails to fulfill its obligations in accordance with B2, then it bears all resulting risks of loss of or damage to the goods, or

b) the buyer fails to give notice in accordance with B7, then it bears all risks of loss of or damage to the goods from the agreed date or the expiry date of the agreed period for delivery,

provided that the goods have been clearly identified as the contract goods.

B6 Allocation of costs

The buyer must pay

a) all costs relating to the goods from the time they have been delivered as envisaged in A4;

b) all costs of unloading necessary to take delivery of the goods from the arriving means of transport at the named place of destination, unless such costs were for the seller's account under the contract of carriage; and

c) any additional costs incurred if it fails to fulfill its obligations in accordance with B2 or to give notice in accordance with B7, provided that the goods have been clearly identified as the contract goods.

B7 Notices to the seller

The buyer must, whenever it is entitled to determine the time within an agreed period and/or the point of taking delivery within the named place of destination, give the seller sufficient notice thereof.

B8 Proof of delivery

The buyer must accept the proof of delivery provided as envisaged in A8.

B9 Inspection of goods

The buyer has no obligation to the seller to pay the costs of any mandatory pre-shipment inspection mandated by the authority of the country of export or of import.

B10 Assistance with information and related costs

The buyer must, in a timely manner, advise the seller of any security information requirements so that the seller may comply with A10.

The buyer must reimburse the seller for all costs and charges incurred by the seller in providing or rendering assistance in obtaining documents and information as envisaged in A10.

The buyer must, where applicable, in a timely manner, provide to or render assistance in obtaining for the seller, at the seller's request, risk and expense, any documents and information, including security-related information, that the seller needs for the transport, export and import of the goods and for their transport through any country.

6.3.2 | Rules for Sea and Inland Waterway Transport

Free Alongside Ship
FAS (insert named port of shipment)

GUIDANCE NOTE

This rule is to be used only for sea or inland waterway transport.

"Free Alongside Ship" means that the seller delivers when the goods are placed alongside the vessel (e.g., on a quay or a barge) nominated by the buyer at the named port of shipment. The risk of loss of or damage to the goods[7] passes when the goods are alongside the ship, and the buyer bears all costs from that moment onwards.

The parties are well advised to specify as clearly as possible the loading point at the named port of shipment, as the costs and risks to that point are for the account of the seller and these costs and associated handling charges may vary according to the practice of the port.

The seller is required either to deliver the goods alongside the ship or to procure goods already so delivered for shipment. The reference to "procure" here caters for multiple sales down a chain ("string sales"), particularly common in the commodity trades.

Where the goods are in containers, it is typical for the seller to hand the goods over to the carrier at a terminal and not alongside the vessel. In such situations, the FAS rule would be inappropriate, and the FCA rule should be used.

FAS requires the seller to clear the goods for export, where applicable. However, the seller has no obligation to clear the goods for import, pay any import duty or carry out any import customs formalities.

A THE SELLER'S OBLIGATIONS

A1 General obligations of the seller

The seller must provide the goods and the commercial invoice in conformity with the contract of sale and any other evidence of conformity that may be required by the contract.

Any document referred to in A1 − A10 may be an equivalent electronic record or procedure if agreed between the parties or customary.

A2 Licences, authorizations, security clearances and other formalities

Where applicable, the seller must obtain, at its own risk and expense, any export licence or other official authorization and carry out all customs formalities necessary for the export of the goods.

A3 Contracts of carriage and insurance

a) Contract of carriage

The seller has no obligation to the buyer to make a contract of carriage. However, if requested by the buyer or if it is commercial practice and the buyer does not give an instruction to the contrary in due time, the seller may contract for carriage on usual terms at the buyer's risk and expense. In either case, the seller may decline to make the contract of carriage and, if it does, shall promptly notify the buyer.

b) Contract of insurance

The seller has no obligation to the buyer to make a contract of insurance. However, the seller must provide the buyer, at the buyer's request, risk, and expense (if any), with information that the buyer needs for obtaining insurance.

A4 Delivery

The seller must deliver the goods either by placing them alongside the ship nominated by the buyer at the loading point, if any, indicated by the buyer at the named port of shipment or by procuring the goods so delivered. In either case, the seller must deliver the goods on the agreed date or within the agreed period and in the manner customary at the port.

If no specific loading point has been indicated by the buyer, the seller may select the point within the named port of shipment that best suits its purpose. If the parties have agreed that delivery should take place within a period, the buyer has the option to choose the date within that period.

A5 Transfer of risks

The seller bears all risks of loss of or damage to the goods until they have been delivered in accordance with A4 with the exception of loss or damage in the circumstances described in B5.

A6 Allocation of costs

The seller must pay

a) all costs relating to the goods until they have been delivered in accordance with A4, other than those payable by the buyer as envisaged in B6; and

b) where applicable, the costs of customs formalities necessary for export as well as all duties, taxes and other charges payable upon export.

A7 Notices to the buyer

The seller must, at the buyer's risk and expense, give the buyer sufficient notice either that the goods have been delivered in accordance with A4 or that the vessel has failed to take the goods within the time agreed.

A8 Delivery document

The seller must provide the buyer, at the seller's expense, with the usual proof that the goods have been delivered in accordance with A4.

Unless such proof is a transport document, the seller must provide assistance to the buyer, at the buyer's request, risk and expense, in obtaining a transport document.

A9 Checking-packaging-marking

The seller must pay the costs of those checking operations (such as checking quality, measuring, weighing, counting) that are necessary for the purpose of delivering the goods in accordance with A4, as well as the costs of any pre-shipment inspection mandated by the authority of the country of export.

The seller must, at its own expense, package the goods, unless it is usual for the particular trade to transport the type of goods sold unpackaged. The seller may package the goods in the manner appropriate for their transport, unless the buyer has notified the seller of specific packaging requirements before the contract of sale is concluded. Packaging is to be marked appropriately.

A10 Assistance with information and related costs

The seller must, where applicable, in a timely manner, provide to or render assistance in obtaining for the buyer, at the buyer's request, risk and expense, any documents and information, including security-related information, that the buyer needs for the import of the goods and/or for their transport to the final destination.

The seller must reimburse the buyer for all costs and charges incurred by the buyer in providing or rendering assistance in obtaining documents and information as envisaged in B10.

B THE BUYER'S OBLIGATIONS

B1 General obligations of the buyer

The buyer must pay the price of the goods as provided in the contract of sale.

Any document referred to in B1 −B10 may be an equivalent electronic record or procedure if agreed between the parties or customary.

B2 Licences, authorizations, security clearances and other formalities

Where applicable, it is up to the buyer to obtain, at its own risk and expense, any import licence or other official authorization and carry out all customs formalities for the import of the goods and for their transport through any country.

B3 Contracts of carriage and insurance

a) Contract of carriage

The buyer must contract, at its own expense for the carriage of the goods from the named port of shipment, except where the contract of carriage is made by the seller as provided for in A3 a).

b) Contract of insurance

The buyer has no obligation to the seller to make a contract of insurance.

B4　Taking delivery

The buyer must take delivery of the goods when they have been delivered as envisaged in A4.

B5　Transfer of risks

The buyer bears all risks of loss of or damage to the goods from the time they have been delivered as envisaged in A4.

If

a) the buyer fails to give notice in accordance with B7, or

b) the vessel nominated by the buyer fails to arrive on time, or fails to take the goods or closes for cargo earlier than the time notified in accordance with B7, then the buyer bears all risks of loss of or damage to the goods from the agreed date or the expiry date of the agreed period for delivery,

provided that the goods have been clearly identified as the contract goods.

B6　Allocation of costs

The buyer must pay

a) all costs relating to the goods from the time they have been delivered as envisaged in A4, except, where applicable, the costs of customs formalities necessary for export as well as all duties, taxes, and other charges payable upon export as referred to in A6 b) ;

b) any additional costs incurred, either because:

(i) the buyer has failed to give appropriate notice in accordance with B7, or

(ii) the vessel nominated by the buyer fails to arrive on time, is unable to take the goods, or closes for cargo earlier than the time notified in accordance with B7, provided that the goods have been clearly identified as the contract goods; and

c) where applicable, all duties, taxes and other charges, as well as the costs of carrying out customs formalities payable upon import of the goods and the costs for their transport through any country.

B7　Notices to the seller

The buyer must give the seller sufficient notice of the vessel name, loading point and, where necessary, the selected delivery time within the agreed period.

B8　Proof of delivery

The buyer must accept the proof of delivery provided as envisaged in A8.

B9　Inspection of goods

The buyer must pay the costs of any mandatory pre-shipment inspection, except when such inspection is mandated by the authorities of the country of export.

B10　Assistance with information and related costs

The buyer must, in a timely manner, advise the seller of any security information requirements so that the seller may comply with A10.

The buyer must reimburse the seller for all costs and charges incurred by the seller in providing or rendering assistance in obtaining documents and information as envisaged in A10.

The buyer must, where applicable, in a timely manner, provide to or render assistance in obtaining for the seller, at the seller's request, risk and expense, any documents and information, including security-related information, that the seller needs for the transport and export of the goods and for their transport through any country.

Free on Board
FOB (insert named port of shipment)

GUIDANCE NOTE

This rule is to be used only for sea or inland waterway transport.

"Free on Board" means that the seller delivers the goods on board the vessel nominated by the buyer at the named port of shipment or procures the goods already so delivered. The risk of loss of or damage to the goods passes when the goods are on board the vessel, and the buyer bears all costs from that moment onwards.

The seller is required either to deliver the goods on board the vessel or to procure goods already so delivered for shipment. The reference to "procure" here caters for multiple sales down a chain ("string sales"), particularly common in the commodity trades.

FOB may not be appropriate where goods are handed over to the carrier before they are on board the vessel, for example goods in containers, which are typically delivered at a terminal. In such situations, the FCA rule should be used.

FOB requires the seller to clear the goods for export, where applicable. However, the seller has no obligation to clear the goods for import, pay any import duty or carry out any import customs formalities.

A THE SELLER'S OBLIGATIONS

A1 General obligations of the seller

The seller must provide the goods and the commercial invoice in conformity with the contract of sale and any other evidence of conformity that may be required by the contract.

Any document referred to in A1 –A10 may be an equivalent electronic record or procedure if agreed between the parties or customary.

A2 Licences, authorizations, security clearances and other formalities

Where applicable, the seller must obtain, at its own risk and expense, any export licence or other official authorization and carry out all customs formalities necessary for the export of the goods.

A3 Contracts of carriage and insurance

a) Contract of carriage

The seller has no obligation to the buyer to make a contract of carriage. However, if requested by the buyer or if it is commercial practice and the buyer does not give an instruction to the contrary in due time, the seller may contract for carriage on usual terms at the buyer's risk and expense. In either case, the seller may decline to make the contract of carriage and, if it does, shall promptly notify the buyer.

b) Contract of insurance

The seller has no obligation to the buyer to make a contract of insurance. However, the seller must provide the buyer, at the buyer's request, risk, and expense (if any), with information that the buyer needs for obtaining insurance.

A4　Delivery

The seller must deliver the goods either by placing them on board the vessel nominated by the buyer at the loading point, if any, indicated by the buyer at the named port of shipment or by procuring the goods so delivered. In either case, the seller must deliver the goods on the agreed date or within the agreed period and in the manner customary at the port.

If no specific loading point has been indicated by the buyer, the seller may select the point within the named port of shipment that best suits its purpose.

A5　Transfer of risks

The seller bears all risks of loss of or damage to the goods until they have been delivered in accordance with A4 with the exception of loss or damage in the circumstances described in B5.

A6　Allocation of costs

The seller must pay

a) all costs relating to the goods until they have been delivered in accordance with A4, other than those payable by the buyer as envisaged in B6; and

b) where applicable, the costs of customs formalities necessary for export, as well as all duties, taxes and other charges payable upon export.

A7　Notices to the buyer

The seller must, at the buyer's risk and expense, give the buyer sufficient notice either that the goods have been delivered in accordance with A4 or that the vessel has failed to take the goods within the time agreed.

A8　Delivery document

The seller must provide the buyer, at the seller's expense, with the usual proof that the goods have been delivered in accordance with A4.

Unless such proof is a transport document, the seller must provide assistance to the buyer, at the buyer's request, risk and expense, in obtaining a transport document.

A9　Checking-packaging-marking

The seller must pay the costs of those checking operations (such as checking quality, measuring, weighing, counting) that are necessary for the purpose of delivering the goods in accordance with A4, as well as the costs of any pre-shipment inspection mandated by the authority of the country of export.

The seller must, at its own expense, package the goods, unless it is usual for the particular trade to transport the type of goods sold unpackaged. The seller may package the goods in the manner appropriate for their transport, unless the buyer has notified the seller of specific packaging requirements before the contract of sale is concluded. Packaging is to be marked appropriately.

A10 Assistance with information and related costs

The seller must, where applicable, in a timely manner, provide to or render assistance in obtaining for the buyer, at the buyer's request, risk and expense, any documents and information, including security-related information, that the buyer needs for the import of the goods and/or for their transport to the final destination.

The seller must reimburse the buyer for all costs and charges incurred by the buyer in providing or rendering assistance in obtaining documents and information as envisaged in B10.

B THE BUYER'S OBLIGATIONS

B1 General obligations of the buyer

The buyer must pay the price of the goods as provided in the contract of sale.

Any document referred to in B1 −B10 may be an equivalent electronic record or procedure if agreed between the parties or customary.

B2 Licences, authorizations, security clearances and other formalities

Where applicable, it is up to the buyer to obtain, at its own risk and expense, any import licence or other official authorization and carry out all customs formalities for the import of the goods and for their transport through any country.

B3 Contracts of carriage and insurance

a) Contract of carriage

The buyer must contract, at its own expense for the carriage of the goods from the named port of shipment, except where the contract of carriage is made by the seller as provided for in A3 a).

b) Contract of insurance

The buyer has no obligation to the seller to make a contract of insurance.

B4 Taking delivery

The buyer must take delivery of the goods when they have been delivered as envisaged in A4.

B5 Transfer of risks

The buyer bears all risks of loss of or damage to the goods from the time they have been delivered as envisaged in A4.

If

a) the buyer fails to notify the nomination of a vessel in accordance with B7; or

b) the vessel nominated by the buyer fails to arrive on time to enable the seller to comply with A4, is unable to take the goods, or closes for cargo earlier than the time notified in accordance with B7, then, the buyer bears all risks of loss of or damage to the goods:

(i) from the agreed date, or in the absence of an agreed date,

(ii) from the date notified by the seller under A7 within the agreed period, or, if no such date has been notified,

(iii) from the expiry date of any agreed period for delivery,

provided that the goods have been clearly identified as the contract goods.

B6 Allocation of costs

The buyer must pay

a) all costs relating to the goods from the time they have been delivered as envisaged in A4, except, where applicable, the costs of customs formalities necessary for export, as well as all duties, taxes and other charges payable upon export as referred to in A6 b);

b) any additional costs incurred, either because:

(i) the buyer has failed to give appropriate notice in accordance with B7, or

(ii) the vessel nominated by the buyer fails to arrive on time, is unable to take the goods, or closes for cargo earlier than the time notified in accordance with B7, provided that the goods have been clearly identified as the contract goods; and

c) where applicable, all duties, taxes and other charges, as well as the costs of carrying out customs formalities payable upon import of the goods and the costs for their transport through any country.

B7　Notices to the seller

The buyer must give the seller sufficient notice of the vessel name, loading point and, where necessary, the selected delivery time within the agreed period.

B8　Proof of delivery

The buyer must accept the proof of delivery provided as envisaged in A8.

B9　Inspection of goods

The buyer must pay the costs of any mandatory pre-shipment inspection, except when such inspection is mandated by the authorities of the country of export.

B10　Assistance with information and related costs

The buyer must, in a timely manner, advise the seller of any security information requirements so that the seller may comply with A10.

The buyer must reimburse the seller for all costs and charges incurred by the seller in providing or rendering assistance in obtaining documents and information as envisaged in A10.

The buyer must, where applicable, in a timely manner, provide to or render assistance in obtaining for the seller, at the seller's request, risk and expense, any documents and information, including security-related information, that the seller needs for the transport and export of the goods and for their transport through any country.

Cost and Freight
CFR (insert named port of destination)

GUIDANCE NOTE

This rule is to be used only for sea or inland waterway transport.

"Cost and Freight" means that the seller delivers the goods on board the vessel or procures the goods already so delivered. The risk of loss of or damage to the goods passes when the goods are on board the vessel.

The seller must contract for and pay the costs and freight necessary to bring the goods to the named port of destination. When CPT, CIP, CFR or CIF are used, the seller fulfils its obligation to deliver when it hands the goods over to the carrier in the manner specified in the chosen rule and not when the goods reach the place of destination.

This rule has two critical points, because risk passes and costs are transferred at different places. While the contract will always specify a destination port, it might not specify the port of shipment, which is where risk passes to the buyer. If the shipment port is of particular interest to the buyer, the parties are well advised to identify it as precisely as possible in the contract.

The parties are well advised to identify as precisely as possible the point at the agreed port of destination, as the costs to that point are for the account of the seller. The seller is advised to procure contracts of carriage that match this choice precisely. If the seller incurs costs under its contract of carriage related to unloading at the specified point at the port of destination, the seller is not entitled to recover such costs from the buyer unless otherwise agreed between the parties.

The seller is required either to deliver the goods on board the vessel or to procure goods already so delivered for shipment to the destination. In addition, the seller is required either to make a contract of carriage or to procure such a contract. The reference to "procure" here caters for multiple sales down a chain ("string sales"), particularly common in the commodity trades.

CFR may not be appropriate where goods are handed over to the carrier before they are on board the vessel, for example goods in containers, which are typically delivered at a terminal. In such circumstances, the CPT rule should be used.

CFR requires the seller to clear the goods for export, where applicable. However, the seller has no obligation to clear the goods for import, pay any import duty or carry out any import customs formalities.

A THE SELLER'S OBLIGATIONS

A1 General obligations of the seller

The seller must provide the goods and the commercial invoice in conformity with the contract of sale and any other evidence of conformity that may be required by the contract.

Any document referred to in A1 – A10 may be an equivalent electronic record or procedure if agreed between the parties or customary.

A2 Licences, authorizations, security clearances and other formalities

Where applicable, the seller must obtain, at its own risk and expense, any export licence or other official authorization and carry out all customs formalities necessary for the export of the goods.

A3 Contracts of carriage and insurance

a) Contract of carriage

The seller must contract or procure a contract for the carriage of the goods from the agreed point of delivery, if any, at the place of delivery to the named port of destination or, if agreed, any point at that port. The contract of carriage must be made on usual terms at the seller's expense and provide for carriage by the usual route in a vessel of the type normally used for the transport of the type of goods sold.

b) Contract of insurance

The seller has no obligation to the buyer to make a contract of insurance. However, the seller must provide the buyer, at the buyer's request, risk, and expense (if any), with information that the buyer needs for obtaining insurance.

A4 Delivery

The seller must deliver the goods either by placing them on board the vessel or by procuring the goods so delivered. In either case, the seller must deliver the goods on the agreed date or within the agreed period and in the manner customary at the port.

A5 Transfer of risks

The seller bears all risks of loss of or damage to the goods until they have been delivered in accordance with A4, with the exception of loss or damage in the circumstances described in B5.

A6 Allocation of costs

The seller must pay

a) all costs relating to the goods until they have been delivered in accordance with A4, other than those payable by the buyer as envisaged in B6;

b) the freight and all other costs resulting from A3 a), including the costs of loading the goods on board and any charges for unloading at the agreed port of discharge that were for the seller's account under the contract of carriage; and

c) where applicable, the costs of customs formalities necessary for export as well as all duties, taxes and other charges payable upon export, and the costs for their transport through any country that were for the seller's account under the contract of carriage.

A7 Notices to the buyer

The seller must give the buyer any notice needed in order to allow the buyer to take measures that are normally necessary to enable the buyer to take the goods.

A8 Delivery document

The seller must, at its own expense, provide the buyer without delay with the usual transport document for the agreed port of destination.

This transport document must cover the contract goods, be dated within the period agreed for shipment, enable the buyer to claim the goods from the carrier at the port of destination and, unless otherwise agreed, enable the buyer to sell the goods in transit by the transfer of the document to a subsequent buyer or by notification to the carrier.

When such a transport document is issued in negotiable form and in several originals, a full set of originals must be presented to the buyer.

A9 Checking-packaging-marking

The seller must pay the costs of those checking operations (such as checking quality, measuring, weighing, counting) that are necessary for the purpose of delivering the goods in accordance with A4, as well as the costs of any pre-shipment inspection mandated by the authority of the country of export. The seller must, at its own expense, package the goods, unless it is usual for the particular trade to transport the type of goods sold unpackaged.

The seller may package the goods in the manner appropriate for their transport, unless the buyer has notified the seller of specific packaging requirements before the contract of sale is concluded.

Packaging is to be marked appropriately.

A10 Assistance with information and related costs

The seller must, where applicable, in a timely manner, provide to or render assistance in obtaining for the buyer, at the buyer's request, risk and expense, any documents and information, including security-related information, that the buyer needs for the import of the goods and/or for their transport to the final destination.

The seller must reimburse the buyer for all costs and charges incurred by the buyer in providing or rendering assistance in obtaining documents and information as envisaged in B10.

B THE BUYER'S OBLIGATIONS

B1 General obligations of the buyer

The buyer must pay the price of the goods as provided in the contract of sale.

Any document referred to in B1 −B10 may be an equivalent electronic record or procedure if agreed between the parties or customary.

B2 Licences, authorizations, security clearances and other formalities

Where applicable, it is up to the buyer to obtain, at its own risk and expense, any import licence or other official authorization and carry out all customs formalities for the import of the goods and for their transport through any country.

B3 Contracts of carriage and insurance

a) Contract of carriage

The buyer has no obligation to the seller to make a contract of carriage.

b) Contract of insurance

The buyer has no obligation to the seller to make a contract of insurance. However, the buyer must provide the seller, upon request, with the necessary information for obtaining insurance.

B4 Taking delivery

The buyer must take delivery of the goods when they have been delivered as envisaged in A4 and receive them from the carrier at the named port of destination.

B5 Transfer of risks

The buyer bears all risks of loss of or damage to the goods from the time they have been delivered as envisaged in A4. If the buyer fails to give notice in accordance with B7, then it bears all risks of loss of or damage to the goods from the agreed date or the expiry date of the agreed period for shipment, provided that the goods have been clearly identified as the contract goods.

B6 Allocation of costs

The buyer must, subject to the provisions of A3 a), pay

a) all costs relating to the goods from the time they have been delivered as envisaged in A4, except, where applicable, the costs of customs formalities necessary for export as well as all duties, taxes, and other charges payable upon export as referred to in A6 c);

b) all costs and charges relating to the goods while in transit until their arrival at the port of destination, unless such costs and charges were for the seller's account under the contract of carriage;

c) unloading costs including lighterage and wharfage charges, unless such costs and charges were for the seller's account under the contract of carriage;

d) any additional costs incurred if it fails to give notice in accordance with B7, from the agreed date or the expiry date of the agreed period for shipment, provided that the goods have been clearly identified as the contract goods; and

e) where applicable, all duties, taxes and other charges, as well as the costs of carrying out customs formalities payable upon import of the goods and the costs for their transport through any country unless included within the cost of the contract of carriage.

B7　Notices to the seller

The buyer must, whenever it is entitled to determine the time for shipping the goods and/or the point of receiving the goods within the named port of destination, give the seller sufficient notice thereof.

B8　Proof of delivery

The buyer must accept the transport document provided as envisaged in A8 if it is in conformity with the contract.

B9　Inspection of goods

The buyer must pay the costs of any mandatory pre-shipment inspection, except when such inspection is mandated by the authorities of the country of export.

B10　Assistance with information and related costs

The buyer must, in a timely manner, advise the seller of any security information requirements so that the seller may comply with A10.

The buyer must reimburse the seller for all costs and charges incurred by the seller in providing or rendering assistance in obtaining documents and information as envisaged in A10.

The buyer must, where applicable, in a timely manner, provide to or render assistance in obtaining for the seller, at the seller's request, risk and expense, any documents and information, including security-related information, that the seller needs for the transport and export of the goods and for their transport through any country.

Cost, Insurance and Freight
CIF (insert named port of destination)

GUIDANCE NOTE

This rule is to be used only for sea or inland waterway transport.

"Cost, Insurance and Freight" means that the seller delivers the goods on board the vessel or procures the goods already so delivered. The risk of loss of or damage to the goods passes when the goods are on board the vessel. The seller must contract for and pay the costs and freight necessary to bring the goods to the named port of destination.

The seller also contracts for insurance cover against the buyer's risk of loss of or damage to the goods during the carriage. The buyer should note that under CIF the seller is required to obtain insurance only on minimum cover. Should the buyer wish to have more insurance protection, it will need either to agree as much expressly with the seller or to make its own extra insurance arrangements.

When CPT, CIP, CFR, or CIF are used, the seller fulfils its obligation to deliver when it hands the goods over to the carrier in the manner specified in the chosen rule and not when the goods reach the place of destination.

This rule has two critical points, because risk passes and costs are transferred at different places. While the contract will always specify a destination port, it might not specify the port of shipment, which is where risk passes to the buyer. If the shipment port is of particular interest to the buyer, the parties are well advised to identify it as precisely as possible in the contract.

The parties are well advised to identify as precisely as possible the point at the agreed port of destination, as the costs to that point are for the account of the seller. The seller is advised to procure contracts of carriage that match this choice precisely. If the seller incurs costs under its contract of carriage related to unloading at the specified point at the port of destination, the seller is not entitled to recover such costs from the buyer unless otherwise agreed between the parties.

The seller is required either to deliver the goods on board the vessel or to procure goods already so delivered for shipment to the destination. In addition the seller is required either to make a contract of carriage or to procure such a contract. The reference to "procure" here caters for multiple sales down a chain ("string sales"), particularly common in the commodity trades.

CIF may not be appropriate where goods are handed over to the carrier before they are on board the vessel, for example goods in containers, which are typically delivered at a terminal. In such circumstances, the CIP rule should be used.

CIF requires the seller to clear the goods for export, where applicable. However, the seller has no obligation to clear the goods for import, pay any import duty or carry out any import customs formalities.

A　THE SELLER'S OBLIGATIONS

A1　General obligations of the seller

The seller must provide the goods and the commercial invoice in conformity with the contract of sale and any other evidence of conformity that may be required by the contract.

Any document referred to in A1 −A10 may be an equivalent electronic record or procedure if agreed between the parties or customary.

A2　Licences, authorizations, security clearances and other formalities

Where applicable, the seller must obtain, at its own risk and expense, any export licence or other official authorization and carry out all customs formalities necessary for the export of the goods.

A3　Contracts of carriage and insurance

a) Contract of carriage

The seller must contract or procure a contract for the carriage of the goods from the agreed point of delivery, if any, at the place of delivery to the named port of destination or, if agreed, any point at that port. The contract of carriage must be made on usual terms at the seller's expense and provide for carriage by the usual route in a vessel of the type normally used for the transport of the type of goods sold.

b) Contract of insurance

The seller must obtain, at its own expense, cargo insurance complying at least with the minimum cover provided by Clauses (C) of the Institute Cargo Clauses[8] (LMA/IUA) or any similar clauses. The insurance shall be contracted with underwriters or an insurance company of good reputation and entitle the buyer, or any other person having an insurable interest in the goods, to claim directly from the insurer.

When required by the buyer, the seller shall, subject to the buyer providing any necessary information requested by the seller, provide at the buyer's expense any additional cover, if procurable, such as cover as provided by Clauses (A) or (B) of the Institute Cargo Clauses (LMA/IUA) or any similar clauses and/or cover complying with the Institute War Clauses and/or Institute Strikes Clauses (LMA/IUA) or any similar clauses.

The insurance shall cover, at a minimum, the price provided in the contract plus 10% (i. e., 110%) and shall be in the currency of the contract.

The insurance shall cover the goods from the point of delivery set out in A4 and A5 to at least the named port of destination. The seller must provide the buyer with the insurance policy or other evidence of insurance cover. Moreover, the seller must provide the buyer, at the buyer's request, risk, and expense (if any), with information that the buyer needs to procure any additional insurance.

A4 Delivery

The seller must deliver the goods either by placing them on board the vessel or by procuring the goods so delivered. In either case, the seller must deliver the goods on the agreed date or within the agreed period and in the manner customary at the port.

A5 Transfer of risks

The seller bears all risks of loss of or damage to the goods until they have been delivered in accordance with A4, with the exception of loss or damage in the circumstances described in B5.

A6 Allocation of costs

The seller must pay

a) all costs relating to the goods until they have been delivered in accordance with A4, other than those payable by the buyer as envisaged in B6;

b) the freight and all other costs resulting from A3 a), including the costs of loading the goods on board and any charges for unloading at the agreed port of discharge that were for the seller's account under the contract of carriage;

c) the costs of insurance resulting from A3 b); and

d) where applicable, the costs of customs formalities necessary for export, as well as all duties, taxes and other charges payable upon export, and the costs for their transport through any country that were for the seller's account under the contract of carriage.

A7　Notices to the buyer

The seller must give the buyer any notice needed in order to allow the buyer to take measures that are normally necessary to enable the buyer to take the goods.

A8　Delivery document

The seller must, at its own expense provide the buyer without delay with the usual transport document for the agreed port of destination.

This transport document must cover the contract goods, be dated within the period agreed for shipment, enable the buyer to claim the goods from the carrier at the port of destination and, unless otherwise agreed, enable the buyer to sell the goods in transit by the transfer of the document to a subsequent buyer or by notification to the carrier.

When such a transport document is issued in negotiable form and in several originals, a full set of originals must be presented to the buyer.

A9　Checking-packaging-marking

The seller must pay the costs of those checking operations (such as checking quality, measuring, weighing, counting) that are necessary for the purpose of delivering the goods in accordance with A4, as well as the costs of any pre-shipment inspection mandated by the authority of the country of export.

The seller must, at its own expense, package the goods, unless it is usual for the particular trade to transport the type of goods sold unpackaged. The seller may package the goods in the manner appropriate for their transport, unless the buyer has notified the seller of specific packaging requirements before the contract of sale is concluded. Packaging is to be marked appropriately.

A10　Assistance with information and related costs

The seller must, where applicable, in a timely manner, provide to or render assistance in obtaining for the buyer, at the buyer's request, risk and expense, any documents and information, including security-related information, that the buyer needs for the import of the goods and/or for their transport to the final destination.

The seller must reimburse the buyer for all costs and charges incurred by the buyer in providing or rendering assistance in obtaining documents and information as envisaged in B10.

B　THE BUYER'S OBLIGATIONS

B1　General obligations of the buyer

The buyer must pay the price of the goods as provided in the contract of sale.

Any document referred to in B1 − B10 may be an equivalent electronic record or procedure if agreed between the parties or customary.

B2　Licences, authorizations, security clearances and formalities

Where applicable, it is up to the buyer to obtain, at its own risk and expense, any import licence or other official authorization and carry out all customs formalities for the import of the goods and for their transport through any country.

B3　Contracts of carriage and insurance

a) Contract of carriage

The buyer has no obligation to the seller to make a contract of carriage.

b) Contract of insurance

The buyer has no obligation to the seller to make a contract of insurance. However, the buyer must provide the seller, upon request, with any information necessary for the seller to procure any additional insurance requested by the buyer as envisaged in A3 b).

B4　Taking delivery

The buyer must take delivery of the goods when they have been delivered as envisaged in A4 and receive them from the carrier at the named port of destination.

B5　Transfer of risks

The buyer bears all risks of loss of or damage to the goods from the time they have been delivered as envisaged in A4.

If the buyer fails to give notice in accordance with B7, then it bears all risks of loss of or damage to the goods from the agreed date or the expiry date of the agreed period for shipment, provided that the goods have been clearly identified as the contract goods.

B6　Allocation of costs

The buyer must, subject to the provisions of A3 a), pay

a) all costs relating to the goods from the time they have been delivered as envisaged in A4, except, where applicable, the costs of customs formalities necessary for export, as well as all duties, taxes and other charges payable upon export as referred to in A6 d);

b) all costs and charges relating to the goods while in transit until their arrival at the port of destination, unless such costs and charges were for the seller's account under the contract of carriage;

c) unloading costs including lighterage and wharfage charges, unless such costs and charges were for the seller's account under the contract of carriage;

d) any additional costs incurred if it fails to give notice in accordance with B7, from the agreed date or the expiry date of the agreed period for shipment, provided that the goods have been clearly identified as the contract goods;

e) where applicable, all duties, taxes and other charges, as well as the costs of carrying out customs formalities payable upon import of the goods and the costs for their transport through any country, unless included within the cost of the contract of carriage; and

f) the costs of any additional insurance procured at the buyer's request under A3 b) and B3 b).

B7　Notices to the seller

The buyer must, whenever it is entitled to determine the time for shipping the goods and/or the point of receiving the goods within the named port of destination, give the seller sufficient notice thereof.

B8　Proof of delivery

The buyer must accept the transport document provided as envisaged in A8 if it is in conformity with the contract.

B9   Inspection of goods

The buyer must pay the costs of any mandatory pre-shipment inspection, except when such inspection is mandated by the authorities of the country of export.

B10   Assistance with information and related costs

The buyer must, in a timely manner, advise the seller of any security information requirements so that the seller may comply with A10.

The buyer must reimburse the seller for all costs and charges incurred by the seller in providing or rendering assistance in obtaining documents and information as envisaged in A10.

The buyer must, where applicable, in a timely manner, provide to or render assistance in obtaining for the seller, at the seller's request, risk and expense, any documents and information, including security-related information, that the seller needs for the transport and export of the goods and for their transport through any country.

New Words and Expressions

encompass	v.	包围，包含
transshipment	n.	转运
clause	n.	条款
supersede	v.	代替
breach	n.	违约
licence	n.	许可
reimburse	v.	补偿
carrier	n.	承运人
premises	n.	场地
mandatory	a.	强制性的，义务的
inspection	n.	保险
advise	v.	通知
procure	v.	采购
incur	v.	产生（费用）
repeat order		回头订单
title to goods		物权凭证
Incoterms		国际贸易术语解释通则
irrespective of		无论是，与……无关
clear goods for export		出口结关

1. customs entry：报关手续。

2. title to goods：货物所有权。"title" 的意思是 "所有权"，因此 "title documents" 是 "所有权单据" 的意思。

3. ... but they can be binding upon buyers or sellers provided that the sales contract specifies that a particular Incoterms will apply.

   本句中的 "binding upon" 为 "对……有约束力" 的意思，而 "provided that" 表示 "在……的条件下"，与英语中的 "on condition that" 的用法相同。

4. The parties are well advised to specify as clearly as possible the point within the named place of delivery, as the costs and risks to that point are for the account of the seller.　当事人应该明确规定交货地点，以及出口商需要承担将货运往该地点之前的风险和费用。

5. ... the seller must provide the buyer, at the buyer's request, risk and expense, assistance in obtaining any export license, or other official authorization necessary for the export of the goods.

   ……出口商，在进口商的请求下，并在由进口商承担风险和费用情况下，协助进口商获得出口许可证和其他出口所必需的官方许可文件。

6. ... pay any additional costs incurred by failing either to take delivery of the goods when they have been placed at its disposal ...　……当货物交付其处置下，如果没有提货，应支付由此所造成的额外费用……

7. the risk of loss of or damage to the goods：货物灭失或损失的风险。

8. Institute Cargo Clauses：《英国伦敦协会海运货物保险条款》，一般简称为《协会货物条款》（Institute Cargo Clause, I. C. C.）。由于国际贸易事业的发展及运输方式的改变，原条款已经不能适合于形势发展的需要，于 1982 年 1 月 1 日修改为《伦敦协会货物条款（A）》[Institute Cargo Clauses(A)]、《伦敦协会货物条款（B）》[Institute Cargo Clauses(B)]和《伦敦协会货物条款 （C）》[Institute Cargo Clauses(C)]，一般统称它们为《伦敦协会货物保险条款》。《协会货物条款》共有 6 种险别，它们是：（1）协会货物条款（A）[简称 ICC（A）]；（2）协会货物条款（B）[简称 ICC（B）]；（3）协会货物条款（C）[简称 ICC（C）]；（4）协会战争险条款（货物）（简称 IWCC）；（5）协会罢工险条款（货物）（简称 ISCC）；（6）恶意损害险（Malicious Damage Clause）。以上 6 种险别中，（A）险相当于《中国保险条款》中的一切险，其责任范围更为广泛，故采用承保"除外责任"之外的一切风险的方式表明其承保范围。（B）险大体上相当于水渍险。（C）险相当于平安险，但承保范围较小些。（B）险和（C）险都采用列明风险的方式表示其承保范围。6 种险别中，只有恶意损害险属于附加险别，不能单独投保，其他 5 种险别的结构相同，体系完整。因此，除（A）、（B）、（C）三种险别可以单独投保外，必要时，战争险和罢工险在征得保险公司同意后，也可作为独立的险别进行投保。我国企业按 CIF 或 CIP 条件出口时，一般按《中国保险条款》投保，但如果国外客户要求按《协会货物条款》投保，一般可予接受。

I Review questions.

1. What are the vital aspects of a transaction?
2. Incoterms are grouped into four categories. What terms are included in each group?
3. What are the differences between FOB, CFR and CIF?
4. What are the derived terms of FOB and CFR and CIF?
5. Under CIF, if the goods are lost or damaged during transit, who is to ask the insurance company to cover the losses?
6. Why is it very important for the seller to send shipping advice to the buyer under CFR?
7. What does CIP mean?
8. What are the differences between FOB/CFR/CIF and FCA/CPT/CIP?
9. What do D terms require the seller to do?
10. Under DDP, does the buyer assume the least liabilities of all trade terms?

II Define the following terms briefly.

1. Incoterms
2. Ex Works
3. DAT
4. CFR
5. CIF
6. CIP
7. FAS
8. AP

III Decide whether the following statements are True or False. Then put T for True or F for False in the brackets at the end of each statement.

1. CFR is the term when the consignment is delivered with all the charges up to arrival at the port of destination paid by the seller. (   )
2. CPT is the most appropriate term when the seller must pay the cost and freight necessary to bring the goods to the named port of destination by a roll-on/roll-off vessel. (   )
3. When the seller pays for the goods to be placed alongside the vessel on the quay or in lighters at

the named port of shipment, the term is FOB. (　　)

4. Under FCA term, the seller has no obligation to contract for carriage. (　　)

5. Under EX-Works term the exporter bears the least risks involved in the shipment of cargoes exported. (　　)

6. Under CFR, the seller must pay the usual freight rate and any additional costs that arise en route. (　　)

7. Under Incoterms 2010, DAT requires the seller to clear the goods for export and import and their related duties.

8. Under Incoterms 2010, DAP, delivered at Place, has replaced the former DAF, DES and DDU rules.

9. If the seller agrees to deliver the goods to a ship, but not to pay for loading them, then the term is FOB. (　　)

10. Under the terms FOB, CIF, and CFR, the risk of loss of or damage to the goods, as well as any additional costs due to events occurring after the time the goods have been delivered on board the vessel, is transferred from the seller to the buyer when the goods pass the ship's rail in the port of shipment. (　　)

Ⅳ Translate the following passage into Chinese.

There are only two terms, which deal with insurance, namely CIF and CIP. Under these terms the seller is obliged to procure insurance for the benefit of the buyer. In other cases it is for the parties themselves to decide whether and to what extent they want to cover themselves by insurance. Since the seller takes out insurance for the benefit of the buyer, he would not know the buyer's precise requirements. Under the Institute Cargo Clause drafted by the Institute of London Underwriters, insurance is available in "minimum cover" under Clause C, "medium cover" under Clause B and "most extended cover" under Clause A. Since in the sale of commodities under the CIF term the buyer may wish to sell the goods in transit to subsequent buyer who in turn may wish to resell the goods again, it is impossible to know the insurance cover suitable to such subsequent buyers and, therefore, the minimum cover under CIF has traditionally been chosen with the possibility for the buyer to require the seller to take out additional insurance. Minimum cover is however unsuitable for sale of manufactured goods where the risk of theft, pilferage or improper handling or custody of the goods would require more than the cover available under Clause C. Since CIP, as distinguished from CIF, would normally not be used for the sale of commodities, it would have been feasible to adopt the most extended cover under CIP rather than the minimum cover under CIF. But to vary the seller's insurance obligation under CIF and CIP would lead to confusion and both terms therefore limit the seller's insurance obligation to the minimum cover.

Ⅴ Translate the following passage into English.

贸易术语，又称价格术语或交货术语，是国际贸易中单价条款的重要组成部分，它代表买卖双方各自特定的义务。每笔商业交易都是以销售合同为基础，而合同中所运用的贸易术语却具有明确物权何时何地从卖方转至买方的作用。贸易术语同时还规定了买卖双方各自承担哪些责任和费用。贸易术语的运用大大简化了合同的谈判，从而节省了时间和费用。

Ⅵ Read the following passages and answer the questions.

Business Law — Commercial Transaction and Bankruptcy

The law of commercial transactions comprises the core of the legal rules governing business dealings. The most common types of commercial transactions involve such specialized areas of the law and legal instruments as sale of goods and documents of title. Despite variations of detail, all commercial transactions have one thing in common: they serve to transmit economic values such as materials, products, and services from those who want to exchange them for another value, usually money, to those who need them and are willing to pay a counter-value. It is the purpose of the relevant legal rules to regulate this exchange of values, to spell out the rights and obligations of each party, and to offer remedies if one of the parties breaches its obligations or cannot perform them for some reason. The law of commercial transactions thus covers a wide range of business activities.

In the 20th century, domestic as well as international commerce has experienced an expansion far beyond any earlier dimensions. With the multiplication of commercial transactions the demand for legal certainty has increased, especially for transactions across national boundaries. The first response to the multitude of practically identical transactions was the standardization of contracts. Printed standard contracts or form lay down those provisions that are essential in the eyes of the drafting party. It depends upon the relative economic strength of the other party whether the departures from the printed form can be negotiated. Apart from standardizing the contract practices of a particular party, the uniform conditions also help to bridge the gap between many different national rules. They are a means of achieving partial uniformity of law for international trade.

The development of uniform legislative rules for international transactions has been another distinctive feature in this century. This trend resulted from the uncertainties to which international commercial transactions that came under two or major national jurisdictional commercial transactional conventions have resulted in the unification of numerous rules, especially in the areas of transportation, industrial property (patents and trademarks), copyright, and commercial paper (bill of exchange and checks). Less successful so far have been attempts in the fields of sale of goods and the conclusion of contract. Despite considerable progress in the field of unification, none of the uniform rules is really worldwide in scope, many being limited to a continent or to narrower regional groups.

The sale is the most common commercial transaction. All the rights that the seller has in a specific object are transferred to the buyer in return for the latter's paying the purchase price to the seller. The objects may be movable or immovable, and tangible or intangible. Not all transfers of goods to another person for any purpose whatsoever constitute a sale. Goods may be transferred for use only (lease), for safe-keeping or storage (bailment), as a present, or in exchange for another goods (barter). A sale is involved only if the seller intends to part with the object completely and conceivably forever and to receive instead a sum of money and the price.

The seller's duties are three: he must deliver the goods, transfer ownership in them, and warrant their conformity to the specifications of the contract. Delivery of the goods sold to the buyer must be at the time and place and in the manner agreed upon by the parties. None delivery is sanctioned by the various legal systems, and delayed delivery is treated differently in various countries. Delivery must be accompanied by transferor of ownership to enable the buyer to enjoy full legal rights over the objects sold. In most countries, ownership in a specific object is transferred with the conclusion of the contract of sale unless the parties agree otherwise. But the parties may delay the transfer of ownership, perhaps until delivery to the buyer, or until payment of the purchase price, or until the buyer receives the goods. Goods sold must conform to the specifications of the contract as to their physical qualities, kinds, and quantity. In most legal systems, if goods of defective quality are detected, the buyer may reject the goods and dissolve the contract of sale. Or he may accept the goods but make a deduction from the purchase price for the defect.

The buyer's duties, by contrast, are simple: payment of the purchase price and acceptance of delivery. If the buyer refuses to take delivery, the seller is entitled to resell the goods at a reasonable price. The proceeds of the resale diminish the seller's loss, but the original buyer remains responsible for the difference. The seller may claim this difference as damages. If the buyer merely delays payment, the seller may claim compensation for any resulting loss.

The duties of seller and buyer are mutual and concurrent. Both the parties assume duties in anticipation of the performance promised by the party. It is a major consequence of the principle of mutuality of obligations that the duties of seller and buyer must be performed in general at the same time unless the parties agree otherwise. The law everywhere protects the time sequence agreed upon by the parties by allowing a party to refuse its own performance as long as agreed advance performance has not been made by the other party. However, the many differences in the sales laws throughout the world are a serious obstacle to an effective and smooth international trade. A considerable degree of unification of sales rule has been achieved by the wide acceptance of certain form contracts, yet they have two important drawbacks: the validity depends on their acceptance by both contracting parties, and they cannot override the mandatory rules of national law. The drawbacks can only be overcome by unifying national legislation. After many years' preparation an international conference at the Hague adopted in 1964 a Uniform Law on International Sale, and a revised Convention on Contracts for the International Sales of Goods was signed in 1980 and entered into force in 1988 in some countries.

The negotiable instrument, which is essentially document embodying a right to the payment of money and which may be transferred from person to person, developed historically from efforts to make credit instruments transferable; that is, documents proving that somebody was in their debt were used by creditors to meet their own liabilities. Thus a promise of A to pay B a certain sum at a specified date in the future could be used by B to pay a debt to C. These "negotiable instruments include promissory notes, checks and drafts (bills of exchange)". These are in fact the most common negotiable instruments in use.

If the debtor or borrower does not make payment after the secured loan has fallen due, the creditor or lender may pursue two different courses. He may enforce his claim for repayment before the courts, or he may enforce his preferred position as a secured lender. The rules to be followed in enforcing a security interest differ considerably from country to country. Very often the lender must sell the charged goods by public sale: occasionally he is permitted to acquire the charged goods himself. If the proceeds of a sale exceed the amount of the secured loan, the surplus must be paid to the borrower, whereas the borrower remains liable for any deficit. All legal systems frown upon clauses that permit a lender to acquire the charged goods automatically on the borrower's failure to pay

Bankruptcy laws were enacted to provide and govern an orderly and equitable liquidation of the estates of insolvent debtors. Purpose has remained an important aim of bankruptcy legislation since the Middle Ages. Modern bankruptcy laws always include detailed provisions for preventive compositions, arrangements, or corporate reorganizations of various types. In fact, the salvage of an enterprise in financial difficulties has become the principal focus of insolvency legislation with particular concern for the maintenance of employment opportunities and the protection of members of the labor force. In addition, the laws may include provisions for the unpaid portions of debts incurred prior to bankruptcy in order to give honest but unfortunate debtors a new start in life.

Since bankruptcy laws aim at the liquidation or rehabilitation of insolvent estates, bankruptcy proceedings involve all nonexempt assets of the debtor, and all creditors entitled to share in the proceeds of the liquidation or in the adjustment of their claim are called to participate. At one time all bankrupts were subjected to severe social and professional sanctions. In recent time, however, great efforts have been made to remove the disgrace attached to bankruptcy.

Liquidation proceedings are often referred to as" straight bankruptcy which is decreed only after the possibility of reorganization has been found not to exist or an attempt reorganization has failed. Modern bankruptcy laws provide for the initiation of liquidation proceedings upon petition by either the bankrupt himself or his creditors. In Common-wealth countries, a single creditor may be a petitioner if the unsecured part of his claim equals or exceeds a specified amount. Otherwise, other creditor must join until aggregate amount of their claims equals the requisite sum.

Please answer the following questions.

1. What is commercial transaction by definition?
2. In what way can standardization of contract be of paramount importance?
3. How do countries differ in transferring ownership in a specific object?
4. Point out the main drawbacks in the unification of sales rules.
5. Name some common negotiable instruments.

Chapter 7

Business Contract
贸易合同

In international trade, business negotiation, which has direct influence on the conclusion and implementation of a contract, plays a basic part in the conclusion of a sales contract and has a great bearing on the economic interest of the parties concerned. After business negotiation and having reached an agreement, the two parties of a transaction sign a written contract which shall function as basis for the performance of rights and obligations by the two parties. Once the sales contract is effectively concluded according to the law, the parties concerned should perform the contract strictly according to the time, the quality and the quantity as stipulated in the contract.

7.1　Business Negotiation

It is conducted for the purpose of reaching an agreement and is a process of discussing the relevant terms and conditions of a transaction between the buyer and seller. Business negotiation is conducted either by correspondence or by face-to-face talk, and involves all kinds of terms and conditions of a sales contract including quality, quantity, packing, shipment, payment, insurance, inspection, claims, arbitration and Force Majeure etc. Generally speaking, business negotiation involves four steps: inquiry[1], offer[2], counter-offer and acceptance, among which, offer and acceptance are two indispensable steps for reaching an agreement and concluding a contract.

7.1.1 ▌ Invitation to Offer

It is either an inquiry made to get information about the terms and conditions of a commodity trading, or a conditional suggestion about the transaction. Inquiry is a usual form of invitation to offer involving quality, quantity, price, packing, shipment, asking for samples and catalogues, etc. Inquiry can be made by the buyer or the seller, and can be made orally or in writing.

7.1.2 ▌ Offer

It is a sufficiently definite proposal for concluding a contract addressed to one or more specific persons indicating the intention of the offeror to be bound in case of acceptance by the offeree.

1. The Constitution of an Offer

(1) The offer is addressed to one or more specific persons. A proposal other than one addressed to one or more specific persons is to be considered as an invitation to make offer, unless the contract is clearly indicated by the person making the proposal. The offeree can be one or more than one physical or legal persons. Commercial ads is not made to specific person and therefore is an invitation to offer which is not an effective offer.

(2) The offer must be definite. A proposal is sufficiently definite if it indicates the goods and expressly or implicitly fixes or makes provision for determining the quantity and the price. But in China, the main terms and conditions of a contract such as name and specifications of commodity, quantity, packing, price, shipment and payment are required in an offer.

(3) The offer must indicate the term of validity.

Usually, offer has a validity period during which the offeror is to be bound so that acceptance by the offeree is effective. If no time is fixed in an offer, acceptance by the offeree should be made within a reasonable time[3], otherwise the acceptance is not effective. The following are ways of fixing the validity period of an offer.

- Fixing the latest date for acceptance. For instance, "our offer is subject to your reply reaching us before September 30", "the offer is valid until September 5 our time".
- Fixing a period of time. For instance, "our offer remains effective for 5 days". when using this kind of method to fix the validity period, disputes may arise as a result of the indefinite statement which does not indicate the starting time of the offer.
- Fixing in general terms. General terms such as "prompt reply', "immediate rely", etc. are ambiguous and indefinite and should be avoided.

2. Withdrawal and Revocation of an Offer

An offer, once accepted, is irrevocable. But rules about whether or not an offer can be withdrawn, altered or revoked differ from country to country. According to the relevant stipulations of the United Nations Convention on Contracts for the International Sales of Goods[4], an offer, even if it is irrevocable, may be withdrawn if the withdrawn reaches the offeree before or at the same time as the offer. Until a contract is concluded an offer may be revoked if the revocation reaches the offeree before he has dispatched an acceptance. However, an offer cannot be revoked under the following circumstances:

(1) If it indicates, whether by stating a fixed time for acceptance or otherwise, that it is irrevocable; or

(2) If it was reasonable for the offeree to rely on the offer as being irrevocable and the offeree has acted in reliance on the offer.

3. Termination

An offer terminates under the following circumstances:

(1) By non-acceptance within the time limit, by non-acceptance within a reasonable time if no

time limit is specified;

(2) When revoked before acceptance;

(3) When rejected by the offeree.

7.1.3 | Acceptance

Acceptance becomes effective when the buyer or the seller unconditionally agrees on the offer made by their counterpart. A contract is concluded once the offer is accepted.

1. The Constitution of an Acceptance

(1) Be made by the offeree.

(2) Be in accordance with the offer.

(3) Be made in the validity period.

To be specific, the acceptance should, the first of all, be made by the right party, that is, offeree. It can be made in words or writing or by action. Examples of actions are: seller's making shipment or buyer's opening of L/C, etc. Secondly, acceptance should be made unconditionally. There should be no conditions of acceptance or any material modification, addition or restriction in the acceptance. According to stipulations of the United Nations Convention on Contracts for the International Sale of Goods, a reply to an offer, which purports to be an acceptance but contains additions, limitations or other modifications is a rejection of the offer and constitutes a counter-offer. However, a reply to an offer which purports to be an acceptance but contains additional or different terms which do not materially alter the terms of the offer constitutes an acceptance[5], unless the offeror, without delay, objects orally to the discrepancy or dispatches a notice to that effect. If he does not so object, the terms of the contract are the terms of the offer with the modification contained in the acceptance. Additional or different terms relating, among other things, to the price, payment, quality and quantity of the goods, place and time of delivery, extent of one party's liability to the other or the settlement of disputes are considered to alter the terms of the offer materially. Thirdly, Acceptance should be made in time. An acceptance would become valid as soon as the acceptance is dispatched (by common law system) or when it is received(by civil law system). According to the Convention, an offer becomes effective at the moment the indication of assent reaches the offer or within the time he has fixed or, if no time is fixed, within a reasonable time. Fourthly, an acceptance should be made by correct means. There are three possibilities in choosing the means of making an acceptance: (1) the means has been specified in the offer (telex, letter, etc.); (2) the means by which the offer has been made is used if it is not specified in the offer; (3) if an oral offer is made, it must be accepted immediately by words unless the circumstances indicate otherwise. The offeree may also indicate acceptance by performing an act such as dispatch of goods or payment of the price.

2. The Withdrawal of Acceptance

According to the relevant article of the United Nations Conventions on Contracts for the International Sale of Goods, an acceptance of an offer becomes effective at the moment the indication of assent reaches the offeror within the time he has fixed or, if no time is fixed, within a reasonable time. An acceptance may be withdrawn if the withdrawn reaches the offeror before or at the same time as the acceptance would have become effective.

3. Late Acceptance

An acceptance, which is made after the period of time for acceptance is late acceptance. A late acceptance is not effective as an acceptance. But there are two exceptions.

(1) A late acceptance is nevertheless effective as an acceptance if without delay the offeror orally so informs the offeree or dispatches a notice to that effect.

If a letter or other writing containing a late acceptance shows that it has been sent in such circumstances that if its transmission had been normal it would have reached the offeror in due time, the late acceptance is effective as an acceptance unless, without delay, the offeror orally informs the offeree that he considers his offer as having lapsed or dispatches a notice to that effect.

(2) All in all, it depends on the offeror as to whether a late acceptance is effective or not.

7.1.4 | Counter-offer

It is a proposal made by the offeree who does not fully agrees on the offer and makes modification or alteration to the offer. Counter-offer is the rejection of the offer and constitutes a new offer.

7.1.5 | Conclusion of a Contract

A contract is concluded when an offer made by a party is accepted by the other party. It is in the nature of an effective contract:

(1) that it must be an agreement freely entered into without any duress or undue influence;

(2) that the parties must have legal capacity to enter into an agreement;

(3) that it must be something that the law will uphold and treat as binding on both parties;

(4) that the signing of written contract: according to the usual practice of international trade, a written contract specifying rights and responsibilities of the parties concerned shall be made after an agreement is reached between the two parties. In some circumstances, the signing of a written agreement constitutes a condition for the contract to become effective.

7.2 The Performance of the Contract

In examining the disposal of goods by the seller in performance of the contract of sale, three issues must be considered: the delivery of the goods, the passing of the property in the goods and the passing of the risk. Normally in overseas sales, in particular on FOB and CIF terms, these three phases do not necessarily coincide and should be clearly distinguished.

7.2.1 | Delivery of the Goods

The goods normally delivered to the buyer when he, or his agent, acquires custody of them or is enabled to exercise control over them. The place and time of delivery are, in export sales, usually defined by the special trade terms, which have been considered earlier.

7.2.2 | Passing of the Property

There are two fundamental rules, namely that where the contract is for the sale of unascertained goods, the property does not pass to the buyer unless and until the goods are ascertained, and where the contract is for the sale of specific or ascertained goods, the property passes at such time as the parties intend it to pass.

7.2.3 | Passing of the Risk

As a rule, the risk shall pass on delivery of the goods.

Under international law, the two concepts of the passing of the risk and the transfer of property are regularly separated and the statutory presumption may be displayed by agreement of the parties. Special arrangements may be agreed upon between themselves. In the absence of them the risk will generally pass in a contract for the sales of goods abroad when the goods leave the custody of the seller.

7.3 The Functions of the Contract in Written Form

1. An Evidence of Formation of Contract

Should any conflict between the two sides arise, reference is generally made to the contract in an effort to resolve the misunderstanding.

2. A Basis for Implementation of Contract

The contract in written form ensures the smooth implementation of the contract. Inconvenience may otherwise arise. So it is very important to stipulate in the contract the rights and obligations of both sides.

3. Sometimes a Prerequisite for Conclusion of Contract

In international trade, usually a contract is concluded provided an acceptance is effective. But under some special circumstances, written contracts are required under some laws.

7.4 Forms of the Written Contract

There are no specific requirements about the forms of contract in international trade. The commonly used forms are: Contract, Confirmation, Agreement, Memorandum, etc. The first two are more commonly used in Chinese foreign trade enterprises which generally have their own printed set format of contract or confirmation.

Once a deal is made, traders may sign two copies of contract face to face. Or the seller may send two copies signed by him to the buyer for counter-signature and the buyer should return one copy to the seller for file.

New Words and Expressions

implement	v.	执行，履行
arbitration	n.	仲裁
inquiry	n.	询价
counter-offer	n.	还盘
offer	v.	发盘
offeree	n.	受盘者
validity	n.	有效期
terminate	v.	终止，结束
modification	n.	修改，改正
purport	v.	意图，目的在于
discrepancy	n.	不符
alteration	n.	变更
liability	n.	责任，职责
withdrawal	n.	撤回
revocation	n.	撤销
performance	n.	履行
phase	n.	阶段
ascertain	v.	确定
statutory	a.	法令的
force majeure		不可抗力
invitation to offer		发盘邀请

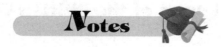

1. inquiry：询盘，询价，也常拼作"enquiry"。询盘旨在了解有关商品和成交条件的信息，对发盘人无约束力。

2. offer：发盘。发盘是一方（发盘人）向一个或一个以上的特定人（受盘人）提出十分确定的订立合同的建议，并表示一旦受盘人接受即受其约束的意旨。

3. reasonable time：合理的时间。所谓的"合理时间"，必须根据具体情况及惯例来定。一般来说，必须在合同中规定交货、发运的时间期限及信用证的有效期。

4. United Nations Convention on Contracts for the International Sale of Goods：《联合国国际货物销售合同公约》。它是与我国进行货物进出口贸易关系最大，也是最重要的一项国际条约。该公约是联合国国际贸易法委员会在 1964 年海牙会议上通过的由国际统一私法研究所拟订的两个统一法，即《国际货物买卖统一法》和《国际货物买卖合同成立统一法》的基础上广泛听取各方意见，将上述两个统一法加以合并，于 1980 年 4 月在维也纳会议上加以修改讨论后通过的。

5. However, a reply to an offer which purports to be an acceptance but contains additional or different terms which do not materially alter the terms of the offer constitutes an acceptance . . .
然而，目的为接受的对发盘的回答如果没有加有实质性地改变原发盘的条件，便构成了接受。

▌ Review questions.

1. What are the three requirements that an offer must meet?

2. Can an offer be withdrawn or revoked after it has been received?

3. Under what circumstances does an offer terminate?

4. What are the four requirements that an acceptance satisfy?

5. What is the process that the performance of a CIF export contract usually goes through?

6. What is the process that the performance of a FOB import contract goes through?

▌ Define the following terms briefly.

1. inquiry

2. offer

3. counter-offer

4. late acceptance

Ⅲ Decide whether the following statements are True or False. Then put T for True or F for False in the brackets at the end of each statement.

1. The quotation can be submitted in written form, and it is not a good practice to send the quotation orally. (   )

2. Any modification to the offer, no matter how minor it is, will make the original offer invalid and thus it constitutes a new offer. (   )

3. Acceptance of the offer commits both the buyer and the seller to the given terms of the sales and constitutes a legally binding contract which cannot be amended unless both parties agree in a written form to make the changes. (   )

4. According to international trade convention, under no circumstances can an offer be revoked once it is made by the offeror. (   )

5. An acceptance can be withdrawn if the withdrawal reaches the offeror before or at the same time with the acceptance. (   )

6. According to the rule in international trade, silence or lack of response to the offer will be considered an acceptance. (   )

7. The two integral links in international trade negotiation are offer and counter offer. (   )

8. An acceptance would become valid as soon as the acceptance is dispatched (by civil law system) or when it is received (by common law system). (   )

9. According to the Convention, a contract is still considered concluded if it is reached orally by both parties. (   )

10. A contract comes into effect at the moment when an acceptance of an offer becomes effective. (   )

Ⅳ Translate the following passages into Chinese.

A contract is an agreement which sets forth binding obligations of the relevant parties. It is enforceable by law, and any party that fails to fulfill his contractual obligations may be sued and forced to make compensation, though most contracts do not give rise to disputes.

The contract is based on agreement, which is the result of business negotiations. There are two types of business negotiations: oral and written. The former refers to direct discussions conducted at the trade fair or by sending trade groups abroad or by inviting foreign customers. Business discussions through international trunk calls are also included in this category.

Written negotiations often begin with inquiries made by the buyers to get information about the goods to be ordered such as quantity, specifications, prices, time of shipment and other terms.

An inquiry is made without engagement on the part of the inquirer. In case of a first inquiry, that is, an inquiry sent to an exporter whom the importer has never dealt with, information should be given in the inquiry as to how the name and address of the exporter have been obtained, the business line and usual practice of the importer, etc. so as to facilitate the exporter's work.

V **Translate the following passages into English.**

谈判是一个动态调整的过程。在进出口贸易中，买卖双方就一共同感兴趣的问题进行磋商，以达成令彼此满意的协议。这是因为交易双方各有自己的目标。例如：卖方欲以较高的价格出售其商品或服务，而买方则想以较低的价格购买同样的商品或服务。双方都想方设法达到自己的目的，这就需要双方之间有一些合作，否则就无法达成协议，从而丧失交易的机会。

这里所说的是争议和合作两个要素：双方因彼此的利益需要而达成某种共识，这是合作的前提；然而，双方的利益截然不同又成为争议的基础。谈判者同时受两个方向的压力：一是冒着谈判破裂的危险而坚持自己的高收益；一是同意双方的要求，达成交易，从而失去获得更高收益的机会。

VI **Read the following passages and answer the questions.**

Negotiation Strategies

Negotiations work wonders. This is particularly so in international business since it is mostly through negotiations that exporters and importers bridge their differences and reach a fair and mutually satisfactory deal.

Exporters entering new markets, particularly small and medium-sized enterprises, often face problems in initial negotiations with importers, agents and buyers in the target markets. These difficulties generally center around pricing questions and particularly the fact that their prices may be considered too high. Although price is not everything but only one of many issues that has to be discussed during business negotiations, too frequently it tends to influence the entire negotiation process. New exporters may be inclined to compromise on price at the beginning of the discussions, thereby bypassing other negotiating strength that they may have, such as the product's benefits, the firm's business experience and its commitment to exporting quality products.

As pricing is often the most sensitive issue in business negotiations, the subject should usually be postponed until all of the other aspects of the transaction have been discussed and agreed upon. It is estimated that about 80% of the issues negotiated are of a non-price nature. Decisions to place orders involving a long-term commitment are in any case rarely made on the basis of price alone but rather on the total export package. This is particularly so in market where consumers are highly conscious of quality, style and brand names; where marketing channels are well structured; and where the introduction of the product in the market is time-consuming and expensive.

By presenting a more comprehensive negotiating package in a well planned and organized manner, exporters should be able to improve the effectiveness of their business discussions and in the long term the profitability of their export operations.

An importer may reject an exporter's price at the outset of the discussions simply to get the upper hand from the beginning of the negotiations, thereby hoping to obtain maximum concessions on other matters. The importer may also object to the initial price quoted to test the seriousness of the offer, find out how far the exporter is willing to lower the price, seek a specific lower price because the product brand is unknown in the market, or demonstrate a lack of interest in the transaction as the product does not meet market requirements.

If the importer does not accept the price, the exporter should react positively by initiating discussions on non-price questions, instead of immediately offering price concessions or taking a defensive attitude. Widening the issues and exploring the real reasons behind the objections to the price quoted will put the talks on a more equal and constructive footing. Only by knowing the causes of disagreement can an exporter make a reasonable counter-offer. This counter-offer need not be based merely on pricing. It can also cover related subjects.

To meet price objections, some exporters artificially inflate their initial price quotations. This enables them to give price concessions in the opening of the negotiations without taking any financial risks. The danger of this approach is that it immediately directs the discussions into pricing issues at the expense of the other important components of the marketing mix. Generally such initial price concessions are followed by more demands from buyers that will further reduce the profitability of the export transaction. For instance, the buyer may press for concessions on quantity discounts, discounts for repeat orders, improved packaging and labeling (for the same price), tighter delivery deadlines that may increase production and transport costs, free promotional materials in the language of the import market, free after-sales servicing, supply of free parts to replace those damaged from normal wear and tear, free training of staff in the maintenance and use of the product, market exclusivity, a long term agency agreement, higher commission rates, better credit and payment terms.

To avoid being confronted by such costly demands, an exporter should try to determine the buyer's real interest in the product from the outset. This can be ascertained through appropriate questions but must also be based on research and other preparations before the negotiations. Only then can suitable counter-proposal be presented.

To achieve a favorable outcome from the negotiations, an exporter should draw up a plan of action beforehand, which addresses a few key issues. Experienced negotiators consider that as much as 80% of their overall time devoted to negotiations should go to such presentations. The preliminary work should be aimed at obtaining relevant information on the target market and the buyers of the product. It should also include developing counterproposals if objections are raised on any of the exporter's opening negotiating points. The preparations should thus involve formulating the negotiating strategy and tactics.

Knowing what the buyer wants or needs requires advance research. Besides customer's preferences, an exporter should assess competition from both domestic and foreign suppliers and be familiar with the prices that they quote. The distributions channels used for the product and the promotional tools and messages required should also be examined. Such information will be valuable when negotiating with buyers. The more that is known about the target market and the buyers for the products concerned, the better placed the exporter is to conduct the negotiations and match the offer to the buyer's needs.

Making counter-proposals also requires detailed information on the costs of the exporter's production operations, freight, insurance, packing and other related expenses. An exporter should carry out a realistic assessment of the quantities that can be supplied and the schedule for supplying them. Every effort should be made to match the export firm's size, financial situation, production capacity, technical expertise, organizational strength and export commitment with compatible buyers. As part of the preparations for negotiations, an exporter should list the potential price objections the buyer may have towards the offer to be presented, along with possible responses.

This is the time for promoting the strength of the export firm as a reliable commercial partner, commitment to long-term business relationships. The buyer should be convinced that the exporter is capable of supplying the type of goods needed on acceptable terms. Once the buyer is convinced that the exporter's firm is a reliable one, negotiations can be directed towards a discussion of the product and its benefits. The attributes of a product tend to be seen differently by different customers. It is therefore essential to find out as soon as possible the buyer's needs and determine how the product can fit them.

In some cases meeting the buyer's requirements is a simple process. For example, during sales negotiations an exporter of cutlery was told by an importer in a major market that the price was too high, although the quality and finish of items met the market requirements. In the discussions the exporter learned that the importer was interested in bulk purchases rather than pre-packed sets of 12 as consumers in that market purchased cutlery either as individual pieces or in sets of eight. The exporter then made a counter-proposal for sales in bulk at much lower price, based on savings in packaging, transport and import duties. The offer was accepted by the importer, and both parties benefited from the transaction. This example illustrates that knowing what product characteristics the importer is looking for can be used to advantage by the exporter.

After covering all of the non-price issues, the exporter can shift the discussions in the final phase of the talks to financial matters having a bearing on the price quotation. This is the time to come to an agreement on issues such as credit terms, payment schedules, currencies of payment, insurance, commission rates, warehousing costs, after-sales servicing responsibilities, costs of replacing damaged goods and so on. Agreement reached on these points constitutes the price package. Any change in the buyer's requirements after his agreement should be reflected in a new price package. For example, if the buyer likes the product but considers the final price too high, the exporter can make a counter-proposal by, for instance, cutting the price but asking the buyer to assume the costs of transport and storage en route.

In international marketing negotiations, it is advisable for small and medium-size exporters not to limit their discussions to pricing issues. Although pricing is a key factor in any business transaction, exporters should give more attention to the full range of marketing factors. They should stress the strengths of their firms and products and match them with the perceived needs of the buyers. Once these issues have been covered, they can consider the question of price and are able to develop a profitable business.

Please answer the following questions.

1. Why do you think price is always the issue that both sides would not take up at the initial stage of the negotiation?
2. Do you think it is safe tactic to inflate price on the negotiating table, why?
3. Why is it important for exporter to determine the real interest of the importer?
4. What should an exporter investigate or research about importer before negotiation?
5. How do you think can an exporter promote the business relations in negotiation?

Chapter 8

Import and Export Documentation
进出口贸易制单

One of the major differences between domestic trade and foreign trade is documentation[1]. Every shipment must be accompanied by a number of correct documents. If they are not the correct ones, the importer will have difficulties in taking delivery of the goods, and delays caused by incorrect documentation may affect future business relations between the trading partners. In the case of documentary letter of credit, any discrepancies between the documents presented and those specified in the credit may lead to refusal by the bank to make payment. Different documents are required for different transactions, depending on the nature of the deal, the term of delivery, the type of commodity, stipulations of credit, regulations and practices in different countries, etc. The International Chamber of Commerce (ICC) classifies four major categories of trade documents.

(1) The commercial documents, principally the invoice, are the seller's description of the goods shipped and the principal means by which the buyer gains assurance that the goods shipped are those ordered.

(2) The transport documents are "documents indicating loading on board or taking in charge".

(3) Insurance documents, represent that the goods are duly insured, hence mitigating the risk if they are lost in transit.

(4) Other documents may include official documents required by governments in order to regulate and control the passage of goods across their borders, they typically include consular documents, import or export licenses, and certificates of origin, inspection certificate, etc.

8.1 Commercial Documents

Commercial documents are generally issued by the importer, exporter or some relevant non-governmental business organizations. They aim to ensure smooth transactions.

(1) Pro forma invoice.

(2) Commercial invoice[2].

(3) Quality certificate.

(4) Weight certificate.

8.1.1 | Pro Forma Invoice

Usually, a pro forma invoice is a structure response to an inquiry. It is issued by exporter under the following circumstances.

(1) An irrevocable letter of credit is required by the exporter. The importer will use it to substantiate the need for a letter of credit to his banker.

(2) The importer's country requires that an import license be issued for each import and must approve the pro forma invoice before making foreign exchange available for payment by the importer.

The invoice clearly states that it is pro forma and if it is accepted the details are normally transferred to a commercial invoice against which payment will be made, although in some cases payment will be made against a pro forma invoice, e. g. where payment for the goods is required before dispatch. Therefore, a pro forma invoice has no legal status. It is only a means to facilitate the buyer to accomplish the above-mentioned tasks.

8.1.2 | Commercial Invoice

It is generally called "the invoice" for short, this document is the general description of the quality and quantity of the goods and the unit and total price. It constitutes the basis on which other documents are to be prepared, and the banks check the conformity between credit terms and documents and the conformity between the documents. A commercial invoice normally includes the following contents: invoice number and the date, name and address of the buyer and the seller; contract number and credit number; description of the goods including name of the commodity, quantity, specifications, etc; unit price, total price, price terms, and commission and discount if any; terms of delivery and terms of payment; packing, shipping marks, etc; and seal or signature of the exporter. It should be noted that the description of the goods in the invoice must comply with the credit while in other documents the goods can be described in general terms, and that total invoice value should not exceed the total amount of the covering L/C.

8.1.3 | Quality Certificate

A quality certificate confirms that the quality/specification of a particular consignment of goods is in accordance with the sales contract at the time of shipment. It may be issued by the exporter or a relevant government department as required under letter of credit or sales contract terms. It is essential that cargo description in the quality certificate conform to its terms found in other relevant documents, such as the commercial invoice, L/C, insurance policy, etc.

8.1.4 | Weight Certificate

The weight certificate is usually requested by the importer to confirm that the weight of the goods is in accordance with the sales contract at the time of shipment. Similar to a quality certificate, it may be issued by the exporter or a relevant government department as required under letter of credit or sales contract terms.

8.2 Finance Documents

In international trade, quite a few finance documents are used to ensure that the exporter receives full and timely payment for the shipment. These documents are usually issued by banks or exporters. As some of the documents have already been discussed about their functions and varieties in the preceding chapters, the subsequent discussion will be mainly about the details that should be contained in these documents.

8.2.1 | Application Form for International Money Transfer

When cash in advance or open account is used, payment may be effected by transferring money through banks. Thus, the overseas buyers need to complete the relevant application form for international money transfer. This kind of form is essentially a request to a bank to make an international money transfer on the remitter's behalf. In other words, an overseas buyer instructs a bank in the buyer's country to transfer an amount of money to an exporter's bank by M/T, T/T or D/T.

8.2.2 | Draft

In the collection method of payment for goods, the exporter uses the banking system to send the importer a draft to get paid. In other words, the exporter uses a draft to draw on an overseas buyer for the sum agreed as settlement in the export contract. By using a draft with other shipping documents through the banking system, an exporter can ensure greater control of the goods, because until the draft is paid or accepted by the overseas buyer the goods cannot be released.

8.2.3 | Application for Documentary Letter of Credit

An application for documentary letter of credit is the form used by the buyer to request his or her bank to open a documentary letter of credit in favor of the seller. It is used to authorize a bank to open a letter of credit.

The following information is always required in the form.

(1) Method of advice: airmail/cable.

(2) Type of credit: whether the L/C is irrevocable or revocable.

(3) Date of expiry.

(4) Applicant's name and address.

(5) Advising/paying/confirming bank.

(6) Amount.

(7) Drafts presented under the credit must be presented for payment/negotiation/acceptance.

(8) Allow partial shipments/transshipment or not.

(9) Port of shipment[3] and port of discharge.

(10) Trade terms.

(11) Description of goods (quality, quantity, packing, etc.).

(12) Price per unit.

(13) Documents required.

(14) Additional conditions.

(15) Bank charges.

(16) Signature.

8.2.4 | Letter of Credit

As one of the most important finance documents used in international trade, accuracy in the content of L/C is of vital importance. Usually, an exporter will be advised of the opening of L/C well before the shipment, so that he could have enough time to check the details contained in it. The details listed below are the ones that require special attention when an L/C is opened by the buyer or checked by the seller.

(1) Method of advice: airmail/cable.

(2) Type of credit: whether the L/C is irrevocable or revocable.

(3) Date of expiry.

(4) Documents required.

(5) Applicant's name and address.

(6) Advising/paying/confirming bank.

(7) Amount.

(8) Drafts presented under the credit must be presented for payment/negotiation/acceptance.

(9) Allow partial shipments/transshipment or not.

(10) Port of shipment and port of discharge.

8.3 Transportation Documents

A single export shipment can involve a lot of different documents to ensure that the goods reach the final consignee. A few commonly used transportation documents are listed below:

(1) Shipping note.

(2) Packing list.

(3) Bill of lading.

(4) Consignment note (rail, road).

(5) Air waybill[4].

(6) Parcel post receipt.

(7) Combined transport documents.

(8) Arrival notification.

8.3.1 | Shipping Note

A shipping note gives information about a particular export consignment when offered for shipment. It serves the shipping company as a delivery or receipt note for particular consignment. Some people also call it Mate's Receipt. Its role in various ports and trades may differ worldwide. Anyway, the cargo description in a shipping note should conform to that found on the commercial invoice.

8.3.2 | Packing List

A packing list provides a list of the contents of a consignment. It is completed by the shipper. Its prime purpose is to give an inventory of the shipped goods. It is often attached to the bill of lading, air waybill, or consignment note. A packing list is especially useful for the consignments which are composite. It is usually required by the customs for clearance purposes. It accompanies the goods through the transit and placed in the container, trailer, etc. Sometimes the credit stipulates for specification list which is similar to the packing list but emphasizes the description of the specifications of the goods. The weight list, weight note, or weight memo[5] are also similar to the packing list in content and function but put emphasis on the weight of the goods and are generally used for goods which are based on the weight for price calculation.

8.3.3 | Bill of Lading

The bill of lading, which can be shortened as "B/L" is the most important document required to establish legal ownership and facilitate financial transactions. It has three major functions.

(1) It serves as a cargo receipt signed by the carrier and issued to the shipper or consignor[6].

(2) It constitutes a contract of carriage between the carrier and the consignor.

(3) It is a document of title to the goods, and the legal holder of the bill of lading is the owner of the goods it covers.

The major contents of the bill of lading include the following.

(1) The carrier, i. e. the shipping company.

(2) The shipper or consignor, it is normally the exporter.

(3) The consignee, it is generally either the importer or made out "to order".

(4) The notify party, i. e. the party to be advised after arrival of the goods at the port of destination. It is often the agent of the consignee or the consignee himself.

(5) A general description of the goods including the name, number of packages, weight, measurement etc.

(6) Shipping marks;

(7) The port of shipment and the port of destination.

(8) Freight, for CIF and CFR it should be "freight prepaid", or "freight paid", for FOB it should be "freight to collect", or "freight to be paid", or "freight payable at destination".

(9) The place where the bill of lading is issued.

(10) The date when the bill of lading is issued which is regarded as the time of shipment and can by no means be later than that stipulated in the credit.

There are quite a few types of bill of lading classified into the following ways.

1. Clean B/L and Unclean B/L

A clean bill of lading is the one that states the goods have been "shipped in apparent[7] good order and condition". It is issued when the goods do not show any defects on their exteriors at the time of loading at the port of shipment. In other words, the consignment must be exactly as written on the bill of lading and not different. The case should be undamaged and sack, if any, should not be torn or stained. Drums of liquid should not be dented or leaking. The number and kind of packages should be the same as on the Bill.

If defects are found on the exteriors of the goods, or the shipping company does not agree to any of the statements in the B/L, the bill will be marked as "unclean", "foul" or "packages in damaged condition". The clauses of this kind are many including: inadequate packaging, second-hand cases, damaged crates etc. Unclean B/L is usually unacceptable to the buyer and banks.

Sometimes certain defects of the goods are unavoidable. For instance, timber often has "split ends". Chemicals cause discoloration on packing. In such cases the exporter must get the agreement of the importer to certain clauses on the Bills of Lading. These clauses must be agreed on before the exporter contract is established and the importer should tell their bank about the agreed clauses.

2. Shipped (on Board) B/L and Received for Shipment B/L

Shipped B/L is issued by the shipping company after the goods are actually shipped on board the designated vessel. Since shipped bill of lading provides better guarantee for the consignee to receive the cargo at the destination, the importer will normally require the exporter to produce shipped B/L and most bill of lading forms are preprinted as "Shipped Bill"

Received for Shipment B/L arises where the word "shipped" does not appear on the bill of lading. It merely confirms that the goods have been handed over to, and are in the custody of the shipowner. The buyer under a CIF contract will not accept such a B/L because, in the absence of the date of shipment, he is in no position to anticipate the arrival of the consignment.

3. Straight, Blank and Order B/L

Straight bill of lading has a designated consignee. Under this bill, only the named consignee at the destination is entitled to take delivery of the cargo. As it is not transferable, it is not commonly used in international trade and normally applies to high-value shipments or goods for special purposes

Blank B/L also called Open B/L or Bearer B/L, means that there is no definite consignee of the goods. There usually appear in the box of consignee words like"to bearer". Anyone who holds the bill is entitled to the goods the bill represents. No endorsement is needed for the transfer of the blank bill. Due to the exceedingly high risk involved, this bill is rarely used.

4. Order B/L

It is widely used in international trade. It means that the goods are consigned or destined to the order of a named person. In the box of consignee, "To order", "To order of the shipper", or "To order of the consignee" is marked. It can be transferred only after endorsement is made. If the B/L is made out "To order of the shipper", the shipper will endorse the bill. If it is made out "To the order of the consignee", the consignee will endorse the bill to transfer it. A blank endorsement is usually required for a "To order" bill.

5. Transshipment B/L

It means the goods need to be transshipped at an intermediate port as there is no direct service between the shipment port and the destination port.

6. Through B/L

In many cases, it is necessary to employ two or more carriers to get the goods to their final destination. In this case, usually the first carrier will sign and issue a through bill of lading. The on-carriage may be either by a second vessel or by a different form of transport.

7. Container B/L

Such type of B/L is becoming more common in use with the development of containerization. It covers the goods from port to port or from inland point of departure to inland point of destination

8. On Deck B/L, Stale B/L

On Deck B/L is issued when the cargo is loaded on the ship's deck. It applies to goods like livestock, plants, dangerous cargo, or awkwardly-shaped goods that can not fit into the ship's holds. In this case, the goods are exposed to greater risks and therefore usually specific insurance must be taken out against additional risks.

It is important that the bill of lading is available at the port of destination before the goods arrive or, failing this, at the same time. Bills, presented to the consignee or buyer or his bank after the goods are due at the port of destination, are described as "Stale Bs/L". As a cargo cannot be collected by the buyer without the bill of lading, the late arrival of this all important document may have undesirable consequences such as warehouse rent, etc., and therefore should be avoided. Sometimes especially in the case of short sea voyages, it is necessary to add a clause of "Stale B/L is acceptable".

In terms of negotiability and non-negotiability, bill of lading can also be categorized into Negotiable B/L and Non-negotiable B/L.

(1) Negotiable bill of lading. Basically the bill of lading is a negotiable document, which allows the goods to be transferred by endorsement.

(2) Non-negotiable bill of lading: In this case, the consignee cannot transfer the property or goods by transfer of the bills. This particular type is seldom found and will normally apply when goods are shipped on a non-commercial basis.

8.3.4 | Consignment Note (for Rail and Road)

Consignment note for rail transport serves as the contract of carriage between the railway and consignor, evidencing the receipt of the goods and the date of acceptance for carriage by the carrier. The consignment note will be delivered with the cargo from the departure station to the consignee at the destination station against payment of the amounts by the consignee. Unlike B/L, it is not a document of title and is not transferable or negotiable. The seller should be responsible for the accuracy of the information in the consignment note. The railway has the right to check if the consignment corresponds with the information in the consignment note.

Road consignment note, similar to rail consignment note in form and contents, stands for the contract for the carriage of goods by road in vehicles, completed by the sender and carrier with the appropriate signatures and/or stamp. Like rail consignment note, it evidences the place and date of taking over the goods and the place designated for delivery. It is not a negotiable or transferable document of title. The consignment note is made out in the three copies signed by sender and carrier. Only the first one is originally kept by the seller, the third copy goes to the carrier and the second copy accompanies the consignment and is finally delivered to the consignee at the destination. In road transport, a separate consignment note sometimes is needed if the goods have to be loaded in different vehicles, or are of different kinds or are divided into different lots. In addition, the seller is liable for all expenses, loss and damage sustained by the carrier by reason of the inaccuracy or inadequacy of certain specified particulars which the consignment note given by him must contain.

8.3.5 | Air Waybill

The air waybill is the consignment note used for the carriage of goods by air. It is basically a receipt of the goods for dispatch and evidence of the contract of carriage between the carrier and the consignor. This document is approximately the equivalent to the sea freight bill of lading, but the air waybill is not a negotiable title to goods in the same way as is an ocean bill of lading although it is widely used as a valuable receipt and evidence of dispatch and can be utilized within the framework of letters of credit, etc. Air waybills are made out in three originals. Normally the exporter would retain No. 1 original, No. 3 would be retained by the airline and No. 2 would automatically go forward with the consignment to the consignee at the destination point. Copies are used as circumstances demand.

Efficient service depends on the accuracy and completeness of the air waybill.

Hence shippers themselves must give clear and complete forwarding instructions to the airline or agent.

8.3.6 | Parcel Post Receipt

Parcel post receipt is issued by the post office for goods sent by parcel post. It is both a receipt and evidence of dispatch and also the basis for claim and adjustment if there is any damage to or loss of parcels. It is not a document of title and goods should be consigned to the party specified. An airmail label should be fixed to a postal receipt in respect of air parcel post dispatch; alternatively the post office should stamp the receipt "air parcel". Overall, parcel post is a cheap method of delivery for small consignments and the post office can provide insurance if required.

8.3.7 | Combined Transport Documents

Combined transport document (CTD) evidences the contract of carriage of goods by at least two modes of transport, issued by a combined transport operator under a combined transport contract. It is quite similar to "through B/L" and combined transport B/L used for ocean transport, but is broader than them. Through B/L and combined transport B/L are always connected with sea, used for any transport combined with sea, while combined transport document can be applied to any kind of combined transport. Several carriers are involved in through B/L, while combined transport document is issued by only one carrier, that is, combined transport operator. combined transport document can be made out either negotiable or non-negotiable.

8.4 Other Documents

International trade involves complex flows of goods and services between many countries. Therefore, a set of documents is used by countries to monitor and control these flows. These usually include:

(1) import license;

(2) foreign exchange authorization;

(3) certificate of origin;

(4) inspection certificate;

(5) consular invoice;

(6) customs invoice.

8.4.1 | Import License and Foreign Exchange Authorization

Many countries use import license and foreign exchange authorization system to restrict imports. Imports have to present pro forma invoices to their licensing authorities or to their central banks, or sometimes to both to apply for the license. If the planned importation is legal and meets current requirements, the license will be issued. Therefore, exporters should not ship to importers who need licenses until the licenses are actually in hand.

8.4.2 | Certificate of Origin

A certificate of origin is a document stating the country of origin of the goods. It is usually required by countries which do not use customs invoice or consular invoice to set the appropriate duties for the imports. It contains the nature, quantity, values of goods shipped and their place of manufacture. No particular format exists internationally. It is a long established document and is required as one of the support documents at the time of importation. It enables the buyer not only to process the importation of the goods, but also permits preferential import duties where appropriate.

In our country, this certificate is generally issued by the Import and Export Commodity Inspection Bureau or China Council for Promotion of International Trade. Nowadays, China enjoys the Generalized System of Preferences (GSP) treatment granted by many countries all over the world. GSP documents may be used when exporting to countries like New Zealand, Canada, Japan, and EU members to get preferential import duties. Commonly used GSP documents include GSP Certificate of Origin Form A, Certificate of Origin of Textile Products, Export Licenses of Textile Products, Shipment Certificate of Textile Products, etc.

8.4.3 | Inspection Certificate

An inspection certificate is a statement issued and signed by the appropriate authority, either a government entity or a private inspection company, providing evidence that the goods were inspected and detailing the results of such inspection.

In many countries, an inspection certificate is issued by an independent inspection company contracted either by the buyer or the seller. For certain commodities or for certain countries, such an inspection certificate must be issued by a government entity.

The inspection certificate contains details of the shipment to which it relates, states the results of the inspection, and bears the signature, the stamp or the seal of the inspection entity.

8.4.4 | Consular Invoice

This is a document obtained by the exporter in his or her country from the governmental representative of the importer's country. It was originally designed to help ensure that fair market values would be listed on the invoices prepared by the exporter. Thus the exporter must prepare and have certified before the foreign consul or representative a document containing all essential details of the sale. After certification the document is forwarded to the buyer for presentation to customs with the customs declaration, ostensibly for use in determining the amount of tariff to be levied.

In recent years, a number of countries including the United States and the Philippines, have eliminated the requirement for the consular invoice. But where they are still required, they must be provided.

8.4.5 | Customs Invoice

Customs invoice is required by the importing country in order to clear the customs, to verify country of origin for import duty and tax purpose, to compare export price and domestic price, and to fix anti-dumping duty, etc. Usually, this invoice is required in exporting to US, Canada, New Zealand, Australia, and some African countries.

New Words and Expressions

documentation	*n.*	编制单据
discrepancy	*n.*	不符，差异
mitigate	*v.*	减轻
dispatch	*v.*	发运
conformity	*n.*	与……一致
commission	*n.*	佣金
consignment	*n.*	一批货，运输
composite	*a.*	拼箱的
adjustment	*n.*	赔偿理算
pro forma invoice		形式发票
M/T		信汇
T/T		电汇
D/T		票汇

quality certificate	质量证书
weight certificate	重量证书
contract number	合同号
shipping mark	运输标志
finance documents	金融单据
shipping note	托运单
packing list	装箱单
bill of lading	提货单
notify party	通知方
consignment note	铁路运单，公路运单
air waybill	航空运单
parcel post receipt	邮政包裹收据
arrival notification	到货通知
receipt note	货运收据
clean B/L	清洁提单
unclean B/L	非清洁提单
shipped on board B/L	已装船提单
straight B/L	记名提单
blank B/L	不记名提单
order B/L	指示提单
transshipment B/L	转船提单
through B/L	联运提单
container B/L	集装箱提单
on deck B/L	舱面提单
stale B/L	过期提单
combined transport documents	联运单据
import license	进口许可证
certificate of origin	原产地证
inspection certificate	检验证
consular invoice	领事发票
customs invoice	海关发票

1. documentation：指的是单据的制作或使用，与表示具体的单据的名词"documents"含义是不同的。

2. commercial invoice：商业发票，可简称"invoice"，就是我们平时讲的"发票"。之所以前面用"commercial"，旨在和"customs invoice"（海关发票）、"consular invoice"（领事发票）等相区分。

3. port of shipment：发货港，装运港，起运港。从严格意义上来讲，最好不要使用"port of delivery"，因为"delivery"的含义为"到货"。

4. air waybill：也可写成"airway bill"，即空运单、空运提单。

5. weight list, weight note, or weight memo：英文虽然使用了三个不同的词，但其含义基本是一样的，译作"重量单"即可，足以涵盖三个词的含义。

6. shipper or consignor：货主，即托运人。

7. apparent：有两个主要的含义，一是"明显的，显而易见的"；二是"外观上，表面上的"。此处为第二种含义。

I Review questions.

1. Under what circumstances is a pro forma invoice used?

2. What are the three basic ways of international money transfer?

3. What are the three functions of Bill of Lading?

4. Which one is widely used in international trade, straight B/L, blank B/L and order B/L? And why?

5. What are the differences between a through B/L and a combined transport document used in international transport?

6. In what way is an air waybill different from a bill of lading?

7. What is the purpose of a certificate of origin to be issued?

II Define the following terms briefly.

1. clean B/L

2. unclean B/L

3. certificate of origin

4. combined transport document

5. consular invoice

6. inspection certificate

III Decide whether the following statements are True or False. Then put T for True or F for False in the brackets at the end of each statement.

1. Commercial invoice constitutes the basis on which other documents are to be prepared. (   )

2. Pro forma invoice has legal status and its details are normally transferred to a commercial invoice.
( )

3. Shipping note is a delivery or receipt note for particular consignment issued by the shipping company, and it does not need to conform to that on the invoice. ( )

4. A packing list gives a list of the contents of a consignment, and is only attached to the Bill of Lading for the Ocean Transportation. ( )

5. Bill of Lading is a title document to the goods and thus is negotiable. ( )

6. The importer will normally require the exporter to produce shipped on board B/L, for it provides better guarantee for both negotiating bank and the consignee. ( )

7. Blank B/L requires no endorsement for the transfer of the blank bill; therefore, it is often used in international trade. ( )

8. Air waybill is not only a receipt of the goods for dispatch and evidence of the contract of carriage between the carrier and the consignor, but also a title document. ( )

9. Certificate of Origin, a document representing the country of origin of the goods, is usually required by countries, which do not use Customs Invoice or Consular Invoice to set the duties for the imports. ( )

10. Consular Invoice and Customs Invoice are adopted by some countries as an instrument to restrict the imports, and are considered some form of non-tariff barriers. ( )

Ⅳ Translate the following passages into Chinese.

Each export shipment requires various documents to satisfy government regulations controlling exporting as well to meet requirements for international commercial payment transactions. The most frequently required documents are the export declaration, the commercial invoice, the bill of lading, the consular invoice, the packing list, and special certifications.

The paperwork involved in successfully completing a transaction is considered by many to be the greatest of all non-tariff trade barriers. There are 125 different forms. A single shipment may require more than 50 documents and can involve as many as 28 different parties and government agencies or require as few as five. Generally, preparation of documents can be handled routinely, but their importance should not be minimized; incomplete or improperly prepared documents lead to delays in shipment. In some countries, penalties, fines, or even confiscation of goods can result from errors in some of these documents. Export documents are the result of requirements imposed by the exporting government, of requirements set by commercial procedures established in foreign trade, and in some cases, of the supporting import documents required by the foreign government. Principal export documents are as follows.

Ⅴ Translate the following passage into English.

在国际贸易中,进出口业务中的一个重要部分就是清楚地了解买卖合同履行当中涉及的各种单据,比如有关单证的作用、局限性和可能出现的问题等。出口商应该保证货物的运输单证完整、准确，并按买卖合同的有关规定准确而迅速地制作单据，否则将会为此付出很大的代价。而进口商应该负责准确填写货物进口的有关表格，以便办理进口许可证和货物的清关手续。单据不符合要求则可能使货物被扣押，存留在仓库或滞留在码头，从而导致货物损坏、损失或发生额外的费用。

Ⅵ Read the following passages and answer the questions.

The Importance of Export Documentation

Documentation is the engine of exports in global trade. Documentation facilitates the movement of freight, transfer of title, processing of payment, and customs clearance. Without documentation, the shipment is at standstill. Even with the continuing advances in technology playing a greater role in international business, documentation is still required by all parties involved in global trade. Why is this so? The answer is surprisingly simple. On an average, customs authorities worldwide physically inspect only from 4 to 8 percent of the cargo that moves through their borders. There are some exceptions, such as Saudi Arabia, but as a general rule, the local customs authorities do not physically inspect most import shipments.

If this statistic is correct, then does customs manage their affairs in all the gateways of the world? How do customs authorities control the merchandise crossing the border and entering into commerce? They do this through the documentation provided by the importer and the importer's customhouse broker. Importers receive their import documentation from the exporter, thereby making documentation the engine that moves the freight through the borders. We cannot stress enough that Export Documents are Import Documents. In the United States, exporters create their documentation at the time the freight is being exported. For a typical export shipment, the only export document actually required by the Bureau of Export Administration, in conjunction with US Customs, is the Shipper's Export Declaration (SED) or a validated Export License. The other documentation created such as the commercial invoice, packing list, certificate of origin, health and sanitary certificate, bill of lading, and certificate of analysis — are all for the account of the importer to meet the customs clearance requirements in their country, thereby making export documentation into import documents. Customs clearance and required import documentation are governed by local laws and vary from country to country. What Korean customs may need to clear a pharmaceutical from the United States is very different from what customs in Brazil, Nigeria or Germany may require. To the US exporter this means it is crucial to have more than one set of criteria for your export documentation needs. The exporter must implement a standard operating procedure (SOP). This SOP must be flexible, particularly for those exporters to meet and identify the specific documentation requirements for each country to which it is exporting. Here are the factors that can vary significantly depending on the country to which you are shipping.

(1) Number of copies.

(2) Notarization.

(3) Legalization/consularization.

(4) Language.

(5) Originals vs copies.

(6) Format of documentation.

(7) Valuation.

(8) Commodity descriptions.

(9) Product labeling.

(10) Other government agency requirements.

(11) Black ink/blue ink.

Standard operating procedures are somewhat arduous to create. However, once the standard is created, it will only require updating. Through the utilization of a database (and there are many available to choose from) a company can electronically store the documentation requirements for each country. Once a shipment is packed and ready for export to a specific country, the document requirements can be retrieved from the database with all of the nuances in place that are unique for the particular destination.

Import shipments accompanied by incomplete documentation are held in storage areas until such time that proper documents are presented to authorities. These delays can expose the shipment to other factors such as bad weather, theft, damage, and/or loss. Additionally, incomplete documentation moves the importer into a reactive position with the local customs authorities. Overseas, as in the United States, the importer is responsible for all declarations made to customs. No importer wants to have customs reject their shipment due to incomplete documentation. Repeated offenses may cause customs to put a "black mark" against the importer. Your buyer's measure of you as a long-term supplier will be dictated by the quality of your documentation capabilities. Your overseas customers will favorably receive complete and accurate documentation. Their customs clearance headaches will be eased as their shipment is delivered timely and safely.

Please answer the following questions.

1. Why does the author think that documentation is the engine of exports in global trade?

2. Why is documentation still required by all parties involved in international trade even with the continued advance in technology, particularly in information technology?

3. In creating a standard operating procedure, what factors should be borne in mind?

4. What adverse consequences might arise from incomplete documentation?

Chapter 9

Description of Commodities and Their Packing

商品描述及包装

9.1 Description of Commodities

To avoid possible conflicts, every effort should be made to describe the goods in the sales contract exactly as the buyer and the seller intend them to be.

9.1.1 | Name of Commodity

This clause is relatively simple. Usually, the parties to the contract just specify the name of the product under the subject "Name of Commodity". This clause is a main component of the Description of Goods. As the basis of a transaction, it concerns the rights and obligations of the buyer and seller. If the goods delivered by the seller are not in accordance with the agreed name of commodity, the buyer reserves the right to lodge a claim, reject the goods or even cancel the contract. Therefore, as a main condition of sale, the name of commodity should be clearly stipulated. When giving the name, try to be specific and adopt the widely accepted name agreed on by both parties.

9.1.2 | Quantity of Commodity

In international trade, as different products have different characteristics and different countries may adopt different systems of weight and measures, units and ways of quantity calculation are varied.

1. The Systems of Weights and Measures

1) Metric system

Primary units under this system are kilogram (kg), meter (m), square meter (sq. m) and litre

(1). Some other derived units are metric ton (M/T), kilometer (km) and so on. This system is widely used by European continent and many other countries.

2) International system

This system is published by international standard metrical organization, and is based on the metric system. Its primary units include kilogram, meter, second, and so on. This is China's legal metrical system.

3) British system

Under this system, primary units are pound and yard. It is adopted by the British Commonwealth. However, announcement of abandoning this system has been made by Britain since it has been a member of EU. It now adopts the metric system.

4) US system

Primary units are the same as the British system, i. e. pound and yard. But there are differences in some derived units. For example, while the British system's long ton, L/T equals to 2200 pounds, the US system's short ton, S/T equals to 2000 pounds. Besides, some capacity units like gallon and bushel are of the same names under the British system and the US system, but the actual capacities are different.

2. Metrical Units

There are two categories of metric units, which are used to show the quantity of commodity in international trade. One is the metric unit, including weight, length, area, volume and capacity; the other is numbers, including some customary units such as dozen, gross, great gross, ream, and some packing units like barrel, bale (cotton), etc.

3. Some Methods for Calculating Weight

In international trade, a lot of products are measured by weight. According to general commercial practices and rules, the following are the methods of calculating weight.

1) Net weight

Net weight means the weight of the product itself. According to international rules and practices, weight is calculated by net weight unless otherwise stated in the contract.

Some products can be weighed only when they are packed, and this weight including package is called gross weight. For some less valued products, we may stipulate in the contract the weight is calculated by gross weight. This is so called gross for net[1]. If net weight has to be used, we must deduct the weight of package, i. e. the weight of tare. The following are some methods of calculating tare.

(1) Real tare. The package is actually weighed.

(2) Average tare. When the packages are in the same sizes, we may select some of them to weigh in the balance, and calculate the average weight.

(3) Customary tare. This is suitable for standardized package. The weight of the package is known to everyone and it is unnecessary to weigh

(4) Computed tare: the weight of the package is agreed upon by both sides.

2) Conditional weight[2]

Some products like wool, cotton, raw silk have unstable moisture contents. In order to determine the moisture contents accurately, the universal conditional weight is used. Conditional weight equals to dry weight plus standard moisture content.

3) Theoretical weight[3]

Some products are of uniform sizes and/or specifications, so the weight of each unit is almost the same. We can get the total weight by multiplying the total number and the weight of each unit.

4. Quantity Clause in Contract

1) The importance of quantity clause

The quantity of commodity is a major indispensable clause in a contract. The United Nations Convention on Contracts for the International Sale of Goods (CISG) states that the seller must deliver goods which are of the quantity required by the contract. If the seller delivers a quantity of goods greater than that provided for in the contract, the buyer may take delivery or refuse to take delivery of the excess quantity. If the buyer takes delivery of all or part of the excess quantity, he must pay for it at the contract rate. If the quantity of goods delivered is less than that provided for in the contract, the seller must replenish the goods within the stipulated time of delivery, and without causing unreasonable losses to the buyer and the buyer reserves the right of claiming damages. Therefore it is very important for both sides to stipulate the quantity clauses correctly.

Units of calculation include weight, number, length, area, volume and capacity. The quantities of many commodities are calculated by weight, gross weight, net weight, conditional weight, theoretical weight, legal weight[4] and net net weight are the commonly adopted ways of calculation. Sometimes, "gross for net" is used for weight calculation.

Since quantity terms may be ambiguous, careful definition in the sales contract is very important. The Metric System, British System, US System and the International System of Units are generally used in international trade nowadays. The implementation and popularization of the International System of Units symbolizes the increasing internationalization and standardization of measurement system. But, confusion and misunderstanding on quantity measures is still not uncommon. An American Pound, for instance, is different from a European pound; similarly, a ton has a different real weight depending on whether it is a short ton, a metric ton, or a long ton.

2) More or less clause

In practice, it is sometimes hard to control strictly the quantity of some bulk cargoes[5] like farm products, mineral products. Besides, owing to changes to supplies and limitation to processing conditions, the actual quantity may be somewhat more or less than the contracted quantity. Under such circumstances, more or less clause is usually stipulated in the contract so that the seller can fulfill the contract more smoothly. The more or less clause is a clause that stipulates that the quantity delivered can be more or less within certain extent (range). The most commonly used way is allowing some percentage more or less. For example, 3000 M/T, 5% more or less at seller's option. However, if the quantity is related with transportation, we may stipulate as "at carrier's option", or "at buyer's option" when the ship is arranged by the buyer.

Settlement for the more or less part is usually based on the contract price. If the parties are concerned about the great changes in price at the time when delivery is made, they may stipulate that settlement for this part is based on the market price at the time when the goods are shipped on board the vessel.

9.1.3 ‖ Quality of Commodity

Terms indicating qualities are frequently even harder to define than weights and quantities. A term for defining one particular degree of quality in one country may have quite a different meaning in another. Some quality standards that are in frequent use in one country or specific industry may not be known or may be interpreted differently in other countries or industries. Furthermore, different commodities have different qualities, and even the same kind of commodity has different qualities. Therefore, great care needs to be taken to specify quality terms to avoid any disputes.

Sometimes, it is important to add a clause like "Quality to be considered and being about equal to the samples" or a "Quality tolerance[6]" clause. It is also useful to clarify the buyer's rights if quality of the goods shipped is lower than intended in the sales contract, for instance, can he reject the shipment and send it back at the seller's expense, or does he get a specified reduction in price? Quality is also an important component of the Description of Goods, serving as the basis of a deal. The goods delivered by the seller should have the agreed quality.

In international transactions, there are different ways of showing quality.

1. Sale by Actual Quality

Sale by actual quality refers to the quality of actual goods, which are usually displayed at the trade fair or the goods at the premises.

2. Sale by Sample

Samples are either offered by the seller or the buyer. They are described as sales by seller's sample, and the sale by buyer's sample respectively

1) Counter sample[7]

When sale is made by buyer's sample, the goods delivered by the seller, may sometimes not be in conformity with the buyer's sample and thus the buyer may refuse to accept the goods. In order to avoid disputes over the quality of goods in the days to come, a wise seller should first send a copied piece of product for confirmation before putting into production. This copied product is called "counter sample" or "confirming sample", on which the seller's delivery will be based.

2) Sealed sample

Before sending samples or delivering the goods to the buyer, the seller may select some samples and seal them in the presence of the buyer or notary. This sealed sample is for checking the quality of the shipments in the future.

3) Safeguard clauses

When sale by buyer's sample, to prevent disputes upon the third party's intellectual properties, safeguard clauses are usually stipulated in the contract. The following is an example:

"It is the buyer rather than the seller who shall be responsible for any disputes arising from the infringement of the third party's intellectual properties. "

4) Reference sample

When sale is made by description, either the seller or the buyer may send a physical sample to the other party to let him know more clearly about the products. This sample is often marked "for reference only". It is not the basis of delivery.

3. Sale by Description

1) Sale by specification

Some indices such as chemical composition, contents, length, sizes, etc can reflect the quality of the goods sufficiently. Describing quality by specification is simple as well as accurate. That is why it is most widely used.

e. g.	Printed Shirting	"Jumping Fish"
	Yarn counts	30×36
	No. of threads	72×69
	Width (inch)	$35/36''$

2) Sale by grade

Some products can be divided into different grades based on different specifications.

e. g.	Fresh Hen Eggs, shell light brown and clean, even in size	
	Grade AA:	$60-65$ gm per egg
	Grade A:	$55-60$ gm per egg
	Grade B:	$50-55$ gm per egg

3) Sale by standard

Standards are formulated either by government or commercial organizations. Some of them are national; others are international. Many countries have their own standards. The typical international standard is ISO Standard. When sale is made by standard, it is important to mark the publication year of the standard, for example, Rifampicin B. P. 1993 (Note: B. P. refers to British Pharmacopoeia)

4) Sale by trademark and brand

Some products may have been sold in the market for many years and enjoy high popularity. Their quality can be represented by their trade-marks and brands, such as Haier, lenovo. However, some well-known brand products cannot be traded only by their marks and/or brands, owing to their varieties and complexities. Take SONY for an example, there are Sony television, Sony DVD, Sony mobile phone, and so on. In this case, detailed quality indices or technical description must be clearly stated.

5) Sale by name of origin

This method is limited only for native products with traditional arts or special local flavor. It is usually used together with brands or specifications.

e. g.　China Plum Wine

6) Sale by description and illustrations

Some products like machinery, instruments, equipments, and transportation tools are complicated in structure. It is difficult to describe the full aspects of their quality, thus sale by descriptions and illustrations is applicable. In the contract, the clause of quality contains not only the name of commodity, the brand but also the instructions to illustrate the structure and functions of the product. Clauses like "quality and technical data to be strictly in conformity with the description submitted by the seller" are to be stipulated.

4. Quality Clause in Contract

In quality clause, the name and specification, grade, or the serial number and date of the sample, etc, should be clearly stated. We may use description or sample separately or together to describe quality, depending on the product features.

We may stipulate in the contract some flexible quality range as follows:

1) Approximate

When sale is made by sample, sometimes it is not easy for the goods shipped to be in complete conformity with the sample, or we are not quite sure of the quality. In this case, clauses like "the quality of the goods shipped to be about equal to the sample" may be stipulated.

2) Flexible quality range for some primary products

(1) Range:

Printed Shirting	"Jumping Fish"	
	Yarn counts	30 ×36
	No. of threads	72 ×69
	Width (inch)	35/36″

(2) Allowing more or less:

e. g.　Duck feather: down content 18% , allowing 1% more or less

(3) Max & min:

Fish Meal	Protein	55% Min
	Fat	9% Max
	Moisture	11% Max
	Salt	4% Max
	Sand	4% Max

3) Quality tolerance

It is very unavoidable for some industrial products such as instruments, mechanical products to have some tolerances. For example, watches go with a tolerance of xx seconds. Some of the tolerances are internationally recognized while others are stipulated by the seller and the buyer in the contract.

For quality differences within the flexible ranges, price is the same as the contract price, with no adjustment. But, if the differences of some products bring fundamental changes to the quality, we may stipulate in the contract that the price is to be increased or reduced accordingly.

9.2 Packing of Commodity

Proper packing can be extremely important depending on the type of product and its description. Ocean voyage may be most damaging to the goods than are not properly packed. Goods subject to breakage have to be crated, and those subject to moisture wrapped in plastic. Others may require some special treatment or coating before shipment, still others have to be refrigerated while in transit. Actually, packing not only serves as a form of protection, but also facilitates loading, unloading and stowage, and prevents pilferage. Furthermore it can promote sales. Therefore, proper packing is contingent on the type of goods and the packages should be fit for any particular purposes expressly or impliedly made known to the seller at the time of the conclusion of the contract. And commodities can be categorized into bulk, nude packed and packed commodities.

Bulk commodities mean the commodity directly shipped and even sold without packages. Bulk shipment is usually applicable for large quantities of commodities that are to be shipped by means of transport with special purposed shipping equipment. Bulk shipment has the advantages of space saving, quick handling and lower freight. But necessary means of transport arc needed and proper handling facilitates and warehouses must be available at the port.

Nude packed commodities mean the commodities to be shipped without any packages or in simple bundles. Some commodities such as steel, rubber and automobiles, etc., can be packed in nude.

Packed commodities— Most of commodities in international trade need certain degree of packing during the shipping, storing and sales process. And packing can be classified into shipping packing and sales packing.

Shipping packaging is also referred to as outer packaging and is used for protecting the commodities against damages to or shortages during the storing and transportation.

Shipping marks on the shipping packages can be classified into Shipping Mark, Indicative Mark and Warning Mark.

Shipping Mark usually consists of a simple design, some letters, numbers and simple words, and mainly contains:

(1) name or code of receiver;

(2) reference number, such as order number, invoice number;

(3) destination;

(4) serial number.

e. g.　　　　WRCCO ---------------------- name of consignee

SC9750 ------------------------ reference number

London ------------------------ destination

No. 4 −20 ---------------------- serial number

Indicative mark consists of simple, noticeable design and words marked on the packages indicating points of attention to be paid during the process of handling, shipment and storing. It is composed of graphs and words, such as HANDLE WITH CARE, THIS WAY UP, KEEP DRY, USE NO HOOK. Warning mark is also called Shipping Mark for Dangerous Commodities, dangerous marks are printed on the shipping packages of the dangerous commodities to give warnings for the handling, shipping and storing personnel to take protective measures according to the characters of the commodities.

Sales packing (also called inner packing or small packing). In addition to the protective role for the commodities, the sales packing also helps to improve the image of commodities, it enables the consumers to easily identify, select, carry and use the commodities, so sales packing has become an important factor directly affecting the sales volume and the price.

Neutral packing is the packing without the name and address of the manufacturer, the origin of country, the trade mark and brand. Neutral packing is adopted to break the tariff and non-tariff barriers of some importing countries or regions, to meet the special demand of the transaction (such as entrepot), and help the manufacturers in exporting countries to increase the competitiveness of their products and expand the exports. Neutral packing is a usual practice in international trade, but in recent years it was restricted by some countries. Exporters should be cautious in adopting it.

Neutral packing[8] is divided into neutral packing with designated brand and neutral packing without designated brand. Neutral packing with designated brand means the brand and/or trade mark designated by the buyer are marked out on the product and/or package, but with no indication of the country of origin. Neutral packing without designated brand means neither brand and/or trade mark nor the country of origin are marked out on the product and/or package.

9.2.1 | Types of Packing

There are different types of packing.

(1) Bale: a heap of material pressed together and tied with rope or metal wire, suitable for paper, wool, cotton, and carpets, etc.

(2) Bag: made of cotton, plastic, paper or jute, ideal for cement, fertilizer, flour, chemicals, etc.

(3) Barrel/Drum: made of wood, plastic or metal used for liquid or greasy cargoes.

(4) Box/Case: wooden in structure and of various sizes, and some are airtight, providing strong protection for cargoes as equipment and car accessories.

(5) Glass container: used for dangerous liquid cargoes such as acids but needs careful handling.

(6) Carton: now a very common form of packing particularly for consumer-type of products. It also aids marketing as words can be printed on them.

(7) Crate/Skeleton case: wooden structure between a bale and a case used for light weight goods of large cubic capacity as machinery.

9.2.2 | Particulars of Attentions

(1) The requirement for packing has changed with the reform of transportation means and packing techniques. For instance, the development of containerization has greatly changed packing techniques for many commodities. Meanwhile, the requirement is constantly changing; some commodities can be either in bulk or packed.

(2) There are varieties of packaging forms; therefore, the packaging form to be adopted should be specified in the contract. Detailed requirements for packing materials and techniques should be clearly stated in the contract, depending on the characteristics of the commodity, means of transportation, the climate in the course of transportation, and the legal requirements of the importing country.

- Packing should be appropriate for the commodity, for instance, cement requires water-proof package, and packages for glassware should be shock-proof.
- Packing should meet the requirements of different means of transportation. For instance, seaworthy packing should be strong and protective against squeezing and bumping, packages for air transportation should be light and compact.
- Laws and regulations of the related countries and the requirements of customers should be considered for the packing. For instance, it is prohibited to use rice straws as packing material in some countries.

(3) There is no uniform interpretation for "seaworthy packing" and "customary packing[9]" in international trade. So in order to avoid any disputes arising from there, it is better not to use these kinds of terms in the contract.

(4) The packing expenses are usually included in the price, and shall be borne by the seller. If the buyer has special requirements for the packing, which is beyond the seller's ability, the expenses can be borne by the buyer.

(5) Packaging decisions should be made more carefully. The first step in selecting a package for a market is to determine national preferences. It is better to select a package already in use in order market. But if a new package is necessary, the firm must evaluate the cost.

(6) In its packaging, the company should be alert to the possibilities of innovation. As consumer behavior changes and income rises, the company might find the appropriate package to be different from what currently exists in that market. The company should identify such trends and lead in packaging.

(7) As different packaging may usually be required by the different markets, which shall make the production and packaging more costly, it is desirable that shapes, sizes, and packaging materials

should be standardized, but differences in colors and aesthetics of the package can be maintained because they create relatively little expense.

(8) The packaging terms in the contract are part of the commodity according to the laws of some countries. Should one party violate stipulations in this respect, the other party shall have the right to reject the goods and claim for the losses. So if specific requirements for packaging are stated in the contract, the seller has to deliver the goods strictly in accordance with the contract. Otherwise, even if the goods are in conformity with the quality, the buyer shall have the right to reject the goods and lodge a claim against the seller.

New Words and Expressions

derived	*a.*	派生的
bushel	*n.*	蒲式耳
deduct	*v.*	扣除
tare	*n.*	皮重
bulk	*n.*	散装（货）
illustration	*n.*	说明书
nude	*a.*	裸装的
entrepot	*n.*	转口贸易
containerization	*n.*	集装箱运输
shock-proof	*a.*	抗震的
seaworthy	*a.*	适合海运的
compact	*a.*	小型的，紧密的
aesthetics	*n.*	美学

to lodge a claim	索赔
the metric system	公制
long ton	长吨
more or less clause	溢短装条款
quality tolerance	品质公差
counter sample	对等样品
shipping mark	运输标志
indicative mark	指示性标志
sales volume	营业额
customary packing	习惯包装
consumer behavior	消费者行为

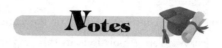

1. gross for net：以毛作净。在国际贸易中，大部分以重量计量的商品都以净重计价，但一些价值较低的农副产品，如粮谷、饲料等有时也以毛重计价。这种以毛重计价的办法称为"以毛作净"。例如：蚕豆，100 公吨，单层麻袋包装，以毛作净。

2. conditional weight：公量。国际贸易中的羊毛、生丝等商品有较强的吸湿性，其所含的水分受客观环境的影响较大，故其重量很不稳定。为了准确计算这类商品的重量，国际上通常采用公量计算的方法，即以商品的干净重加上国际公定回潮率与干净重的乘积。

3. theoretical weight：理论重量。对于某些按固定规格生产和买卖的商品，只要其规格一致，每件重量大体是相同的，一般可以从其件数推算出总量，称为理论重量。

4. legal weight：法定重量。法定重量是商品重量加上直接接触商品的包装物料的重量，如销售包装等的重量。而除去这部分重量所表示出来的纯商品的重量，则为净净重，即"net net weight"。

5. bulk cargo：散装货。指不易包装、不能包装、不值包装或只能散装的商品，如矿砂、煤、粮食、石油等。

6. quality tolerance：品质公差。指公认的商品主要品质指标的误差。要求所交货物的品质指标在公认的误差范围内，即为符合合同，否则买方可以拒收。公认的品质公差不计价格增减。

7. counter sample：回样，对等货样。买方提出的货样，卖方无十分把握提供与其完全相同的货物时，自行按买方样品仿制或略加修改，提出货样要求买方重新考虑，此种样品称为"回样"。

8. neutral packing：中性包装。是指既不标明生产国别、地名和厂商名称，也不标明商标或牌号的包装。中性包装包括无牌中性包装和定牌中性包装两种。

9. customary packing：习惯包装。此系国际贸易合同中关于商品包装的用语，指商品常规包装。由于含义不明确，各国理解不一，容易引起争议

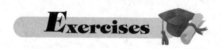

I Review questions.

1. What should you note when specifying the name of commodity in sales contract?

2. What are the units of calculation in quantity used in international trade?

3. Give an example to illustrate more or less clause.

4. How do we indicate the quality of commodity in sales contract?

5. Give an example to illustrate quality tolerance clause.

6. What are the functions of shipping marks? What are the parts included in a standard shipping mark?

7. Shall the buyer have the right to reject the goods and lodge a claim against the seller if the goods delivered are in conformity with the quality but the packing of the goods is not strictly in accordance with the contract?

8. Give examples to illustrate the point that packing should be appropriate for the characteristics of the commodity and meet the requirements of different means of transportation.

9. In what case can the packing expenses be borne by the buyer?

Ⅱ Define the following terms briefly.

1. conditional weight
2. more or less clause
3. quality tolerance
4. indicative marks
5. neutral packing

Ⅲ Decide whether the following statements are True or False. Then put T for True or F for False in the brackets at the end of each statement.

1. In terms of systems of weights and measures, China adopts US system due to its being widely applied in the international trade. (   )

2. Metric units are used to show the quantity of commodity in international trade, and they only include metric unit of weight, length, area, volume and capacity. (   )

3. "Gross for net" is often stipulated in the contract to indicate the weight of the less valued products is calculated by gross weight. (   )

4. The more or less clause is a clause that stipulates that the quantity delivered can be more or less within certain extent (range). (   )

5. If the parties are concerned about the great changes in price at the time when delivery is made, they may stipulate that settlement for this part is based on the market price at the time when the goods are shipped on board the vessel. (   )

6. Counter sample can help avoid disputes over the quality of goods in the future transaction. (   )

7. Sale by description and illustration is applicable to those products, which are complicated in structure. (   )

8. Quality tolerance will be stipulated in the contract to indicate that so long as both parties agree, quality difference can be tolerated. (   )

9. Neutral packing is adopted to break tariff and non-tariff barriers of some importing countries, and tend to be widely adopted by many countries. (   )

10. If one party violates stipulations in packing terms, the other party shall have the right to reject

the goods and claim for the losses. (   )

Ⅳ Translate the following passages into Chinese.

Packing for sales, or inner packing, or small packing, will not only protect, but also prettify commodities. It provides some necessary information about the quality, function, origin, usage and some other things about the commodities. Inner packing plays a very important part in sales promotion. Various forms of inner packing have been developed to meet the demands of consumers and marketing competition, including suspensible packing, transparent packing, portable packing, window packing, gift packing, etc.

Inner packing should be artistically attractive. With the development of consuming taste and science and technology, inner packing becomes something like a kind of art. Good inner packing may impress consumers with creative designs and suitable colors. Of course, it should also help to make itself easy for people to carry and use the commodities.

Ⅴ Translate the following passage into English.

在某些情况下，要满足买主的需要，做起来还是很简单的。例如，在促销谈判中，一个主要市场上的进口商告诉餐具出口商，虽然他的餐具质量和精加工都能满足市场的需要，但是价格太高。在洽谈中，出口商了解到进口商对散装货感兴趣，而不愿意购买预先包装好的12件一套的餐具，因为那一市场上的消费者购买餐具，或是单件零买，或是买一套8件。这时，出口商根据散装货在包装、运输和进口税等方面节省的费用的基础上，提出还盘。对于散装供货，价格可以减低很多。进口商接受了这一还盘，双方都从这一交易中获得了利益。这一例子说明，了解到进口商寻求的产品特点是什么，对出口商大有用处。

Ⅵ Read the following passages and answer the questions.

WTO arbitrators found today that the European Union's ban on US beef and beef products has resulted in lost annual US exports of beef to the EU in the amount of 116. 8 million. The EU's ban, which covers beef and beef products from animals treated with growth hormones, was previously found to be unjustified under WTO rules. Decades of scientific research by both US food safety regulators and international bodies such as the World Health Organization have proven the safety of the growth hormones used in US beef production.

"The arbitrator's decision today confirms that under WTO rules, the EU must pay a price for failing to comply with its WTO obligations," said United States Trade Representative Charlene Barshefsky. "The EU's WTO inconsistent ban on US beef is harming US farmers and processors, and is denying EU consumers access to the world's highest quality beef. The EU must understand that as a result of its failure to comply with its WTO obligations, the United States will act firmly and swiftly under its WTO rights to sharply raise tariffs on imports from the EU in an amount equivalent to the trade damage. Despite taking this action, the United States remains willing as it always has been to negotiate a resolution of the issue with the EU."

Pursuant to the arbitrators' decision, the United States will exercise its WTO rights by imposing 100 percent tariffs on a list of EU products with an annual trade value of 116. 8 million. The list of products and other details regarding the tariff increase will be announced in the near future.

This dispute over the EU'S beef policies dates back to the 1980s. In December 1985, the EU adopted a directive on livestock production restricting the use of natural hormones to therapeutic purposes, banning the use of synthetic hormones, and prohibiting imports of animals, and meat from animals, to which hormones had been administered. The EU adopted this policy even though the safety of consuming beef from cattle treated with certain hormones has been thoroughly researched since the 1950s. On all occasions of FDA testing, the six hormones subject to this trade dispute have always been found to be safe. The clear international scientific consensus is that these approved and licensed products are safe when used in accordance with good veterinary practices. Even the EU's scientists have agreed with these findings. At present, US beef is shipped to 138 countries.

That EU's 1985 directive was later declared invalid by the European Court of Justice on procedural grounds and had to be re-adopted by the Council, unchanged, in 1988 (the Hormone Directive). These measures became effective January 1, 1989, notwithstanding US attempts to resolve this issue bilaterally and multilaterally, including through dispute settlement under GATT.

On December 24, 1987, the President of the United States announced an increase in duties on selected European products in response to the Hormone Directive and related measures, but immediately suspended this action to promote a negotiated solution of the issue. The USTR enacted the increase in duties in January 1989 when the EU began implementing the hormone ban against imports from the United States. The USTR subsequently modified the application of increased duties on a number of occasions. During the early 1990s, the United States continued to encourage resolution of this dispute and worked in the FAO/WHO Codex Alimentarius to develop principles that reinforce the pre-eminent role of science in establishing high food safety standards.

Following entry into force of the WTO Agreement on the Application of Sanitary and Phytosanitary Measures (SPS Agreement) on January 1, 1995, the United States and, later, Canada, proceeded with formal WTO dispute settlement procedures against the hormone ban. On May 20, 1996, the WTO's Dispute Settlement Body (DSB) established a dispute settlement panel (the WTO panel) to examine the consistency of the EU's hormone ban with the its WTO obligations.

On August 18, 1997, the WTO panel issued its report, finding that the hormone is not based on scientific evidence, a risk assessment, or relevant international standards in contravention of the EU's obligations under the SPS Agreement. The Appellate Body issued its report on January 16, 1998 affirming that the hormone ban is not consistent with the EU's obligations under the SPS Agreement. On February 13, 1998 meeting, the DSB adopted the Panel and Appellate Body reports on hormones.

The EU subsequently requested four years to implement the DSB recommendations and rulings. An arbitrator determined that the reasonable period of time for implementation was fifteen months, and would expire on May 13, 1999.

The EU took no actions to implement the DSB recommendations and rulings by the May 13, 1999 deadline. Accordingly, on May 17, 1999, the United States exercised its WTO rights by requesting authorization to suspend tariff concessions on EU goods with an annual trade value equivalent to annual lost exports of US beef, estimated by the United States as equal to $202 million.

Please answer the following questions.

1. According to Barshefsky, what is the US government about to do in response to the EU's ban on US beef and beef products?
2. What was banned by the EU's directive adopted in 1985?
3. Concerning the EU's obligations under the SPS Agreement, what was found in the report issued by the WTO panel in 1997?
4. Why did the US government ask for suspension of tariff concessions on EU goods in 1999?

Chapter 10

International Cargo Transportation
国际货物运输

Transportation is fundamental to the development and operation of an industrial society. It permits the specialization of work and effort necessary to achieve efficiency and productivity. Geographically distant resources become accessible with transportation. The economic growth of any society in any part of the world is directly related to the availability of transportation. A society without an advanced transportation system remains primitive.

Transportation plays a major role in the production process. It allows the entrepreneur to assemble more easily the raw material and labor inputs needed to make a specific product. The same transportation system moves intermediate products to other producers for subsequent use in their production process, and it moves finished products to consumers.

The most important contribution that transportation has made to the production process is that, by widening the market areas that a producer can reach, it has encouraged the introduction of more efficient, large-scale production techniques. Substantial economies of scale have been achieved, and these have resulted in reduced per-unit production costs. This saving in per-unit production costs has often more than offset the per-unit transportation cost involved in reaching more distant markets.

As a society, we enjoy a richer and more leisurely life than we would if small communities had to be totally self-sufficient. Transportation has also allowed us to trade with countries throughout the world; and this commercial intercourse has helped to eliminate many barriers between nations.

10.1 Modes of Transport

The freight system includes several distinct forms of transportation, called modes. The modes differ in terms of operating characteristics and capabilities, giving them comparative advantages and disadvantages. The five major modes are water, rail, truck, pipeline, and air. Each mode enjoys what might be called natural product province. For example, water transportation is usually used to move goods of low-value, and in large quantity. Low value reduces the transportation urgency, and large quantity is especially suited for the volume loading and unloading machinery used at dockside. All the modes and their representative carriers play important roles in the overall transportation system.

10. 1. 1　Sea Transport（Ocean Transport）

Ocean transport is the most widely used mode of transportation in international trade, with advantages of easy passage, large capacity and low cost. However, it is slow, vulnerable to bad weather and less punctual if compared with road or air transport.

1. Kinds of Vessels

There are different types of cargo vessels designed to suit the needs of shipping different cargoes.

（1）General cargo vessels: to carry various types of cargoes.

（2）Oil tankers: responsible for the movement of the world's oil.

（3）Container vessels: designed to carry from 200 to over 4,000 standard containers of 20 feet in length.

（4）Oil/Bulk/Ore（OBO）vessels: multi-purpose ships designed for switching between bulk shipments of oil and bulk grain, fertilizer and ore.

（5）Ro/Ro vessels[1]: designed for loaded trailers or any vehicles to be driven onto the vessel to facilitate faster loading and unloading.

（6）LASH[2]（Lighter Abroad Ship）: designed to carry lighters on which cargoes are loaded, ideal for shallow waterways.

（7）Refrigerated ship: for carrying perishable cargoes.

（8）Timber ship: with spacious holds and heavy lifts for carrying timber or wood logs.

According to the ways of operation, merchant vessels can be divided into liners and tramps. Comparatively speaking, liners proved to be a more economical means of international cargo distribution.

A liner is vessel that operates over a regular route, stops at fixed ports according to an advertised schedule. Its freight is relatively fixed with loading and unloading charges included. It is suitable for cargo of small quantity.

A tramp does not follow regular routes or fixed schedule, but travels when cargoes are available, ideal for cargo of a completed shipload. Its freight is determined by market. Tramps can be divided into voyage charter[3] and time charter[4]. A voyage charter is the hire of a ship for a particular voyage that can be further divided into single voyage charter, consecutive voyage charter and so on. A time charter is the charter of a ship for a definite period of time.

2. Freight Rate

In practice, most shipping companies calculate freight rates on a weight or measurement basis. The following rules are applicable in relation to the calculation of freight.

（1）For items marked with "W", the freight thereon is to be calculated per metric ton on weight（weight ton）.

（2）For items marked with "M", the freight is to be calculated per cubic meter on measurement of the cargo (measurement ton).

(3) For items marked with "Ad Val. [5]", the freight is to be calculated on the basis of price or value of the cargo concerned.

(4) For items marked with "W/M", the freight is to be calculated on the basis of either weight ton or measurement ton, subject to the high rate.

(5) For items marked with "W/M or Ad Val.", the highest rate is applicable.

(6) Where different articles are contained in one package, the higher rate of freight is applicable, while the same kind of commodity in different packing is subject to different rates.

In addition to the basis of freight rates, there are all kinds of surcharges that can not be ignored, such as Extra Charges on Heavy Lifts, Extra Charges on Over Lengths, Additional on Optional Discharging Port, Direct Additional, Transshipment Additional, Port Additional and so on.

10. 1. 2 Rail Transport

Rail transport is a major mode of transport in terms of capacity, only second to ocean transport. It is capable of achieving high speed and is most economical especially if it provides the complete trainload for a shipper on a regular basis. Besides, it is less prone to interruption by poor weather. But it is confined to railroads and therefore less flexible.

Rail transport can be divided into international combined rail transport and domestic rail transport. The most important document for rail transport is consignment note. Once the forwarding railway station has accepted the goods for carriage together with the consignment note, the contract of carriage comes into existence.

10. 1. 3 Air Transport

Air transport is one of the youngest forms of distribution. The most obvious advantage of airfreight is quick transit. Quick, reliable transits eliminate need for extensive warehouse accommodation and reduce the risk of stockpiling, obsolescence, deterioration and capital tied up in warehouse and stock provisions. Low risk of damage and pilferage with consequent very competitive insurance premium is another advantage. Air freight is ideal for consumer-type cargoes such as fresh flowers and fruits which deteriorate easily, fashionable articles that have a short selling life, seasonal goods or merchandise of high value to low weight ratio. However, air transport is subject to a high operating cost and initial cost of aircraft when compared to overall capacity. Average aircraft capacity is only 2,000 −25,000 kg.

10. 1. 4 Road Transport

The road vehicle, used between countries connected by roads, is a low capacity but very versatile unit of transport, very flexible in its operation. It has a high distributive ability of offering a door-to-door service. Road transport is ideal for general merchandise and selective bulk cargoes in small quantities. But besides limited capacity, road transport has relatively high operating cost. There is also a high risk of pilferage and damage although the driver accompanies the vehicle throughout the transit. One of the problems facing road transport is the complication, in relation to customs examination and possible duty payments when a vehicle is involved in crossing several frontiers.

10. 1. 5 | Inland Waterway Transport

The inland waterway system is usually linked to the seaport and thereby acts as a distributor and feeder[6] to the shipping services. In some countries, especially underdeveloped ones, inland waterways are a major form of distribution as the road and rail systems are unable to cope or are nonexistent in many areas. Inland waterway transport can relieve port congestion through overside loading and discharge. This eliminates the cargoes passing through the port warehouse which can prove costly in tariffs and time-consuming through customs processing. It also has the advantage of low rate, and is suitable for a range of commodities extending from general cargoes to bulk shipment of timber, coal, oil, chemicals and so on. However, the transits are slow compared with road or rail.

10. 1. 6 | Container Transport

Containerization is a method of distributing merchandise in a unitized form, suitable for ocean, rail and multinational transport. It is the most modern form of physical international distribution and overall is highly efficient in terms of reliability, cost, quality of service, advanced technology and so on.

1. Features of Container Transport

Features of container transport can be summarized as follows:

(1) If offers a door-to-door service under FCL/FCL[7] (Full Container Load/Full Container Load), door to container freight station (cfs) service under FCL/LCL[8] (Full Container Load/Less than Container Load), cfs to cfs service under LCL/LCL, or cfs to door service under LCL/FCL conditions.

(2) It can be handled quickly and easily by standardized equipment and can thus save labors and loading and unloading charges.

(3) The low risk of cargo damage and pilferage enables more favorable cargo premiums to be obtained, compared with break-bulk cargo shipments.

(4) Less packing is required for containerized consignments. In some cases, particularly with specialized ISO (International Standards Organization) containers such as refrigerated ones of tanks, no packing is required. This produces substantial cost savings in the international transit and raises service quality.

(5) Faster transits, coupled with more reliable maritime schedules, and ultimately increased

service frequency, produce savings in warehouse accommodation needs, lessen risks of obsolescent stock and speed up capital turnover.

A substantial volume of world trade is moved in maritime ISO containers. The range of container types continue to increase and this is aiding the expansion of business. Furthermore, as port modernization proceeds, the size of container vessels capable of being handled at container berths is on the increase. New ports are also being developed by some countries to facilitate the development of their trade. These on-going developments have lowered transportation costs and permits more competitive rates.

2. Options for Container Freight Calculation

There are several options for container freight calculation.

(1) Rate can be generally formulated based on container capacity and the origin and destination of the merchandise. This is irrespective of the commodity inside the container.

(2) Another kind of rate will embrace the inland transportation cost, applying to full container load (FCL).

(3) A further type of container rate is based on the commodity inside the container. Hence the rate will vary with the commodity in the container (FLC).

(4) A very substantial volume of goods that is conveyed in containers is less than container load (LCL). A consignment comprising various LCL cargo is assembled and loaded into a container, with each individual LCL attracting a separate rate.

When calculating the W/M ship option rate, the volumetric rate will apply when the goods are of a low weight but high volume. Conversely the actual weight rate will prevail when the goods have a high weight but small volume. Usually, the freight rate is higher under FCL. The small importers are urged to use the LCL container service when possible as it offers regularity of service coupled with competitive rates and reliable transits.

10. 1. 7 | International Multimodal Transport

Following the containerization of international transport, a brand new mode of transport "International Multimodal Transport" has been introduced in the transport industry. International multimodal transport means the carriage of cargo by at least two modes of transport on the basis of a multimodal transport contract from a place at which the cargoes are collected in one country to a place designated for delivery in another country. Although different modes of transport (sea, air, rail, etc.) are combined, only one multimodal transport operator is responsible for taking the cargo from the consignor and delivering them to the consignee. This adds simplicity to the transport. The use of containers in multimodal transport means high efficiency, better quality of transport, lower cost and less time being required for cargo movement between the point of origin and the place of delivery. Multimodal transport document is the only document used, which also adds to the economy and simplicity of the documentation process.

10.1.8 | Parcel Post Transport

Parcel post transport is relatively a simple method of transportation. It is becoming more and more popular with the development of international postal network and the improvements in the quality and range of services. It is a cheap mode of delivery for small consignments like samples and the post office can provide insurance if required. It includes surface parcel post and air parcel post.

10.1.9 | Pipeline Transport

Pipelines are used for transporting commodities, such as crude oil and gases etc., long distances over land and under the sea. Rising fuel costs make pipelines an attractive economic alternative to other forms of transport in certain circumstances. Safety in transferring flammable commodities is another important consideration.

10.2　Shipping and Forwarding Agents

Large exporters are able to afford their own export shipping staff and try to handle all shipping themselves. But it is more economical for small exporters to use forwarding agents.

Forwarding agents are experts on the availability of different modes of transport for different kinds of markets, on the cost of transport and on the suitability of each mode.

A forwarding agent should act as export traffic department in general. An agent's jobs are:

(1) booking space;

(2) arranging documentation;

(3) collecting cargo;

(4) dealing with customs entries and other formalities;

(5) arranging payment and insurance;

(6) grouping a number of consignments;

(7) giving advice on markets, import/export regulations and export packing.

10.3　Clause of Shipment

When negotiating a transaction, the buyer and the seller should reach an agreement on time of shipment, port of shipment and port of destination, shipping advice, partial shipment and transshipment, dispatch and demurrage, etc. and specify them in the contract of sale. Clear stipulation of shipment clause is an important condition for the smooth execution of the contract.

10. 3. 1 │ Time of Shipment

Time of shipment is the deadline by which the seller makes shipment of the contracted goods. There are basically two ways of setting the time of shipment. One is specifying clearly a period of time. The other is setting a time period between the shipment and the deadline by which the relevant L/C must reach the seller. For example, shipment is to be made days after the seller receives the L/C. When stipulating the time of shipment, both parties should consider the availability of goods, ships and shipping space, the opening date of L/C and nature of the cargo. Avoid ambiguous phrases as "Immediate Shipment", "Prompt Shipment", "Shipment as soon as possible". Normally, the L/C should arrive at least 15 days before the time of shipment to permit sufficient time to check the L/C and make necessary shipping arrangements.

10. 3. 2 │ Port of Shipment and Port of Destination

Port of shipment is the port where goods are shipped and depart, while port of destination is the port at which goods are ultimately discharged. Both of them should be specified in the contract: Normally, one specific port of shipment and one specific port of destination are stipulated, but sometimes two or more of each are stated to meet special requirements. In case a decision cannot be made, several alternatives should be listed, such as "One port out of London/Hamburger/Rotterdam as the port of the destination at the buyer's option" or perhaps a general scope is stated such as "EMP (European Main Port)", "China Port", and so on. As "EMP" or "China Port" is too vague, we'd better try to avoid using them. In choosing port of shipment and port of destination, try to make them as clear as possible; provide some flexibility by allowing optional ports especially when it is hard to make a final decision; take into account port regulations, facilities, charges and possible sanctions; and be alert to the possibility of different ports having the same name.

10. 3. 3 │ Shipping Advice

When the goods are shipped on board the vessel, the seller needs to give the buyer prompt notice of the port of shipment, the date of sailing, the name of carrying vessel, the estimated time of arrival of the vessel and send the buyer the copies of the necessary documents to enable the buyer to get ready to take delivery of the goods. In the event of the seller failing to send shipping advice to the buyer within the prescribed time period, the seller would bear the consequential cost incurred. Upon FOB terms, the seller should send notification of cargo readiness to the buyer 30 days or 45 days before the time of shipment so that the buyer can charter ships, and send them to the shipment port to take cargoes in time. On the other hand, after receipt of the notification of cargo readiness from the seller, the buyer should inform the seller within the agreed time the name of the nominated vessel and the date of the vessel taking cargoes so as to enable the seller to arrange shipment.

10.3.4 | Partial Shipment and Transshipment

Partial shipment means shipping the commodity under one contract in more than one lot. It should be defined in the clause of shipment whether "Partial shipment is (or is not) allowed". Meanwhile, the time and quantity of each shipment should be specified, such as "shipment during March — June in four equal monthly lots". The seller should strictly follow the regulation, or otherwise, the buyer has the right to reject goods. Transshipment means when there is no direct ship between the port of shipment and the port of destination, or no suitable ships available at that particular period, the goods have to be transferred from one ship to another at an intermediate port. The clause must also specify whether "transshipment is (or is not) allowed". In addition, it should also be indicated who pays the cost of transshipment.

10.3.5 | Lay time, Demurrage and Dispatch

Lay time[9] is the time allowed for the completion of loading and unloading, and is usually expressed by days or hours.

There are several ways of stipulating lay time.

(1) Days or Running Days: including bad weather days, Sundays or any other holidays, unfavorable to the shipper.

(2) Weather Working Days of 24 hours: excluding Sundays, holidays and rainy days, favorable for shipper but unfavorable for ship-owner.

(3) Weather Working Days of 24 consecutive hours[10]: excluding the bad weather time period, suitable for ports that operate day and night.

As lay time concerns the interests of ship-owner, consignor or consignee, it is important to make it clear in the contract. Vague phrases as "to load/discharge in customary quick dispatch" should be avoided. If loading and unloading are not completed within the agreed lay time, demurrage should be paid to the ship-owner to compensate for the cost sustained at an agreed rate by the party that charters ships. On the other hand, if loading and unloading are completed in advance, the ship-owner will pay dispatch money as a reward to the party who charters ships. Demurrage and dispatch are considered as a way of encouraging timely shipment, and are sometimes specified in the shipment clause.

New Words and Expressions

entrepreneur	*n.*	企业家
offset	*v.*	补偿，抵消
pipeline	*n.*	（石油、天然气等）输送管道
vulnerable	*a.*	易受（攻击、伤害等）的，脆弱的
tramp	*n.*	不定期船
distribution	*n.*	分销，分配
consecutive	*a.*	连续的
surcharge	*n.*	附加费
stockpiling	*n.*	储备
obsolescence	*n.*	废弃，过时
feeder	*n.*	支线运输
demurrage	*n.*	滞期费
dispatch	*n.*	速遣费
intermediate products		中间产品
finished products		最终产品，制成品
oil tanker		油轮
OBO vessel		散油三用轮
Ro/Ro vessel		滚装船
LASH		子母船，驳船载轮
freight rate		运费表
weight ton		重量吨
measurement ton		尺码吨
Ad Val.		从价运费
Additional on Optional Discharging Port		选择卸货港附加费
Port Additional		港口拥挤附加费
tie up		把（资金）占用，把（财产）冻结
break-bulk cargo		零散货
multi-modal transport		多式联运
lay time		装卸时间

1. Ro/Ro vessel：全名为"roll on/roll off vessel"，滚装船。系集装箱船的一种。装载集装箱的卡车或拖车可以从通向船尾舱口的倾斜面直接驶入船内，待船抵达目的港后，原车又从船尾开出，码头和船上均无需起重机。对于海上航程较短，特别是从内地运出的货物来说，采用滚装船最为适宜。

2. LASH：原文为"lighter aboard ship"，子母船。每一子母船可混合承载数十艘子船（驳船）及集装箱。每一子船相当一大型集装箱，是一特种的平底驳船。母船到港后，无需停靠码头，可利用船上特设的起重设备，将子船由船尾卸入港中，再由拖船将子船拖至起驳地点进行起卸。

3. voyage charter：程租船，航次租船。船东按与租船人商妥的条件和费率将船租给租船人，将整船货物或不足一船的货物自某一港口或若干港口运至指定的目的港。租船人按租船合同规定将货物装船后，就可以在卸货港等待提货。

4. time charter：期租船。船东将整艘船租给租船人使用一个固定时期，租船人可按租船合同规定的条件自行调度，每月按船舶吨位付给租金，与实运货物数量无关。租船人自己负责运输工作，而船东应负责使船舶在租赁期间处于良好航行状态。

5. Ad Val.：从价。全称为"ad valorem"，系拉丁文，相当于英文"according to value"。指按商品价格，而不是按商品数量计算运费或征收关税的方法。从价计收运费或关税的商品通常是贵重货物，如丝绸、金银、宝石、有价证券、美术作品等。

6. feeder：支线。"feeder service"意为"支线运输"。在国际集装箱运输方面，远洋集装箱船只停靠基本港口，如上海、神户、香港等。各基本港口地区的其他港口称为支线港口（feeder port）。由支线港口以小型近海集装箱船将出口的集装箱货物运到基本港口，以及由基本港口将进口的集装箱货物运到支线港口的运输，统称支线运输。

7. FCL/FCL：整装整拆，亦称CY/CY。系集装箱运输货物的作业方式之一。出口商在自己的地方将货物装入集装箱，收货人在自己的地方开箱取货。即起运地的装箱作业由托运人负责，目的地的拆箱作业由收货人办理，与船运公司无关。

8. FCL/LCL：整装分拆，亦称CY/CFS。在这种集装箱运输作业方式下，船运公司在出口地的集装箱堆场接受已由托运人装妥货物的集装箱，运到进口地的集装箱货物集散站后，打开集装箱取出货物分交给各收货人。即起运地的装集装箱的工作由托运人自行负责，而目的地的开集装箱的工作由船运公司负责。

9. lay time/lay days：装卸货时间。指租船合同中租船人与船东对船舶装卸货所规定的天数。如实际装卸货日数超过规定天数，租船人应付滞期费；不足规定天数的，船东应付速遣费。

10. weather working days of 24 consecutive hours：连续24小时晴天工作日。这一术语表示以实际的昼夜连续24小时为一个晴天工作日。只要港口气候条件适于进行正常装卸作业，即使港口规定的工作时间是每天8小时，其余的16小时也算作装卸时间。

I Review questions.

1. What is the difference between a liner and a tramp?
2. What are the advantages of air transport?
3. Please explain the calculation of the liner freight.
4. What are the features of container transport?
5. What does FCL/LCL mean?
6. What are the characteristics of international multimodal transport?
7. How is the time of shipment specified in a sales contract?
8. Who would bear the consequent cost incurred if the seller failed to send shipping advice to the buyer within the prescribed time period?
9. Why are optional ports allowed?
10. Under what cases should transshipment be allowed?
11. What are the ways of stipulating lay time?
12. Why is demurrage and dispatch money stipulated in the contract?

II Define the following terms briefly.

1. voyage charter
2. time charter
3. dispatch money
4. demurrage

III Decide whether the following statements are True or False. Then put T for True or F for False in the brackets at the end of each statement.

1. The majority of exporters will not make use of intermediaries such as freight forwarders to facilitate the efficient and cost effective transport of goods. (   )
2. Merchant vessels can be divided into liners and tramps, and trampers proved to be a more economical means of international cargo distribution. (   )
3. For terms marked with "W/M", the freight is to be calculated on the basis of either weight ton or measurement ton, subject to the higher rate. (   )
4. Consignment note, the most important document for rail transport, is negotiable document that can represent the title to goods. (   )
5. Containerization, the most form of physical international distribution, can substantially reduce costs and raise service quality in the international transit. (   )

6. Bulk cargoes, or shipments that can be carried in conveniently sized containers due to their nature, can be transported in a variety of specialist vessels, depending on the nature of the consignment, whether it be sugar, coal, timber, foodstuffs or vehicles and so on. (   )

7. In most cases, while port of shipment and port of destination are stipulated in the contract, two or more of each are stated to provide more options for either buyers or sellers. (   )

8. Under FOB terms, the seller should notify the buyer of the cargo readiness at least 30 days before the time of shipment so that the buyer can have enough time to charter ships and send them to the shipment port in time. (   )

9. In stipulating the lay time in the contract, there are several ways to prescribe lay time, but in our country, the way of stipulating "weather working days of 24 consecutive hours" is usually adopted. (   )

10. When the charterer fails to load or unload the goods within the stipulated period of time, he has to pay demurrage to the shipowner. (   )

Ⅳ Translate the following passage into Chinese.

With large quantities of goods to export, the large companies employ their own staff for handling the shipping and dispatching of their goods overseas. Small exporters find it easier to use the services of shipping and forwarding agents, or freight forwarders as they are sometimes called. They are experts on the availability of the different modes of transport for different markets, on the cost, and on the suitability of each mode. Their job involves: booking space, arranging documentation, and in many cases, collecting the goods from the factory and carrying them to the dock, airport, railway station or road collection point. Shipping and forwarding agents deal with customs entries and other formalities. They arrange payment of freight charges and insurance, if necessary, and handle collection of necessary documents. They may also help by "consolidating" or grouping together a number of consignments to make transportation more economical.

Ⅴ Translate the following passage into English.

对运输功能起着积极作用的一个因素是商业的全球化。越来越多的公司寻求在世界上任何地方购买货优价廉的生产投入物,而整个世界都是他们产品的潜在市场。在这个世界范围的环境中,生产投入物和制成品的运输向分销经理们提出了特殊的挑战。对所有公司来说,有竞争力地为世界市场服务将需要一个更为复杂的物流体系。

Ⅵ Read the following passages and answer the questions.

Economists and governments agree these days on the crucial importance of foreign direct investment. They see it both as the global market's "seal of approval" on a country's policies and prospects, and as a force, especially in developing countries, for far-reaching economic change. This consensus is surprising when you remember that FDI remains politically sensitive in many poor, and some not-so-poor, countries. But the benefits are so great that reservations on this account have been put aside. The point about FDI is that it is far more than mere "capital": it is a uniquely potent bundle of capital, contacts, and managerial and technological knowledge. It is the cutting edge of globalization.

The outlook for FDI — in total, and country by country — is therefore a matter of great interest. Forecasting it, however, is far from easy. The determinants are complicated, and not always susceptible to measurement. Up to now, so far as this column is aware, detailed forecasts have not been attempted. In a report published this week, the Economist Intelligence Unit (EIU), a sister company of the Economist, has ventured into this uncharted territory. It provides a forecast for FDI extending to 2005 for no fewer than 60 countries (accounting for virtually all of the world's actual and projected flows of FDI).

The main difficulty arises from the fact that FDI depends closely on what the EIU calls the business environment — a necessarily broad term that includes, on the firm's definition, 70 separate indicators. Some of these are political, and to the extent that they can be measured at all have to be gauged through surveys that ask investors questions such as, "Is the quality of the bureaucracy and its ability to carry out government policy very high, high, moderate, low or very low?" It is one thing to compile this kind of evidence into a backward-looking aggregate which can then be tested for its ability to explain past movements in FDI. It is quite another to use it for forecasting — because to do that the researcher has to predict how political and other conditions will change.

There is no alternative but to blend together different kinds of information. First, take whatever evidence economists can yield about the way the forces driving FDI — size of host-country market, expected growth, input costs, geography and natural resources, and the policy framework — have worked in the past. Next, add conventional forecasts of relevant economic aggregates. Third, unavoidably, make more qualitative and speculative assessments of changes in other, "non-economic", conditions. All is that this study tries to do. It is academically impure, because it has to be. But the workings and the supporting information are in plain view, and the results are very interesting.

Global FDI flows are projected to shrink markedly this year, from $1.1 trillion in 2000 to less than $800 billion. Almost all of the reduction is forecast to be in FDI to rich countries, driven by the slowdown in America and by the diminishing pace of mergers and acquisitions (which are a principal driver of FDI in the developed economies). FDI to poor countries merely pauses, at around $220 billion. In subsequent years, flows recover across the board, but growth in flows to poor countries continues to outpace, modestly, growth in flows to rich ones. As a result, the developing countries' share of global FDI inflows rises slightly, to 29%, by 2005. By then, the global stock of FDI will have risen to more than $10 trillion, according to the report, from less than $6 trillion last year.

The United States, unsurprisingly, is expected to dominate the rankings in 2001−2005, much as it does today, accounting for more than 25% of global inflows. The analysis shows that America's business environment is about as good as one would infer, statistically speaking, from its income. Britain, in contrast, is one of 14 countries with a somewhat better business environment than its income would lead you to expect. Britain is expected to remain the world's second-biggest recipient of FDI, accounting for more than 9% of the total in 2001–2005. In terms of FDI per head, Britain currently ranks seventh, behind Ireland, Belgium, Hong Kong Special Administrative Region of China, Sweden, Singapore and the Netherlands. On this measure, the United States ranks fourteenth.

The study's most encouraging finding is that scores of business environment are rising almost everywhere. FDI is a competitive undertaking, but not a zero-sum game: rising scores for business environment drive the totals higher. Comparing 2001–2005 with 1996–2000, the EIU marks down only two economies, Hong Kong Special Administrative Region of China and Malaysia, and in neither case by enough to alter the overall assessment — "very good" for Hong Kong Special Administrative Region of China and "good" for Malaysia. Thailand, Poland, Hungary and Mexico are among those expected to move in the other direction, from "moderate" to "good"; likewise Germany, Denmark and France, from "good" to "very good".

If all goes well, the process may entrench itself, with FDI fueling improvements in business conditions, and improving conditions spurring additional FDI. The report scotches the view that the world is anywhere near a natural ceiling on FDI: the scope for further investment is increased, rather than diminished, by the trends it describes and predicts. If the EIU is right, globalization is continuing to gather momentum, and has much further yet to run.

Please answer the following questions.

1. Why is FDI of crucial importance to many nations in the eyes of today's economists and governments?
2. Why is forecasting FDI not an easy matter?
3. How many factors must be considered in order to describe the business environment of FDI?
4. What is the first step in arriving at a forecast on FDI according to the text?
5. What is the main reason for the forecast reduction of FDI to developed countries?
6. Will the scope for further growth of FDI be expanded, diminished, or remain uncertain, as held by the report published by EIU?

Chapter 11

Insurance (I)

保险 (一)

A brief survey of insurance literature[1] reveals differences of opinion concerning how the term should be defined. In whatever way the term is defined, insurance is a social device in which a group of individuals transfer risk and provides for payment of losses from funds contributed by all members who transferred risk. Those who transfer risk are called the insureds. Those who assume risk are called insurers.

11.1 Risk Transfer

Insurance is a risk transfer mechanisms, whereby the individual or the business enterprises can shift some of the uncertainty of life onto the shoulders of others. In return for a known premium, usually a very small amount compared with the potential loss, the cost of that loss can be transferred to an insurer. Without insurance, there would be a great deal of uncertainty experienced by an individual or an enterprise, not only as to whether a loss would occur, but also as to what size it would be if it did occur.

For example, a house-owner will realize that each year several hundred houses are damaged by the fire. His uncertainty is whether in the coming year his house will be one of those damaged, and he is also uncertain whether, given[2] that he will be one of the unlucky ones, his loss will amount to a hundred dollars or so for the redecoration of his kitchen or whether the house will be gutted and cost him thousands of dollars to repair. Even though the probability of his house becoming one of the loss statistics is extremely low, the average house-owner will nevertheless select to spend, say $50 to $60 on house insurance, rather than face the extremely remote possibility of losing a house worth $200,000.

In the case of business enterprises, the values exposed to loss[3] are usually much higher, and the premium charged is likely to be substantially higher than that for a house. Even in these circumstances the majority of firms prefer to pay a known cost or premium for the transfer of risk, rather than face the uncertainty of carrying the risk of loss.

11.2　The Common Pool

The insured's premium is received by the insurer into a fund or pool for that type of risk, and the claims of those suffering losses are paid out of this pool. Because of the large number of clients in any particular fund or pool, the insurance company can predict, with reasonable accuracy[4], the amount of claims likely to be incurred in the coming year. There will be some variation in claims costs from year to year and the premiums include a small margin to build up a reserve upon which the company can draw in bad years.

The main stimulus to enterprise is the release of funds[5], now available for investment in the productive side of a business, which would otherwise need to be held in easily accessible reserves[6] if the firms would probably create reserve funds for emergencies which might put their whole future viability in jeopardy. The premium payable to an insurer, however, would only be a small proportion of the fund required because of the pooling arrangements, and so most of this money could be invested in new plants, buildings or stock.

11.3　Transportation Insurance

In overseas trade the geographical gaps are great, and the transport multi-modal — that is to say, we must combine road, rail, sea and air in almost all cargo movements to some extent. Similarly the time lag is great between production and consumption. In bridging both the geographic gap and the time gap serious risks have to be run. And it is in this framework that the insurance underwriters[7] operate to carry the risks which otherwise would have to be borne by the producers.

Cargo insurance is one of the main branches of insurance. These are usually listed as fire, marine, life and accident. The term "marine" used to refer to the insurance of ships and their cargoes. Today the movement of cargoes is frequently effected partly by other modes of transport, in association with shipping. Where cargo is concerned, "transportation insurance" seems a better term to use today than marine insurance. Goods do not go overseas solely by sea — air transport takes an increasing share by road, rail and inland waterway, while import cargo moves to the hinterland in the same way.

Cargo insurance therefore is an activity aimed at moving the burden of risk from the shoulder of the exporters and importers, and placing it upon the shoulders of specialist risk-bearing underwriters. Trade would not cease if there were no method of insurance available, but the losses would be suffered by those who were unfortunate, and not shared out equally among all traders.

1. Principles of Insurance

Transportation insurance, like all forms of insurance, conforms to certain basic principles. When firms seek cover for goods and units of carriage they must follow these principles. There are three main principles of insurance, two subsidiary principles and a doctrine.

Insurable interest[8] holds that no one may insure anything unless he has an interest in it, which means that the thing insured is preserved he will derive a benefit from its preservation, but if it is in any way damaged or lost the assured will be adversely affected. You can insure your own car, if it is damaged you will have to pay for it to be repaired and consequently you will suffer a loss. For this reason the insuring of anything by people who are not "interested" in it is held to be "against public policy". This means that crime would be encouraged.

Every contract of insurance requires an insurable interest to support it, or otherwise it is invalid and any claim made upon it will not be entertained. The time of an event may be crucial to the question of insurable interest. The interest passes with the documents. [9] In cargo insurance we know who has an interest in the cargo at any particular point of time, if we know the terms of sale[10] which have been arranged. We can work out who will suffer loss by discovering at what point the property passes from one person to another.

The person who is going to suffer the loss is the one who has the insurable interest at any moment. This means that goods may be shipped at the port of origin by a shipper or freight forwarder under a policy taken out to cover them, and the buyer takes over the policy which has been issued when he takes over the ownership of the goods. If they fail to complete the voyage undamaged, he can claim on the insurance even though it was not in his name.

Utmost good faith is a very important principle[11]. The people who decide what premium is fair for a particular cover do so on the basis of written statements made in a proposal form. If this statement is untrue, then the premium agreed on will not be a fair one. Suppose I say that a crate contains copper, when in fact it contains platinum. The premium required to cover the cheaper metal will be unfair premium for the more valuable cargo. The mis-statement is a fraud, and the policy is voidable by the party who is misled. Even if the mis-statement was unintentional, the underwriter would still be decided and the policy voidable.

Indemnity holds that a contract of insurance is one which restores a person who suffered a loss into the same position as he was in before the loss occurred. A person with a third-hand[12] Ford car will receive sufficient compensation to buy another third-hand Ford car, not enough to buy a brand-new Ford car. This principle cannot apply to life or personal accident insurance — for of course a life, or a limb, cannot be restored.

In a normal policy of insurance the compensation payable is sufficient only to restore the insured to the position he was in before the loss occurred — not to a better position. Cargo policies are often issued for an agreed value and are therefore called "valued" policies. It means that the compensation to be paid will be at an agreed figure, often at invoiced cost plus freight and forwarding charges plus the insurance premium plus an agreed percentage such as 10 percent. This represents a profit that could have been earned on the capital tied up in the transaction.

2. Sub-principle of Insurance

Contribution[13] is a sub-principle which is associated with indemnity. It holds that a person cannot be allowed to insure twice for the same risk, and claim compensation from both insurers.

Therefore, if two policies do cover the same event, the insurance companies contribute pro rata[14] to the loss, and the insured is only restored to the indemnity position. This is unlikely to happen very frequently in cargo insurance.

Subrogation[15], the sub-principle, also relating to indemnity, is of enormous importance in cargo insurance. The word "subrogate" means to "take the place of another". Imagine a situation where A has insured his cargo with B, who will pay up for the loss suffered. However, because C was negligent, a legal action by A against C would almost certainly lead to an award of damages against C. A would thus be compensated twice, and this would be a breach of the principle of indemnity. To prevent this happening, B, the insurer, is substituted for A, the insured, in any legal action against C. The insurer is entitled to the advantage of every right of the insured which will diminish the loss he has been forced to bear.

The doctrine of proximate cause — when an insurance policy is made out to cover a certain risk, a claim becomes payable only if that risk occurred as the proximate (closet) cause of the loss[16] suffered. The proximate cause is the direct cause of the loss.

New Words and Expressions

survey	n.	概览
insurer	n.	保险人
gut	v.	损害
pool	n.	统筹资金
margin	n.	保证金
stimulus	n.	刺激
jeopardy	n.	危险
multi-modal	a.	多种方式的
hinterland	n.	内地，内陆
conform	v.	一致，符合
cover	n.	保险
subsidiary	a.	附带的，次要的
doctrine	n.	信条
crucial	a.	决定性的
utmost	a.	极度的，最大的
platinum	n.	白金
voidable	a.	可使无效的
unintentional	a.	非故意的
indemnity	n.	损失赔偿

contribution	*n.*	分摊
subrogation	*n.*	代位，取代
breach	*v.*	违反，不履行
negligent	*a.*	疏忽的，玩忽的
insured	*n.*	被保险人
diminish	*v.*	减少，降低
forwarding charges		交货费用
pro rata		按比例
proximate cause of the loss		导致损失的直接原因

Notes

1. literature：文献，说明书。

2. given：此处为"假设"之意。

3. value exposed to loss：遭遇损失的价值。

4. with reasonable accuracy：较为准确地。此处的"reasonable"作"适度"解释。

5. release of funds：腾出资金。

6. held in easily accessible reserves：留作可以随时使用的储备资金。

7. underwriter：保险公司。

8. insurable interest：可保险权益，可保利益。指投保人对保险标的具有的法律上承认的利益。

9. The interest passes with the documents. 权益随单据转移。谁持有单据，谁就具有可保险权益

10. terms of sale：价格条件。从上下文来看，实际指的是价格条件，如 FOB、CIF、CFR 等。根据这些价格条件，保险公司可确定投保是否享有可保险权益。

11. principle of utmost good faith：最大诚信原则。最大诚信是订立各种保险合同须遵守的基本原则，要求投保人或被投保人在订立合同之前及在合同有效期内必须保持最大限度的诚信，双方都应互不欺骗隐瞒。

12. a third-hand (something)：经过两次倒手的东西。

13. contribution：根据某些保险单规定的条款照比例分摊损失的份额。

14. pro rata：拉丁文，意为"按比例"，相当于英语中的"proportionally"。

15. subrogation：代位追偿。指保险人在赔付被保险人的损失之后，被保险人应将保险标的损失后的权利转让给保险人，并以被保险人的身份向对此项损失负部分或全部责任的第三者进行追偿。

16. proximate cause of the loss：导致损失的直接原因。保险人一般只对承保风险为近因而造

成的损失负赔偿责任，而对保险责任范围以外的风险造成的保险标的的损失不承担赔偿责任。

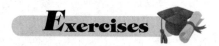

I Review questions.

1. Explain the risk transfer mechanism in insurance.
2. What are the functions of the common pool insurance?
3. What are the four basic principles of insurance?
4. What are the two sub-principles relating to indemnity of insurance?

II Define the following terms briefly.

1. insurable interest
2. indemnity
3. proximate cause
4. contribution
5. subrogation

III Translate the following passages into English.

One of the more important risks involved in an export transaction is that of loss or damage to goods during their physical movement from seller to buyer. In most instances, full protection from this risk can be provided through special transportation insurance, such as marine insurance. Protection can be provided to cover all transport risks from the time the goods leave the seller's warehouse or factory — whether located inland or at a port of exit from his or her country — until they reach the final destination stipulated by the foreign buyer. In its most basic form, such insurance provides the means to reimburse the owners of goods being transported to overseas markets for any losses or damages incurred for which the carriers cannot legally be called upon to make payment. In addition to legal owners, non-owners often have an interest in seeing that a shipment is adequately protected.

From the point of view of the parties involved in an international marketing transaction — that is, the seller and buyer — a deciding factor in the question of who needs transportation insurance, and when to insure, is insurable interest. Generally speaking, insurable interest depends on whether a company will benefit from the safe arrival of the carrier and its cargo or whether the firm will be injured by its loss, damage, or detention. This covers a wide range of situations in that not only do the owners of the carrier and cargo have such an interest, but also many certain non-owners. For instance, in certain situation the seller can have an insurable interest as a non-owner even though the buyer already has become the legal owner of the goods.

IV Translate the following passage into English.

决定保险费率的因素有许多：首先船只的年龄，类型，旗帜，船主及管理都是应考虑的重要因素。其次，还与运输方式及包装的坚固与否有关。空运和海上集装箱运输通常要求较少的包装。它还与所运载的货物类型有关。有些产品比其他产品更加易受损伤。另外，还必须考虑所提供的险别以及运输此类货品的经验。显然，保险范围越广，保险费率也就越高。例如，对玻璃品投保包括破碎险在内的一切险，其保险费率就高于不包括破碎险的情形。

V Read the following passages and answer the questions.

Winning the Service Game

From past business experiences, we have gleaned five critical principles that services must follow to deliver service quality.

(1) Never divorce the customer from thoughts about what a service business really is or how it should be managed. Customers are part of your firm.

(2) Select, train, and reward employees for delivering service quality as your own market research indicates that quality is defined by your customers.

(3) Pay as much attention to the backroom people and operational details as to the front-line and procedures. Service is in the details and if service quality is poor, your customer won't care from whom that service comes.

(4) In trying to meet customer expectations and needs, integrate internally across functions, to ensure that all functions present the same seamless quality orientation to the customer.

(5) Coordinate 1−4 above to promote a "service culture" as your service guarantees. You can really only manage service quality through culture because you can't be there during every transaction.

We can build a winning service through the following means.

1. Organization by Mastering the Rules of the Game

Using industrial models to manage service-based corporations makes as little sense as using farm models to run factories.

The message is simple: Service organizations can outperform the competition if they master what we offer as the "rule of the service game." We emphasize service game because it is indeed a very different game from manufacturing. Daniel Bell's book made this most clear to us when he described the steps in the evolution of the nature of work.

Step 1: the agrarian "game against nature", in which the game was human versus the land.

Step 2: the industrial "game against fabricated nature", in which the game was between human and machine.

Step 3: the preindustrial services "game between persons", in which the game is between a clerk and a customer or a professional and a client.

Each of these games requires different resources and rules.

2. The Three Tiers of a Winning Service Organization

Competitive advantage in services derives from unique ways of conceiving and managing service operations. Here we offer a unique view of service organizations — one that treats a service business as comprised of three tiers: a customer tier, a boundary tier, and a coordination tier. This three-tiered model stands in sharp contrast to traditional functional ways of slicing up organizations — like into marketing, human resources, and operations management. And we connect success in service to the effective management and integration of these tiers. So we discuss here how to strategically and holistically manage the hundreds of things that must be done well across these three tiers to win the service game.

3. The Customer Tier

Customers are the foundation of any service organization. They are the scorekeepers in the service game. Some colleagues of ours have suggested that figure skating is now the sport that offers the most appropriate metaphor for the nature of competition in today's world. It is, instead, an individual organization trying to delight and impress a panel of judges, and the judges are your customers. You can successfully bash the other organizations but still lose the service game if you only — ring up 4s and 5s with your customers. In figure skating, 10s are perfection — and that is what is required to win the service game.

Management practice should be based on a deep knowledge of customer characteristics in three areas: expectations, needs, and competencies. Our experience is that today's managers have learned a lot about expectations but little about needs and competencies.

The distinction between expectations and needs is important because customers are generally aware, or easily become aware, of what they expect, but they are generally unaware of what they need. At a minimum, service organizations must meet their customers'expectations merely to be able to stay in the game with their competitors. You must determine the specific expectations your customers have for your service if you want to remain in the service game.

A critical management challenge is to define the business's strategic focus relative to the expectations of the customers you want to keep. Each service organization must be fitted to its market and its customers'particular definition of service quality. This "strategic view of service quality" — in which the organization is designed around the expectations of the customers you must want to keep — is the central principle on which all the other rules of the game are based.

Once customer expectations have been identified and met, respecting customers' subconscious needs is the key to differentiation in a service business. This is what it takes to win the game. We have come to believe that service organizations must meet three key customer needs to deliver service excellence.

(1) Security: the need to feel secure and to feel unthreatened by physical, psychological, or economic harm.

(2) Esteem: the need to feel that one's self-esteem is maintained and enhanced by others.

(3) Justice: the need to feel fairly and justly treated.

A focus on customer needs helps us understand why customers react the way they do, especially how they react to service failures and why they are typically slow to use services.

Customers not only bring expectations and needs to the organization to be fulfilled; they also bring competencies. Organizations that can capitalize on customer competencies can be big winners. In service organizations, customers are producers as well as customers. Customers are no less a part of a firm's human resources than its employees. If your customers are sufficiently talented, they can do all sorts of things for you, from codesigning your services to codesigning your human resources management practices. Having the "best customers" can be a source of competitive advantage.

The customer tier, then, deals with three important customer characteristics: their expectations, their needs, and their competencies. Once these are understood, the people who deal with customers, those who manage the service encounter, come into play. We call the people who interface with customers members of the boundary tier.

4. The Boundary Tier

The second tier of service organization is where the customer meets the organization. This has been called the "moment of truth". Much of the game between persons that is played at the boundary occurs face-to-face between service providers and customers.

The people who deliver service play some special roles within the boundary tier and deserve special attention. Service characteristics like intangibility and customer contact require service employees to display more initiative, to cope more effectively with stress, to be more interpersonally flexible and sensitive, and to be more cooperative than their colleagues who work in manufacturing.

The make-it-or-break-it role service employees play is that of linking customers to the organization. The boundary tier — especially but not exclusively the employees at the boundary tier — is the glue that binds customers to the firm. Because service employees are both physically and psychologically close to the customers they serve, they play at least two important roles for the organization.

(1) Impression managers: For many customers, the service employee is the organization. This means that boundary employees' behavior and the experiences their behavior creates for customers are service quality in customers' eyes.

(2) Gatekeepers of information: Boundary employees, being in constant interaction with customers, are an endlessly useful source of insights into customer attitudes, information on competitor strategies, and ideas about how to enhance service quality.

It is important to know how to recruit, hire, pay, train and appraise front-line employees. However, we will always emphasize that attention to these workers and their individual abilities, attitudes, and motivations is only one of many rules for winning the service game. We will avoid what we call the "human resource trap", which is the mistake many companies make of putting all the burden for service quality on how people at the moment of truth treat customers. We will also stress the importance of non-personal service characteristics (like the physical facility, billing accuracy, and timeliness) and the support that must be given to front-line employees to enable them to contribute most effectively to winning the service game. As with a figure skater who is provided with just the right music and wardrobe, performance by service workers can be only as perfect as the supporting element permit.

5. The Coordination Tier

Coordination is management's responsibility, and in service firms, it may be management's most important task. It includes the coordination of the activities of customers who are often on site helping to coproduce the service and the integration of the customer and boundary tiers. Key coordination problems are to ensure that:

(1) clear strategic decisions have been made about who the target market is or should be and that internal functioning of the organization is effectively coordinated to pursue that market;

(2) the boundary tier has the logistical systems, and staff support to meet the customer tier's expectations and needs;

(3) the needs and expectations of those who work at the boundary tier are being met.

The toughest challenge here is to get the various subsystems of the service organization … e. g. operations, marketing, human resources management … to act as one system. Each function has its own driving internal logic, which may be at odds with its organizational counterparts. For example, marketing may feel compelled to do whatever is necessary to keep costs down. The coordination objective is to meld these various competing logic into one compelling, organization-wide service logic driven by a dedication to meeting customers' expectations and representing their needs.

We emphasize coordination through the creation of a service climate and culture as the most effective means for dealing with the unique challenges of service system integration. That is, the coordination problem reduces to the creation, maintenance, and enhancement of a climate and culture for service excellence. A service culture is an atmosphere, tone, or milieu pervaded by a service imperative. No single thing or even several things can make service quality happen. Hundreds of things must be put in place for employees to believe that their own business believes in service quality … and it is this belief by employees that translates into service quality for customers. In summary, we propose that managers must think about service organizations as being comprised of three tiers: the customer tier, the boundary tier, and the coordination tier. This way of thinking about service organization has some unique features. First, customers are included as part of the organization, not regarded as external to it. They belong. Customers are portrayed as the foundation of the organization. It is worth repeating: there is no business organization without customers; service organizations exist because of customers.

Please answer the following questions.

1. In order to guarantee service quality, what should a service business do?

2. What a role does the customer play in a service organization? What should a service organization

do with the customer to win the service game?

3. What do customer characteristics include?

4. What are the customer's needs?

5. Why is the coordination tier so important?

Chapter 12

Insurance (II)

保险（二）

In international trade, goods traveling long distances to another country, out of the direct physical control of both the buyer and the seller, may face all kinds of risks or losses and therefore must be insured against loss or damages at each stage of their journey. In this way, whatever mode of transport is being used, neither the exporter nor the customer suffers any loss. Obviously, cargo insurance is a contract whereby the insurer (insurance company), on the basis of a premium paid, undertakes to indemnify the insured against loss from certain risks or perils to which the cargo insured may be exposed. It is an indispensable adjunct of international trade. Without adequate insurance and protection of the interests of those with goods in transit, international trade can not be guaranteed.

12.1 Marine Cargo Insurance

12.1.1 | Types of Risks, Losses and Expenses Covered

1. Types of Risks

Two types of risks are covered by ocean marine insurance.

1) Perils of the sea

One is the perils of the sea, including both natural calamities and unexpected accidents. Natural calamities include heavy weather, lightening, Tsunami, earthquake, volcanic, eruption and so on. Accidents refer to fire, explosion, vessel being stranded, grounded, sunk or capsized, collision or contact of vessel with any external object other than water, etc.

2) External risks

The other type of risks is external (extraneous) risks including general external risks and special external risks. General external risks include theft and pilferage, contamination, leakage, breakage, sweating and/or rain water damage, short-delivery and not-delivery, shortage in weight, clashing and so on. Special risks include war, strike, failure to deliver due to some special laws or regulations.

2. Types of Losses

Two types of losses are covered by marine cargo insurance. One is total loss and the other partial loss.

1) Total loss

Total loss is divided into actual total loss and constructive loss. Actual total loss means the complete loss of the insured cargo in value. It, within the meaning of definition, may be construed in three distinct ways: (1) when the subject matter is totally destroyed, (2) when the subject matter is so damaged as to cease to be a thing of the kind insured, (3) when the assured is irretrievably deprived thereof. A constructive total loss occurs when the cost of salvaging the shipment would be more than the salvaged value of the merchandise. The shipment insured is reasonably abandoned as any further efforts at salvage would be fruitless. [1] Most insurance policies provide for the payment of a total loss up to the insured amount.

Where there is a constructive total loss, the assured may either treat the loss as a partial loss, or abandon the subject matter insured to the insurer and treat the loss as if it were an actual total loss. Where the assured elects to abandon the subject matter insured to the insurer, he must give notice of abandonment. If he fails to do so, the loss can only be treated as a partial loss.

2) Partial loss

Partial loss means the total loss of part of the insured cargo. It can be divided into general average and particular average.

General average is based upon a relationship between the shipowner and all the shippers who have cargo aboard the same vessel on a particular voyage. All these parties are bound together in the "adventure". Sometimes, when the whole ship was threatened by a peril of the sea or some other hazard, in order to save the ship and some of the cargo, part of the cargo or vessel have to be sacrificed, then an act of general average would be declared. According to maritime law, those interests whose property was saved must contribute proportionally to cover the losses of the one whose property was voluntarily sacrificed. [2] As for the act of general average, there needs certain criteria to be met. Namely, the act must be:

- Extraordinary

For there to be a general average loss, there must be an "extraordinary" sacrifice or expenditure which is made for the benefit of all the parties to the common adventure. The former is a physical act, while the latter is a financial outlay, but both are losses in general average.

- Voluntarily and reasonably made

"Voluntary made" infers that the action of making a sacrifice is intentionally made on willingness rather than on the orders of others. "Reasonably made" infers that the master of a vessel must act reasonably when making a sacrifice for which others will eventually be partly liable. Similarly, any expense incurred must be governed by the same criteria of reasonableness.

- In time of peril

A loss may be claimed in general average act which causes that loss to take place "in time of peril". The peril must be real and actually exist. If the perils were not real or were later proved mistaken, any claim against damages caused by the act would not be entertained by the underwriter.

- Successful

The action of the ship's master should be successful in saving the voyage the ship is no longer listing because the jettisoned cargo righted the ship; the tugboat successfully kept the ship from running aground, the fire was successfully put out. If, however, making the general average sacrifice or expenditure, no property in the venture is saved, there would be no forthcoming contributions, because nobody has benefited from the general average act.

Particular average means a partial loss suffered by part of the cargo. It occurs when a storm of fire damages part of the shipper's cargo and no one else's cargo has to be sacrificed to save the voyage. The cargo owner whose goods were damaged or lost should refer to his insurance company, provided his policy covers the specific type of loss suffered.

3. Expenses

Ocean marine insurance also covers some expenses incurred in reducing the loss of the subject matter insured either by the insured himself or a party other than the insurer and/or the insured.

Take for example, "salvage charges" which means charges recoverable by salvor independently of contract. They do not include the expenses of services in the nature of salvage rendered by the insured or his agents, or any person employed for hire by them, for the purpose of averting a peril insured against. Such expenses, where properly incurred, may be recovered as particular charges or as a general average loss, according to the circumstances under which they were incurred.

12.1.2 | Ocean Marine Cargo Clauses of CIC

Ocean Marine Cargo Clause of the People's Insurance Company of China was constituted in 1972 and revised in 1976 and 1981.

There are mainly two types of insurance coverage, basic coverage and additional coverage. Basic coverage mainly includes FPA, WPA and All Risks. Additional coverage includes general additional coverage and special additional coverage.

1. FPA

Free from Particular Average (FPA) of China Insurance Clause (CIC)[3] became effective in January 1, 1981. FPA (Free from Particular Average) is a limited form of cargo insurance cover under which no partial loss or damage caused by natural calamities is recoverable. It only provides coverage for total losses and general average emerging from the actual "marine perils" like vessel being stranded, grounded or sunk.

China Insurance Clauses are very similar to Institute Cargo Clauses (ICC, effective January 1, 1982) made by the Institute of London Underwriters and widely used around the world. ICC (C), for example, has the same coverage as CIC FPA except for damage of package during loading and /

or unloading.

2. WPA

WPA (With Particular Average) is a wider cover than FPA. It provides extensive cover against all loss or damage due to marine perils throughout the duration of the policy, including partial loss or damage which may be attributed to natural calamities like heavy weather. This coverage provides protection against damage from seawater caused by "heavy weather". ICC (B) has the same coverage plus damage of package during loading and/or unloading. ICC (B) and (C) provide cover against specified risks only.

3. All Risks

All Risks is the most comprehensive of the three basic coverages under which the insurer is responsible for all total or partial loss of, or damage to the goods insured either arising from sea perils or general external causes. However, it does not cover loss, damage or expense caused by delay, inherent vice or nature of the goods insured, or special external risks of war, strike, etc.

ICC (A) provides cover against all risks that are not specifically excluded and is similar to All Risk of CIC.

4. General Additional Risks

General additional risks include TPND (Theft, Pilferage and Non-delivery), Fresh Water Rain Damage, Risk of Shortage, Risk of Intermixture and Contamination, Risk of Leakage, Risk of Clash and Breakage, Risk of Odor, Damage caused by Heating and Sweating, Hook Damage, Risk of Rust, etc. These additional risks cannot be covered independently and should go with FPA or WPA and are included in All Risks coverage.

5. Special Additional Risks

Special additional risks include War Risk, Strike Risk, Failure to Delivery Risk, Import Duty Risk, On Deck Risk, Rejection Risk, etc., among which war risk and strikes risk are more common. These additional coverages are usually taken out together with FPA, WPA and All Risks.

Exporters cannot get whatever coverage they want from the insurance company. Even if they can, subject matters should be insured in the appropriate category. Experienced exporters know the losses they expect. The insurance should be both economical and effective.

For instance, cargo like mineral ores will face little or no risk of partial loss and FPA or ICC(C) will be sufficient. On the contrary, cargo such as shoes, bikes and most manufactured goods will face perils of the sea and extraneous risks, so AR or ICC (A) will be most appropriate. Wood logs need the coverage of FPA or ICC (B) since they could be lost (during the loading and /or unloading as well) but not damaged, while plywood should be covered by WA or ICC (B) since it can be lost and/or damaged, but less prone to damage or loss by extraneous risks than finished products.

12.1.3 | Institute of London Underwriters and Institute Transit Clause

Institute of London Underwriters is a professional organization founded in 1884 representing the interests of underwriters. Its Technical and Clause Committee has produced and will continue to produce special clauses, institute clauses, which are widely used. When a new institute clause is applied, if it has not been included in the insurance policy, it will be added to other clauses by sticking to the policy a separate slip of paper with the new clause. Institute Transit Clause covers the goods from the time they leave the warehouse named in the policy, continues while goods are in transit and terminates either when the goods reach their final warehouse or on the expiry of 60 days after discharge overside from the overseas vessel whichever is earlier. [4]

12. 1. 4 Major Types of Policy

1. Time Policy

A time policy usually runs for a period of time usually not exceeding 12 months. In adopting a time policy, the most important issue is whether the loss occurred at a time in which the policy was running because sometimes it is difficult to prove in case where it is alleged that the conditions giving rise to the loss (eg, a hole in the ship) occurred during the policy, although the final consequence (the foundering of the vessel) occurred afterwards.

2. Voyage Policy

This is a policy that operates for the period of the voyage, and the cover for cargo is from warehouse to warehouse. The policy will not be applied to the situation where the actual voyage and/or ports are different from those in the policy.

3. Mixed Policy

This is a policy that covers the subject matter for the voyage within a time period. It is used to cover the cargo from warehouse to warehouse with a time limit. The cargo has to be warehoused within 60 days after discharge or the policy will no longer cover the cargo.

4. Floating Policy

This is an arrangement by which a large initial sum of insurance is granted. Each time a shipment is made, the insured declares this and the value of the shipment is deducted from the outstanding sum insured. The premium is paid in advance.

This arrangement provides the policy holder with a large reserve of cover for cargo. It is often used by a dealer with several consignments of goods to insure, and such a policy is represented by certificates for each separate consignment.

Floating policy is the total of several voyage policies. In other words, it is one policy that can be used up. Although valid usually for a year, it is not a time policy.

5. Open Policy

This is an arrangement in which terms such as types of risks to be covered, validity of the insurance contract, rate, premium, maximum value of each shipment and geographical limits, etc are worked out when the contract is signed. Each shipment is covered once the insured declares the details. The inssured may be authorized to issue against payment a preprinted insurance certificate which is valid after completion of shipment details and his signature for documentation purposes. The insurance certificate is pre-signed by the insurer.

12. 1. 5 | Premium

Premium is generally based on the value of goods covered and the statistical probability of loss. The premium is calculated upon the insurance amount and the rate.

12.2　Insurance of Land, Air and Postal Transportation

A high volume of business is now conveyed by rail and road. It is essential that adequate cover be obtained for the land carriage. Again, the insurance broker or a trade association can give valuable advice. Insurance coverage for land transportation can be divided into two categories: Land Transportation Risk, almost equivalent to WPA, and All Risks for land transportation, almost equivalent to Marine All Risks.

By the nature of air movements, short transit times, lighter packing required, quick clearance at destination points and, in most places, stricter theft-pilferage control, a significant number of export dispatches are sent by air these days. While an air disaster is spectacular and concentrates the public attention exceptionally, it is true that air traffic is one of the safest methods of moving goods. Obviously, the speed and ease of handling air freight makes an insurance risk attractive to the insurer and premium rates attractive to the insured. There are also two types of coverage: Air transportation risk and air transportation All Risks. Air transportation risk is similar to WPA, while air transportation All Risks is similar to Marine All Risks.

Parcel post insurance covers the losses of or damage to the parcels caused by natural calamities, fortuitous accidents or external risks. It includes Parcel Post Risk and parcel post All Risks. On the basis of these two basic coverages, some additional risks may be added if circumstances require.

12.3　Insurance Procedures

12. 3. 1 | Insurance Clause in Sales or Purchase Contract

Insurance clause is one of the important parts of international sales or purchase contract. The contracts are different when different trade terms are chosen.

In FOB, CFR OR FCA, CPT contract, the insurance clause may simply be stipulated as:

"Insurance: To be covered by the Buyer. " If the buyer entrusts the seller to effect insurance, items like amount insured, risk covered, clause applied and so on should be clearly stipulated in the contract.

In CIF or CIP contract, the clause should make it clear as to who is responsible for effecting insurance, the risks covered, the methods of ascertaining the insurance amount, and the insurance clauses adopted. Ambiguous clauses such as "usual risks" or "customary risks" should be avoided.

The following is an example of an insurance clause in a CIF contract: "Insurance to be covered by the Sellers for 110% of total invoice value against All Risks, as per and subject to the relevant ocean marine cargo clauses of the People's Insurance Company of China, dated 1/1, 1981. "

12. 3. 2 | Insurance in Practice

1. Export Insurance

When transaction is made on CIF and CIP basis, the export enterprises would effect insurance contract by signing contract with the local insurance company. They should insure the goods against the risks for the amount stipulated in the contract when the goods are ready and the date of shipment as well as the name of vessel has been determined. They should first fill in the application form and pay the premium, on which the insurance policy or insurance certificate issued by the insurance company is based.

The date of insurance policy/certificate should not be later than the date of B/L. The insured amount should cover the price of the goods, the transaction costs and the expected profit, etc. This is called additional insurance. If the insured amount is not clearly stated in the contract, according to the usual practice, it is the CIF or CIP price plus 10% CIF or CIP price. If the buyer asks for increased percentage of addition, it is generally acceptable. But the additional premium should be borne by the buyer.

The insurance document is one of the major export documents. It can be transferred by endorsement.

2. Import Insurance

When imported goods are transacted on FOB, CFR, FCA and CPT basis, the import firms shall effect insurance by themselves. In order to simplify the procedures and avoid failure of insurance, open policies are adopted, i. e. the insured and the insurer sign a long-term insurance contract which covers the goods insured, risks, responsibilities, premium rate and the way of settlement of claim. The insured shall inform the insurer in written form of the information concerning the name of the vessel, the sailing date and route, the name and quantity of the goods, and the amount insured. The insurance company shall then be reliable automatically as soon as the ship departs.

Those firms which do not sign any open policy with the insurance company shall effect insurance contract. Upon receiving shipping advice from the buyer abroad, these firms should carry out insurance procedures immediately.

3. Insurance Amount and Premium

The insurance amount is the highest amount for which the insurer shall compensate. The premium is calculated upon the insurance amount and the rate.

$$\text{insurance amount} = \text{CIF(CIP) price} \times (1 + \text{percentage of addition})$$
$$\text{premium} = \text{insurance amount} \times \text{premium rate}$$

4. Claim for Losses

1) Advice of losses

When the insured knows the losses, he should inform the insurance company or its agent appointed in the policy of the losses. Upon receiving the advice, the latter should immediately take correspondent measures like inspecting the losses, putting forward rescue proposals, identifying liabilities and issuing inspection report of losses.

2) Claim for damages on the carrier and other parties concerned

Apart from informing the insurer of the losses, the insureds should ask the carrier and other parties concerned such as the customs for evidence of losses of or damage to the goods. If it is their fault, claim should be made in written form immediately.

3) Take suitable measures

The insured should take suitable measures to remedy the goods or put them in order. Moreover, the insured should do as the insurer required

4) Prepare documents for claim

Insurance documents, shipping documents, invoices, inspection report and evidence of damage and losses, etc. should be prepared to support the claim.

New Words and Expressions

undertake	v.	承诺
indemnify	v.	补偿
peril	n.	危险，风险
indispensable	a.	不可缺少的，必需的
adjunct	n.	环节，附件
tsunami	n.	海啸
strand	v.	搁浅
capsize	v.	倾覆

collision	n.	碰撞
extraneous	a.	外部的，外来的
contamination	n.	污染
leakage	n.	渗漏
salvage	v.	救济，拯救

mode of transport	运输方式
theft and pilferage	偷窃
Actual Total Loss	实际全损
Constructive Total Loss	推定全损
General Average	共同海损
Particular Average	单独海损
FPA	平安险
WPA	水渍险
All Risk	一切险
ICC（Institute Cargo Clauses）	协会货物保险条款
TPND（Theft，Pilferage and Non-delivery）	偷窃提货不着险
Fresh Water Rain Damage	淡水雨淋险
Risk of Intermixture and Contamination Risks	混杂污损险
Risk of Clash and Breakage	碰损破碎险
Risk of Odor	串味险
Hook Damage Risk	钩损险
Risk of Rusk	锈损险
Failure to Delivery Risk	交货不到险
On Deck Risk	舱面险
Institute Transit Clause	伦敦保险协会条款
floating policy	大保单
open policy	预约保单

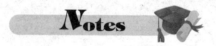

1. The shipment insured is reasonably abandoned as any further efforts at salvage would be fruitless. 因进一步拯救已是徒劳无益，便合理地放弃这批所保的货物。

2. According to maritime law, those interests whose property was saved must contribute proportionately to cover the losses of the one whose property was voluntarily sacrificed.   按照海运法，货物得救的受益方必须按照比例分摊那些自动牺牲货物的当事人的损失。

3. China Insurance Clause（CIC）：中国保险条款。中国的国际货物运输保险使用的都是中国保险条款（CIC）。在国际保险市场上比较通用的保险条款是伦敦保险协会条款（ICC）。这一条款在 1981 年 1 月 2 日生效的新条款中做了比较重大的改革，将原来的平安险、水渍险和一切险的传统险别分别改为（A）、（B）、（C）三种险别。"（A）险"负责一切外来风险造成的损失；"（B）险"负责条款列举的自然灾害和意外事故、抛弃、冲击落海及装卸事故等造成的损失；"（C）"险比"（B）险"则少了地震、火山爆发、电击、水损和装卸事故造成的损失。在投保时，可由双方来确定何种保险条款。

4. Institute Transit Clause covers the goods from the time they leave the warehouse named in the policy, continues while goods are in transit and terminates either when the goods reach their final warehouse or on the expiry of 60 days after discharge overside from the overseas vessel whichever is earlier.　伦敦保险协会条款对货物的投保从货物离开保单上列明的仓库开始算起，一直包括货物的整个运输期间；当货物到达目的地仓库或者卸载越过船舷 60 天以后终止，其中以较早者为准。

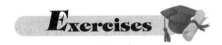

I Review questions.

1. Why is insurance indispensable to international trade?

2. What is constructive total loss and what is the difference between actual total loss and constructive total loss?

3. What are the three basic coverages in Ocean Marine Cargo Clauses of CIC（China Insurance Clauses）?

4. What kind of loss is covered by WPA, but not by FPA? Explain the two types of ocean risks.

5. What is constructive total loss and what is the difference between actual total loss and constructive total loss?

6. What losses or damages are not covered by All Risks?

7. Under which insurance coverage will the insurer cover the loss caused by leakage?

8. How is insurance procedure going on?

II Define the following terms briefly.

1. constructive total loss

2. general average

3. premium

4. open policy

III **Decide whether the following statements are True or False. Then put T for True or F for False in the brackets at the end of each statement.**

1. General external risks include theft and pilferage, failure to deliver due to government restriction and leakage, breakage, etc. (   )

2. General average may be taken as the losses caused by the natural calamities. (   )

3. In ocean marine insurance. FPA is the most restrictive cargo insurance cover under which no partial loss or damage is recoverable. (   )

4. Special additional coverage, such as war risks, strikes and so on must be effected together with FPA, WA or AR. (   )

5. All Risks can cover all the losses that are caused by various kinds of risks. (   )

6. Floating Policy is the same as the Open Policy in some cases. (   )

7. Premium is calculated upon the insurance amount and the rate, therefore, it cannot exceed the insured amount of goods. (   )

8. Land transportation Risk is almost equivalent to WPA, and All Risks for land transportation is almost equivalent to Marine All Risks. (   )

9. Ocean marine insurance covers two types of losses: partial loss and total loss. (   )

10. Ocean marine insurance covers ship and their cargo only on the high seas and not on inland waterways. (   )

IV **Translate the following passages into Chinese.**

The international trade is subject to many risks. Ships may sink or consignments be damaged in transit, exchange rates may alter, buyers default or governments suddenly impose an embargo. Therefore, exporters and importers have to insure themselves against many of these risks.

The history of insurance goes back as far as the twelfth century, when marine insurance was known to exist in North Italy. In the fourteenth century, Italian merchants came to Britain and brought their system of insurance to safeguard ships and cargo with them. In those days, of course, there were no insurance companies; merchants would group together and write their names under a promise to pay for ships or cargoes lost in storms or taken by pirates, and this is how the term "underwriters" came into existence. If the ship was lost, the financial loss was spread and no single merchant risked all his money.

V **Translate the following passage into English.**

不论何时发生了实际的损失, 对与货物有关的一方来说, 能够得到公正、有效和迅速的理赔是极为重要的。保险单实际掌握在谁的手中, 索赔权通常就属于谁。索赔者应得到由专家出具的鉴定说明书, 把证明书、提单副本、商业发票、保险单和一封要求予以偿付的说明函一起邮寄给保险公司立案。解决一项索赔并不是一件容易的事, 需要的是耐性、证据和知识。

VI Read the following passages and answer the questions.

What Is Not Insured

To have a clear idea of what "All Risks" really means, one must understand the meaning of "risks" and "external" as these terms are used in insurance. A "risk" is something that may happen, but not something that must happen. It is, in other words, a possibility that may arise as fortuity, an accident, and not something inevitable. This means that marine insurance does not cover the kind of damage that can be expected to occur under normal conditions because of the nature of the goods themselves.

Inherent vice is specifically excluded from coverage "All Risks" clauses, and it is an implied exclusion in all insurance policies, whether or not it is specifically mentioned.

Delay is another exclusion that is usually specifically stated, and it is implied in all policies in any case. This means that if goods are delayed in transit and there is a loss because the delay causes them to spoil or lose market value, this loss is not covered. In the case of especially sensitive products, such as meat or butter, it is possible to have the policy changed to pay for physical damage caused by delay, but even then the delay usually must be the result of fortuitous named perils.

1. Other Exclusions

Clearly, it is as important to understand what market insurance does not cover as to understand what it does. All insurance is written within a framework of basic conditions, or implied warranties, which doe not appear in the policy, but which have been backed up over the years by court decisions. If these conditions are violated, the insurance may be invalidated, and the underwriter would have the option of rejecting claims.

Perhaps the most important principle of insurance is Utmost Good Faith. This means that the inssured is obligated to disclose to the insurer all facts relevant to the risk when applying for the insurance. If, for example, an exporter misrepresents the kind of packing used and breakage occurs, the insurance company may well refuse to pay for the damage.

All insurance policies also carry the implied conditions that the insured must follow the generally established trade usages for the particular product, and that he will not contribute to the loss through willful fault or negligence. Another implied warranty is that the venture must be legal.

Insurance contract may explicitly limit the coverage for particular goods or circumstances. Thus, the following losses could be excluded in a contract: leakage or hook losses on goods packed in bags, spontaneous combustion fires in cotton; solidification of palm and coconut oil, unless heated storage is provided.

2. Choosing the Right Coverage

Most exporters will probably want to have the widest form of coverage they can get . . . "All Risks" coverage. But because of the nature of their goods, underwriters may agree to provide only a more limited form of cover. Moreover, even though an exporter can get All Risks coverage, he may well decide that it is uneconomical. An experienced exporter will come to know the losses he can expect, and may find it cheaper to write them off as trade losses than to pay the relatively high All Risks premium.

Products should be insured in the appropriate category. A good rule of thumb is that an exporter should insure for the coverage accepted in his particular trade. Now let's examine which type of insurance cover an intelligent exporter would choose for the following items.

(1) A consignment of shoes.

(2) Logs of wood.

(3) Wooden toys.

(4) Heavy machinery.

(5) Plywood.

(6) Bicycles.

Probably, you will give the following answers.

(1), (3), (4) and (6) would probably be insured All Risks because they are prone to be damaged in transit. Most manufactured goods fall into this category. (2) would be insured FPA, for while it could be lost it is not likely to be damaged. (5) on the other hand would be insured WPA because it could be damaged in transit, but is less prone to damage than the finished products mentioned. Normally, the insurance company will advise the exporter in this respect.

Please answer the following questions.

1. Do you think All Risks can insure goods against all potential risks?

2. Do you agree that delay in transit is another insurance exclusion?

3. Can you list a few of other exclusions?

4. What factors should be considered in choosing an appropriate coverage?

Chapter 13

Inspection, Claim, Force Majeure and Arbitration

商品检验、索赔、不可抗力及仲裁

13.1 Inspection

13.1.1 Importance of Commodity Inspection

In international trade, the quality and quantity of the goods delivered by the seller should be in conformity with the terms of the contract and should be packed in the manner required by the contract. In this sense, inspection of commodity and the issuance of certificate of inspection are necessary steps in the transfer of the goods.

Inspection may be made by the seller and the buyer themselves. But on most occasions, the seller does not transfer the goods to the buyer face to face. In addition, during the long-distance transit, loading and unloading operation, losses of or damage to the goods may occur owing to the various kinds of risks or the carriers' fault. For the purpose of identifying liabilities and ascertaining facts, inspection by authoritative, impartial inspection bodies is required, by whom the certificates of inspection are issued. These certificates have been the major basis for transferring the goods, making payments, lodging and settling claims in international trade.

Besides, CISG (United Nations Conventions on Contracts for the International Sale of Goods) and the laws of various countries have made similar stipulations on buyer's right of inspection.

13.1.2 Time and Place for Inspection

The time and place in which the inspection is to be made differs from country to country. Generally speaking, the time and place in which the inspection is to be made in international trade are closely related to the trade terms and the nature of commodity of a contract; the industry customs and practice and the state's statue etc. The manner in which inspection is to be made can be outlined as follows:

1. Inspection at the Factory

The inspection is to be made, because of the dispatch of the goods at the factory, by the inspector of the factory at the exporting country or, as required by the contract, by both the inspector of the factory and the inspector of the buyer. Risks in transit in respect of the quality and the quantity of the goods shall be borne by the buyer.

2. Inspection at or Before the Shipment

The final quality or weight of the goods delivered shall be subject to the Quality and Weight Certificate issued by the agreed inspection authority before the goods is placed on board the vessel at the port of shipment. Quality and Weight Certificate issued under such circumstances is also called Shipping Quality and Shipping Weight. An inspection certificate issued by the competent authority to the seller shall indicate that the quality or weight of the goods delivered by the seller conforms to the contract, and that the buyer shall not have the right to reinspect the delivered goods.

3. Inspection at the Importing Country

The final quality or weight of the goods delivered shall be subject to the Quality and Weight Certificate issued by the agreed inspection authority at the port of destination. Quality and Weight Certificate issued under such circumstances is also called Landed Quality and Landed Weight.

4. Inspection at the Port of Shipment of the Exporting Country and Re-inspection at the Port of Destination or Importing Country

Certificate issued by the inspection authority at the port of shipment shall be one of the documents to be presented by the seller to the bank for negotiation, but shall not be the final proof for the quality and weight of the goods. Re-inspection shall be made at the agreed time by the agreed inspection authority at the port of destination. In case the quality or weight of the goods is found to be inconsistent with the contract, and such an inconsistency is caused by the seller, then the re-inspection certificate can be used as a final evidence by buyer for the recovering damages from the seller.[1] This kind of method is widely used in international trade. While this arrangement looks better than the previous two, it also has a problem, for example, if the quality or weight of the goods changes during the transit, then inspection results at ports of shipment and destination would be different. Sellers and buyers might have different arguments about the difference. A seller would argue that his responsibilities end where the goods are delivered. For example, for FOB, he is responsible only for loading the goods according to the contract and once the goods pass over the ship's rail, all risks pass over to the buyer. A buyer can argue that the seller is responsible for the goods to be marketable when they arrive at the port of destination.

In practice, for small differences (e. g. , 0.5% of weight), inspection result at the port of shipment is considered final or the difference is divided between the buyer and the seller. When the difference is big, it needs to be settled by negotiation or by arbitration.

5. Weight Inspection at the Port of Shipment and Quality Inspection at the Port of Destination

It is also referred to as Shipping Weight and Landed Quality. The Weight Certificate issued by the inspection authority at the port of shipment shall be used as the final evidence for the weight of the contracted goods, while Quality Certificate issued by the inspection authority at the port of destination shall be used as the final proof for the quality of the goods. This kind of approach is widely accepted by the traders who are dealing with bulk commodities.

13. 1. 3 | Inspection Authority

There are mainly two types of inspection body: governmental and non-governmental. The governmental inspection bodies such as the Food and Drug Administration (FDA)[2] in the USA specialize in inspection of particular merchandise (grain, drug, etc.). The international inspection of commodity is mainly undertaken by nongovernmental bodies which have the same legal status as notary organizations. The notable bodies are Society Generale De Surveillance S. A. (SGS) in Geneva, Swiss[3], Underwriters Laboratory (UL)[4] in the USA, Lloyd Surveyor[5], B. V. in Britain and Japan Marine Surveyor& Sworn Measurer's Association (NKKK)[6], etc.

According to the Law of the People's Republic of China on Import and Export Commodity Inspection and the Regulations for the Implementation of the Law of the People's Republic of China on Import and Export Inspection, the State Commodity Inspection Authorities are in charge of the inspection of import and export commodities throughout the country.

13. 1. 4 | Inspection Standard

Inspection on import and export commodities performed by the commodity inspection authorities shall cover quality, specifications, quantity, weight, packing and the requirements for safety and hygiene. The commodity inspection authorities shall conduct inspection according to the following standards.

(1) If the compulsory standards or other inspection standards which must be complied with are specified by law or administrative regulations, the inspection shall be performed according to the standards as specified by laws and administrative regulations.

(2) In the absence of the compulsory standards or other inspection standards which must be complied with as specified by laws or administrative regulations, the inspection shall be performed according to the standards agreed upon in the international trade contracts. If the trade is conducted against the sample, the inspection shall be performed simultaneously according to the sample provided.

(3) If the compulsory standards or other inspection standards which must be complied with as specified by law or administrative regulations are lower than the standards agreed upon in the international trade contract, the inspection shall be conducted according to the standards agreed upon

in the international trade contract. If the trade is conducted against the sample, the inspection shall be performed simultaneously according to the sample provided.

（4）In the absence of compulsory standards or other inspection standards which must be complied with as specified by laws and administrative regulations, and in case inspection standards are either not agreed upon or agreed upon unclearly in the contract, the inspection shall be conducted according to the standards of the manufacturing country, or relevant international standards or the standards designated by the state inspection agency.

13. 1. 5 | Inspection Certificate

Inspection certificate can be used to prove whether the quality, weight (quantity) or packing etc. of the goods delivered by the seller are in accordance with the contract. It also serves as evidence where the buyer rejects goods that do not conform to the contract or claims compensation from the seller. etc, and as one of the documents to be presented to the bank by the seller. Where the inspection result shown in an inspection certificate is not in accordance with the contract or the L/C, the bank shall have the right to refuse negotiation.

Most frequently used certificates are: Inspection Certificate of Quality, Weight, Quantity, Origin, Value, Damaged Cargo, and Health. For commodities such as frozen meat or leather, Veterinary Inspection Certificate might be required to prove that the commodity is free from diseases of animals. When feathers or other biological products are traded, Sanitary or Disinfection Inspection Certificate is required to prove that the commodity is free from harmful bacteria. It should be clearly stated in the contract what certificates are needed according to the nature of the goods and the laws of the importing country.

13. 1. 6 | An Example of Inspection Clause in Contract

"It is mutually agreed that the Inspection Certificate of Quality and Quantity (weight) issued by the Manufacturer (or xxx Surveyor) at the port of shipment shall be part of the documents to be presented for negotiation under the relevant L/C. The Buyer shall have the right to re-inspect the quality and quantity (weight) of the cargo. The re-inspection fee shall be borne by the Buyers. Should the quality and/or quantity (weight) be found not in conformity with that of the contract, the Buyers are entitled to lodge with the Sellers a claim which should be supported by survey reports issued by a recognized surveyor approved by the Sellers.[7] The claim, if any, shall be lodged within xx days after arrival of the cargo at the port of destination."

13.2 Claim

There are generally three types of claim: claim regarding selling and buying, claim regarding transportation, and claim regarding insurance. In this section, we will only focus on the claim regarding selling and buying.

13. 2. 1 Liabilities of Breach of Contract

1. Breach of Contract

(1) Breach of contract committed by the seller mainly covers: ① the seller fails to deliver the goods; ② the documents relating to goods are incomplete; ③ the goods do not conform with contract, etc.

(2) Breach of contract committed by the buyer mainly covers: ① the buyer fails to pay the price; ② the buyer fails to take delivery of the goods, etc.

2. Liabilities of Breach of Contract

(1) CISG Article 25 provides that "A breach of contract committed by one of the parties is fundamental if it results in such detriment to the other party as substantially to deprive him of what he is entitled to expect under the contract, unless the party in breach did not foresee and a reasonable person of the same kind in the same circumstances would not have foreseen such a result. [8]" The injured party may declare the contract voided and claim damages.

(2) If, however, the breach of contract is non-fundamental, the injured party can only claim damages but cannot declare the contract voided.

(3) The British law divides the breach of contract into breach of condition and breach of Warranty.

Breach of Condition refers to the breach of the major terms of the contract, the injured party may declare the contract voided and claim damages. Breach of Warranty means breach of the minor terms of the contract, the breach of which gives rise to a claim for damages, but not to a right to reject the goods and treat the contract as repudiated.

13. 2. 2 Claim Clause in Contract

Clauses in respect of claim in an import and export contract can be fixed as follows:

1. Discrepancy and Claim Clause

Discrepancy and claim clause also includes, besides stipulating that if any party breaches a contract the other party is entitled to lodge claim against the party in breach, other aspects in respect of proofs presented when lodging a claim and effective period for filing a claim etc.

2. Proofs

Clause in this respect stipulates the relevant proofs to be presented and the relevant authority competent for issuing the certificate. The proofs should be complete and clear, and the authority should be competent for issuing the relevant certificate. Otherwise, claims could be refused by the other party. Proofs include legal proof which refers to the sales contract and the relevant governing laws and regulations and fact proof which refers to the facts and the relevant written evidence in respect of the breach.

3. Period for Claim

Period for claim refers to the effective period in which the claimant can make a claim against the party in breach. Claims beyond the agreed effective period can be refused by the party in breach. Therefore, claim period should be reasonably fixed. Generally speaking, a period that is too long may put the seller under heavy responsibility and a period that is too short may make it impossible for the buyer to file a claim. In addition, a detailed stipulation in respect of the starting date for making a claim should also be included in the clause. For instance, "Claim should be filed by the buyer within 15 days after the arrival of the goods at the port of destination", "Claims should be made by the buyer within 10 days after the discharging of the goods at the port of destination", "Claim should be made within 15 days after the arrival of the goods at the business place of the buyer", "Claim should be made within 10 days after the inspection" etc. Most of the contracts concerning the sale of general goods include only the "discrepancy and claim" clause, but contracts for bulk commodities or machines and equipment will include both "discrepancy and claim" clause and "penalty clause".

4. Penalty

Clause in respect of penalty in a contract should stipulate that "any party who fails to perform the contract shall pay an agreed amount as penalty for compensating the other party for the damages. Penalty clause is fixed where the seller fails to make timely delivery; the buyer fails to open the relevant L/C or the buyer fails to take delivery on time, and the penalty ceiling is also included in the contract.

Most of the claims are related to imports. A claim is usually filed by the buyer against the seller who has delivered goods that does not accord with the contract.

13.2.3 | Claim

1. Claims Against the Seller

A claim may be filed by the buyer against the seller where the seller fails to make timely delivery or refuses to make delivery; where the goods delivered by the seller is not in accordance with the contracted quantity, quality, specifications; and the goods are damaged due to improper packing etc.

When a buyer files a claim, attention should be paid to the following.

(1) Proofs for claiming: When filing a claim against the seller, the buyer should present adequate proofs and give sufficient reasons, and documents such as statement of claim, inspection certificate issued by the inspection authority, invoice, packing list, copy of B/L etc should be presented. Under a FOB or CFR contract, an insurance policy should be included. When lodging a claim against the shipping company, the buyer should also present a tally report issued and signed by

the master or tally clerk of the harbor authority and a damage and/or short-landed memo issued and signed by the master. And additional document such as combined inspection report issued and signed by the insurance company and the buyer should be included for any claim that may be filed with the insurance company.

(2) Claim period: Claim should be made within the validity of the contract. If extension of the validity is necessary for commodity inspection, then the claim period can be extended after getting approval from the other party.

(3) Seller's responsibility for settlement: If imports incur losses or damages that are caused by the shipping company, the insurance company or the seller, then the buyer can file a claim against the responsible party. If losses or damages are caused directly by the seller, then the buyer should lodge a claim directly with the seller.

Usually, the buyer shall be given a reasonable opportunity for inspecting goods before he accepts or pays for the goods. The fact that the buyer has received goods does not denote that he has accepted the goods. Acceptance of goods occurs when a buyer, after having a reasonable opportunity to inspect the goods, indicates that he will take them. The basic duty of the buyer is to accept and pay for the goods if they conform to the contract. But if goods, after inspection, do not accord with the contract, then the buyer can either reject the goods that are not in accordance with the contract or accept the goods and reserve the right for claiming compensation for losses or damages. To reject goods, the buyer must notify the seller of the rejection and specify the defect or nonconformity. If a buyer treats the goods as if he owns them, the buyer is considered to have accepted. For instance if a buyer resells the defective goods delivered by the seller to a third party even though he knows it is defective, then an acceptance exists. If a buyer accepts any part of a commercial unit of goods, he is considered to have accepted the whole unit. By accepting goods, the buyer does not forfeit or waive remedies against the seller for any non-conformity in the goods. If the buyer wishes to hold the seller responsible, he must give the seller timely notice that the goods are nonconforming, and the buyer is obliged to pay for the goods that are accepted.

Under certain circumstances a buyer is permitted to revoke the acceptance. A buyer may revoke acceptance of nonconformity goods where the nonconformity substantially impairs the value of the goods and the buyer accepted them without knowledge of the nonconformity due to the difficulty of discovering the nonconformity or the buyer accepted the goods because of assurance by the seller.

2. Claim Against the Buyer

If the seller incurs losses or damages caused by the buyer's failure to perform the relevant obligations stipulated in the contract, the seller is entitled to claim compensation from the buyer.

If a seller files a claim, then the buyer should:

(1) carefully check the documents presented by the seller so as to ensure that the documents are authentic, inspection result is correct and the issuing party is competent.

(2) make a thorough investigation so as to find out the responsible party. If the shipping or the insurance company is responsible, the claim should be handed over to them. The buyer should compensate the seller for his losses or damages where the buyer is held responsible, and the buyer

should reject claim that is unreasonable and ill-founded on the part of the seller.

（3）correctly and reasonably decide the losses or damages incurred and work out a rational settlement to the claim.

13.3　Force Majeure

13. 3. 1 ｜ Definition of Force Majeure

A force majeure event is one that can generally be neither anticipated nor brought under control. Certain natural disasters and social disturbances are considered force majeure.

If possible, specific events should be clearly agreed upon and listed in contract to avoid any dispute if a specific event should be considered force majeure.

A force majeure event should have the following features.

（1）It happens after the contract is signed.

（2）It is not due to the negligence of the buyer or the seller.

（3）Neither the buyer nor the seller can control the situation.

A force majeure clause is mainly a protection for the seller to enable him to avoid his contractual obligations without paying a compensation or penalty, although it protects the buyer as well.

13. 3. 2 ｜ Consequences of Force Majeure

1. Termination of Contract

In cases of natural disasters or other events that have made it impossible to fulfill the contract, the contract can be terminated.

2. Postponement of Contract

In cases of events（such as transportation stoppage caused by an earthquake）that will only delay the fulfillment of a contract, the contract can be postponed but not terminated since it is still possible for the seller to carry out his contractual obligations.

13. 3. 3 ｜ Cautions When Drafting the Clause

1. Determine the Scope

The kinds of events that are to be considered as force majeure should be specified as clearly as possible. For instance, some people include social disturbances or strikes as force majeure events, but some other people disagree. If the scope of the events is not clearly defined, there might be difficulties in using the clause.

There are basically three ways to set the scope.

(1) General stipulation: "generally recognized force majeure causes".

(2) Specific listing: "war, flood, storm, heavy snow".

(3) Specific listing plus general stipulation: "war, flood, storm, heavy snow or any other causes beyond their control and other generally recognized force majeure causes".

2. Specify the Consequences.

Since there are different consequences of a force majeure, the clause should specify when the contract can be terminated and when it can only be postponed. For example, the contract can be cancelled only if the force majeure lasts over one month.

3. Designate the Agency to Issue Certificate

A force majeure should be verified by government authorities or a chamber of commerce at the location where the event takes place. The clause should specify which agency is to be the issuer.

4. Set the Time Limit of Notice to the Other Contractor

In case of a force majeure event, the party who wants to quote the clauses should inform the other party of his decision within a reasonable time limit.

13.3.4 | Cautions When Quoting the Clause

(1) Decide if an accident is within the scope according to the contract terms

(2) Notify the other contractor as soon as possible (The other party should reply quickly if he agrees or disagrees).

(3) Supply the certificate issued by the correct agency.

13.4 Arbitration

Disputes in international trade arise either from the breach of the contract by the intentional act of a party or from the breach of the contract by the negligence or fault of a party. When disputes arise between exporter and importer, they can be settled through friendly consultation, arbitration, or litigation. Friendly negotiation is an important tool in the process of dispute settlement, and undoubtedly the one most commonly relied on. The majority of the disputes are settled this way, while arbitration is the next best alternative.

13.4.1 | Definition of Arbitration

Arbitration means a method of resolving disputes arising from the two-side of parties who voluntarily render their disputes to a third party (an ad hoc arbitration tribunal or a permanent arbitration body) agreed by themselves to deal with in accordance with certain arbitration rules and make a final decision binding on each of the parties based on the arbitration clause concluded previously by them or based on arbitration agreement the parties have reached after the disputes arose.

13. 4. 2 | Characteristics of Arbitration

1. Voluntary

The litigants submit themselves voluntarily to an arbitrator. The arbitrator is a private, disinterested person, or nonofficial government organization chosen by the parties to a disputed question.

2. An Arbitration Agreement

It is in written form between the parties concerned, which is prerequisite for arbitration. An arbitration agreement is a contract between two or more parties whereby they agree to refer the subject in dispute to others and to be bound by their award. [9]

3. Simpler in Procedures, Less Costly and Time-consuming Than Litigation

The proceedings are much simpler, and cost less money and time than legal actions

4. The Award is Final and Binding on Both Parties

Neither party may bring a suit before a law court or make a request to any other organization for revising the arbitral award. The characteristic of finality of arbitral award is the basic element of the modern commercial arbitration recognized all over the world.

13. 4. 3 | Location of Arbitration

Location is not only a matter of convenience. It is also related to the application of the law system under which the disputes are settled. The location can be anywhere in the seller's country, the buyer's country or a third country. The arbitration place is the first important place in recognition and enforcement of an arbitral award. Therefore, no matter where the arbitration takes place, the location must be politically and professionally acceptable.

13. 4. 4 | Arbitration Bodies

There are two forms of arbitration: institutional arbitration and ad hoc arbitration. What the major difference between an ad hoc arbitration and an institutional arbitration falls on the fact that it is unnecessary for an ad hoc arbitration to have an institutional arbitration body to administer a case. That is to say, arbitration body is not the element that all forms of arbitration or arbitration clause must have. Generally speaking, it is not essential to stipulate an arbitration body in an arbitration clause for an ad hoc arbitration. But things are different in China, and there is no ad hoc arbitration in China at present. So in China, it is necessary to indicate an arbitration body, otherwise the arbitration clause may be considered as an invalid clause. The China International

Economic and Trade Arbitration Commission in Beijing, and its chapters in Shenzhen and Shanghai, and liaison offices in Dalian, Fuzhou, Changsha, Chendu and Chongqing accept arbitration cases according to arbitration rules and regulations, and use the unified Arbitration Rules and Panel of Arbitrators.

13.4.5 | Arbitration Award

An award is the decision made by the arbitration tribunal. It must be in written form with or without explanations or reasons. The arbitration award is final and binding upon both parties. Neither party may bring a suit before a law court or make a request to any other organization for revising the arbitral award. But if one party refuses to obey the award, the other can ask a court to enforce the implementation of the award. There is another situation where a lawsuit can be filed in respect of award of arbitration, that is the procedures of arbitration are illegal.

13.4.6 | Arbitration Fees

Fees can be borne by the losing party of the dispute, can be divided between the two parties or can be paid according to the award.

New Words and Expressions

inspection	n.	检验
liability	n.	责任
authoritative	a.	权威的
impartial	a.	公平的
dispatch	n.	发运
authority	n.	机构
inconsistency	n.	不符
hygiene	n.	卫生
compulsory	a.	义务的
simultaneously	ad.	同时地
veterinary	n.	兽医
disinfection	n.	消毒
claim	v.	索赔
breach	n.	违约
detriment	n.	破坏

non-fundamental	*n.*	非实质性的，非根本性的
repudiate	*v.*	拒绝接受
claimant	*n.*	索赔者
penalty	*n.*	惩罚，罚金
denote	*v.*	意味着
authentic	*a.*	真实的
ill-founded	*n.*	不可靠的，无根据的
arbitration	*n.*	仲裁
ad hoc	*a.*	临时的
litigant	*n.*	诉讼当事人
prerequisite	*n.*	前提
time-consuming	*a.*	费时的
chapter	*n.*	分会，分支机构
award	*n.*	裁决
quality certificate		质量证书
weight certificate		重量证书
shipping weight		装运重量
landed quality		到达质量
be competent for		有……资格
bulk commodities		大宗货物
tally clerk		码头点货员
short-landed memo		货物短缺证明
to lodge claim against		向……提出索赔
binding upon		对……有约束力

Notes

1. In case the quality or weight of the goods is found to be inconsistent with the contract, and such an inconsistency is caused by the seller, then the re-inspection certificate can be used as a final evidence by buyer for the recovering damages from the seller. 如果货物的质量和重量与合同不符，而且此不符是由出口商造成的，进口人可以凭复验证书向出口人索赔。

2. The Food and Drug Administration（FDA）：美国食品药物管理局（美国官方检验机构）。

3. Society Generale De Surveillance S. A.（SGS）in Geneva, Swiss：瑞士日内瓦通用鉴定公司。它属于非官方检验机构。非官方检验机构主要是指由私人创办的，具有专业检验、鉴定技术能力的公证行或检验公司。

4. Underwriters Laboratory（UL）：美国担保人实验室（美国半官方检验机构）。它是指有一定权威的，由国家政府授权，代表政府行使某项商品检验或某一方面检验管理工作的民间机构。

5. Lloyd Surveyor：英国劳埃氏公证行，也是非官方检验机构。

6. Japan Marine Surveyor& Sworn Measurer's Association（NKKK）：日本海事鉴定协会（非官方检验机构）。

7. Should the quality and/or quantity（weight）be found not in conformity with that of the contract，the Buyers are entitled to lodge with the Sellers a claim which should be supported by survey reports issued by a recognized surveyor approved by the Sellers.   如果货物的质量与数量与合同不符，买方有权向出口商提出索赔，索赔须凭出口人同意的检验机构所开具的检验报告为准。

8. A breach of contract committed by one of the parties is fundamental if it results in such detriment to the other party as substantially to deprive him of what he is entitled to expect under the contract，unless the party in breach did not foresee and a reasonable person of the same kind in the same circumstances would not have foreseen such a result.   一方当事人违反合同的结果如使另一方当事人蒙受损失，以至于实际上剥夺了他根据合同有权期待得到的东西，即为根本性违反合同，除非违反合同的一方并不预知而且同样一个通情达理的人处于相同情况中也没有理由预见会发生这种结果。

9. It is in written form between the parties concerned is prerequisite for arbitration. An arbitration agreement is a contract between two or more parties whereby they agree to refer the subject in dispute to others and to be bound by their award.   当事人之间签订的书面合同是仲裁的前提条件，仲裁协议是两个当事人或以上者之间的合同，他们同意将有争议的问题交由第三方来处理，并受仲裁裁决的约束。

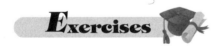

Exercises

▌ Review questions.

1. What is the importance of commodity inspection?

2. What are stipulations on the options of inspections on the part of buyers?

3. Can you name a few of inspection standards?

4. What does CISG article 25 stipulate for liabilities of breach of contract?

5. What will the buyer do if he or she lodges a claim against seller?

6. What cautions should the relevant parties need to have when drafting the clause of force majeure?

7. What are characteristics of arbitration?

8. What does it mean by saying that award is the final and binding on both parties?

II Define the following terms briefly.

1. inspection certificate
2. penalty
3. claim
4. force majeure
5. arbitration
6. arbitration award

III Decide whether the following statements are True or False. Then put T for True or F for False in the brackets at the end of each statement.

1. When Shipping Quality and Shipping Weight are referred to in the contract, the buyer shall have the right to re-inspect the delivered goods. (   )
2. In most cases, inspection at the port of shipment of the exporting country and re-inspection at the port of destination or importing country is widely carried out in international trade. (   )
3. For one contract, only one method and one standard should be used to ensure the consistency in inspection. (   )
4. Inspection certificate can be used to only prove whether the quality of the goods delivered by the seller is in accordance with the contract. (   )
5. Any party that fails to perform the contract may be free from the obligation of compensating the other party for the damages so long as that party has paid the penalty. (   )
6. All natural disasters and social disturbances can be universally taken as force majeure by all the countries in the world. (   )
7. Consequences of force majeure are all that the contract shall be terminated or cancelled. (   )
8. Arbitration agreement should be in the written form, and reached by both parties. (   )
9. An arbitration award is final and binding upon both parities, therefore, if one party does not get satisfied with the award, it cannot refer the case to the court, so long as the arbitration procedures are legal. (   )

IV Translate the following passages into Chinese.

Breach of a contract occurs where any party of a contract does not follow the stipulations of the contract. The sales contract shall have a legal binding force upon the contracting parties. Any party who has violated the contract shall be legally held responsible for the breach, and the injured party is entitled to remedies according to the stipulations of the contract or the relevant laws. Remedies can be outlined as follows:

Seller's remedies:

(1) Cancel the contract, and withhold delivery of any undelivered goods: When a buyer breaks contract, the seller has the right to cancel the contract and to hold up his own performance of the contract. If the seller is in the process of manufacturing the goods, the seller may complete

manufacture of the goods or stop manufacturing. But the seller would be justified in completing the manufacture of goods that could be resold readily at the contract price, but the seller would not be justified in completing specially manufactured goods that could not be sold to anyone other than the buyer who ordered them.

(2) Resell the goods: The seller may resell the goods to the third party, and recover damages. The seller must make any resale in good faith and in a reasonable commercial manner. If the seller does so, the seller is entitled to recover from the buyer as damages the difference between the resale price and the price the buyer agreed to pay in the contract. In the meanwhile, the seller may also recover incidental damages such as storage charges and sales commissions etc. The seller may make a profit at the resale if the goods bring more than the contract price. In such circumstances, the seller may keep the profit and does not have to give the profit to the buyer.

(3) Recover from the buyer the profit the seller would have made on the sale or the damages the seller sustained. The seller may recover as damages the difference between the contract price and the market price at the time and place the goods are to be delivered to the buyer.

(4) Require the buyer to return the goods. If the buyer is insolvent, then the seller has the right to require the buyer to return any goods, the insolvent buyer obtained from the seller.

Ⅴ Translate the following passage into English

仲裁原则的适用：在买卖合同中，应订明进行仲裁的所在国及适用的仲裁规则。适用我国的仲裁规则，是指适用《中国国际经济贸易仲裁委员会仲裁规则》，应注意，所采用的仲裁规则与仲裁地并非绝对一致，按国际仲裁的一般做法，原则上采用仲裁所在地的仲裁规则，但有的法律上也允许双方当时人在合同中约定，采用仲裁地点以外的其他国家（地区）仲裁机构的仲裁规则进行仲裁。

Ⅵ Read the following passages and answer the questions.

Arbitration Agreement

According to the relevant law of USA, the arbitration agreement is in the nature of a contract, subject to the general rules of contract law. The agreement must be in writing but it need not be signed. There must be consent to the arbitration by both parties.

If a party claims that an entire agreement, which contains an arbitration clause, is invalid because it was induced by fraud, the question frequently arises whether the arbitrator(s) have any authority to act. If the agreement is invalid, the arbitration clause is necessarily invalid. The courts have almost unanimously overruled this argument, and held that the arbitrator(s) must decide whether the agreement was induced by fraud or invalid for any other reasons. The rationale for this holding is that the agreement as a whole and the arbitration clause are separable. Consequently, the situation is different when the validity of the arbitration clause alone is in dispute. In that case, resort must be had to the courts. Illegality of a part of the contract does not vitiate the arbitration clause.

If the potential defendant resists the institution of arbitration proceedings, the aggrieved party may apply for a court order to compel arbitration. This is not necessary where the applicable rules of arbitration allow the arbitration to proceed if the defendant, after due notice, defaults.

If a party disregards the arbitration agreement and commences a legal action in court, the defendant may apply to the court for a stay of court proceedings.

Conversely, when arbitration is improper, the court may order a stay of arbitration. This applies, generally, where an issue is not arbitrable.

The award must be rendered within the time period fixed by the agreement or the rules of the organization under whose auspices the hearing has taken place. An award rendered after the expiration of that time is a nullity.

The award needs not, and as a rule does not state the grounds of the decision of the arbitrator(s). This rule differs from the arbitration law of many countries. Most arbitrators adhere to this practice. It eases their workload and may avoid attacks on the award. On the other hand, it is often disappointing to the unsuccessful party, which would like to know why it lost. Mistakes of law or fact are permissible, but irrationality is not.

According to relevant law of England, "arbitration agreement" is defined as a "written agreement to submit present or future differences to arbitration, whether an arbitrator is named therein or not". This definition covers both (1) an arbitration clause by which the parties agree to submit future disputes to arbitration (sometimes called an "agreement to refer") and (2) an agreement to submit a particular dispute or disputes to arbitration. An oral agreement or refer, or an oral submission to arbitration, is valid but is outside the scope of the Arbitration Acts.

The arbitration agreement needs not be contained in one document. An exchange of letters, telegrams, faxes, emails and so forth, will be sufficient provided that the exchanges reveal a clear arbitration agreement. There is no statutory requirement that the "arbitration agreement" should be signed by the parties.

The Rules of the London Court of International Arbitration (hereinafter referred to as LCIA) recommends the following model clause to parties who wish to have disputes referred to arbitration under the LCIA Rules: "Any dispute arising out of or in connection with this contract, including any question regarding its existence, validity or termination, shall be referred to and finally resolved by arbitration under the LCIA."

It will be observed that the model clause is not linked with a choice of English law as governing the contract. However, the LCIA advises parties to express in their contract the law of the country by which it shall be governed, by adding, "the governing law of this contract shall be the substantive law of ...". In addition, the LCIA recommends the parties to specify that the place and language of the arbitration and the number of arbitrators.

The place of arbitration shall be (city)...; the language of the arbitration shall be ...; and the tribunal shall consist of (a sole or three) arbitrator(s)...; (In the case of a three member tribunal) the following words may be added: "... two of them shall be nominated by the respective parties."

Every person who has general contractual capacity may conclude an arbitration agreement. An infant is not bound by an arbitration clause in a contract which is not for his benefit. A bankrupt may make an arbitration agreement.

In Brazilian law a distinction is made between the agreement to refer an already existing dispute to arbitration (submission) and the agreement to refer future disputes to arbitration (arbitral clause). It is always necessary in the case of an arbitral clause to conclude a submission once the dispute has arisen. However, the Brazilian courts adhere to the view that if a party refuses to conclude the submission in such a situation he cannot be compelled to do so. In other words, the arbitral clause, although regarded as an agreement to agree, is wholly unenforceable in Brazil. The refusal to conclude the submission can, at the most, lead to a liability for damages on the part of the recalcitrant party.

It should be added that the arbitral clause must be in writing, although there is no specific requirement as to the form of the writing itself.

The submission must contain the following matters.

(1) The name, profession and domicile of each of the parties.

(2) The name, profession and domicile of each of the arbitrators.

(3) The subject matter of the dispute in full detail.

(4) A declaration concerning the liability for the payment of the experts and the costs of the procedure.

Any person who has the capacity to include contracts in general can agree to arbitration. This means that no arbitration agreement can be concluded by persons who are under an absolute incapacity: minors (younger than 16 years), insane and deaf and dumb not being capable of expressing their will.

The fact that a party is a foreigner does not limit his capacity to agree to arbitrate in Brazil. According to relevant law of Greece, there is no longer any distinction between the arbitral clause and the submission. Disputes can be submitted to arbitration by means of an agreement in writing, provided that the parties have the right to dispose of the subject matter of the dispute. An arbitral clause is valid if it concerns a determined legal relationship. Thus, a clause referring to arbitration "any dispute which may arise between the parties in the future" is invalid under Greek law as it is not linked with a determined legal relationship.

Arbitration is based on an agreement of the parties, voluntarily entered into. The arbitration agreement, as well as any amendment to it, must be in writing. The Supreme Court has held that the signature of all parties must be placed upon each original copy of the agreement; an exchange of letters, telegrams and the like does not meet the requirement of the written form.

In any case, the lack of a written arbitration agreement can be cured if the parties to the agreement appear before the arbitrators and participate in the arbitral proceedings without raising an objection to this effect.

The capacity to conclude an arbitration agreement is determined by civil law: a person who is capable of being a party to a contract is capable of being a party to an arbitration agreement. A legal person can validly resort to arbitration through the persons authorized to represent it.

An agent can conclude an arbitration agreement for a principal only if he has received a written power from the latter, specifically mentioning that the agent is authorized to conclude arbitration agreements for the principal.

The captain of a commercial vessel, however, or a ship-owner's agent, can validly insert an arbitral clause into a bill of lading issued on behalf of the ship-owner, without the requirement of a specific power.

Please answer the following questions.

1. What form should the arbitration agreement have according to the relevant law of the US?
2. Why is the arbitration clause so important to the arbitration?
3. In what situation is award rendered invalid? Can you describe a few cases to illustrate the situation?
4. How will make arbitration agreement valid according to the relevant law of England?
5. Are there any differences on the stipulations of law of Brazil and law of Greece in respect of arbitration agreement?
6. What does the Supreme Court spell out in terms of arbitration agreement?

Chapter 14

Import and Export Procedures

进出口贸易流程

Once a contract is concluded, both the seller and the buyer should perform their obligation. The seller must deliver the goods, hand over any documents relating to them and transfer the property in the goods, as required by the contract. The buyer must pay the price for the goods and take delivery of them as required by the contract.

The specific procedures of implementing the contract may be different since the terms and conditions included in each contract vary. This chapter is to outline the import and export procedures.

14.1　Import Procedures

14.1.1 ┃ Import License

As with export license, import license is needed by many countries. In order to import, an importer must obtain an import license from the government agency. Importers should find out whether a license is needed and can be obtained before he starts the negotiation.

14.1.2 ┃ Sales Contract

Negotiation is the step that precedes signing the sales contract, and the agreed terms of document will help determine the rights and obligations of both the importer and the exporter. Once this agreement is signed, all the terms should be strictly observed. Therefore, it is of great importance that all the terms should be expressly agreed upon by the importer and the exporter and that the quality of goods should conform to the stipulations of the contract and the requirements of the related laws. [1] When the sale is by description, the goods should comply with the description; when the sale is by sample, the goods should be in accordance with the sample in terms of quality; when the sale is by sample as well as by description, the goods will correspond with both the sample and the description.

14. 1. 3 | Letter of Credit

If L/C is requested by the relevant parties as a means of payment, the importer should open the L/C in time in favor of the exporter who could usually arrange production or shipment after receiving this important document. The L/C application should be made to fit the sales contract terms. Otherwise, the exporter will ask the importer to amend the L/C. That will cause extra work and cost and may delay the shipment.

While requesting for an amendment to L/C, Exporter should immediately notify the applicant in the shortest possible time. If such a request is made according to the contract terms, the applicant should apply to the L/C issuing bank for amendments. If the amendment request would change some of terms agreed upon by both sides, it is necessary for the importer to decide whether he can accept the request. If he agrees, he might ask the exporter to pay the amendment fee.

14. 1. 4 | Arrange Shipment and Insurance

If the importer conducts the transaction on the basis of FOB or FCA, it is responsible for arranging shipment. After being notified of cargo readiness on the part of exporter, the importer needs to book shipping space or charter a vessel and timely inform the exporter of the progress to facilitate smooth delivery of the goods. If necessary, importer can also go to the loading port to supervise the shipment. Similarly, under FOB, FCA, CFR and CPT terms, the cargo insurance should be effected by the importer, who should ask the exporter to advise the shipment in time so that the goods can be covered by insurance without delay. [2]

14. 1. 5 | Document Examination and Payment

When L/C is used, the exporter will present to the negotiating bank the relevant document to get payment after the shipment is made. In consequence, the issuing bank will pay for the documents if the bank confirms that all the documents are acceptable, then, the bank will notify the importer to make the payment and get the documents. Under documentary collection, the importer himself should examine the documents presented by the exporter to confirm if they meet the requirements of the sales contract . If no problems exist, payment should be made in the pre-agreed manner.

14. 1. 6 | Customs Clearance

The imported goods must go through customs, and therefore, importers should submit some documents like invoice, B/L, inspection certificate etc. Some forms must be filled out. The customs officer will examine the goods against the documents.

14. 1. 7 | Taking Delivery and Reinspection

With the shipping documents, the importer can now take delivery of the goods from the carrier. After that, reinspection should be carried out to confirm if the goods are up to the standard set in the sales contract. After the inspection is conducted, if problems such as weight shortage, inferior quality or wrong shipment are found and attributed to the exporter, the importer should make claims against the exporter. If the loss or damage is due to the negligence of the carrier, the claim should be made against the carrier. If the loss or damage has been caused by the risks that are covered by insurance, the claim should be made against the underwriter.

14. 1. 8 | Settlement of Disputes

If a claim cannot be settled between the parties involved through negotiation, the dispute should be submitted to arbitration if that has been agreed upon. Otherwise, a lawsuit might be filed.

14. 2　Export Procedure

Contracts for export in our country are in most cases signed under CIF term on Letter of Credit. A lot of work needs to be done in carrying out this kind of contract. The whole export process usually involves about eight procedures including: cargo readiness, Letter of Credit, booking space or ship and document and payment. The following is a brief account of the possible steps in an export transaction.

14. 2. 1 | Export License

A great number of countries have export controls over some or all merchandises. Therefore, before exporting these merchandises, exporters should make sure whether they can get export licenses from the government.

14. 2. 2 | Sales Contract

Once sales contract is signed, all the terms should be strictly observed. Therefore, it is important that all the terms should be expressly agreed upon by the exporter and the importer. Generally speaking, a sales contract must be made in written form.

14. 2. 3 | Cargo Readiness

Immediately after the contract is signed, the exporter should seek to ensure the goods are to be made ready for shipment before the stipulated delivery time. Therefore, lots of coordination is involved between sales and marketing, scheduling, production and shipping. The quantity, quality, packaging and marking of the goods must strictly follow the stipulation in the sales contract.

If the goods need to be inspected before shipment, the inspection should be conducted in time and necessary inspection certificates must be made available. It should be noted that an inspection certificate usually stipulates a validity period and shipment should be made within the stipulated period. Otherwise, another inspection would be needed before the goods are consigned[3].

14. 2. 4 | L/C

If the payment is to be made by L/C, the exporter should ask the importer to open the L/C in time, e. g. 30 days or more before the date of shipment, depending on the nature of individual contracts. With large orders or orders produced according to the special requirement of the importer, the exporter may wait until the L/C is opened to arrange the cargo readiness. After receiving the L/C, the exporter must check the L/C against the sales contract.[4] Only when all the terms in the L/C are consistent with the terms of the sales contract can the exporter proceed to ship the goods.[5] If there is anything in the L/C that has not been agreed upon by the exporter and the importer, it might cause disputes, especially in payment, the exporter should ask the importer to amend the L/C.

14. 2. 5 | Export Declaration and Customs Clearance

Exporters should now declare the export goods to the customs by filling in certain customs forms and submitting appropriate documents such as commercial invoice, export license, copy of sales contract[6] and inspection certificates, etc. The customs will inspect the export shipment and decide if the shipment can be cleared through customs[7]. Once the goods are cleared, shipment can be made anytime.

14. 2. 6 | Shipment

Shipment should be made according to the contract terms. Usually, the exporter shall book the shipping space or ship by filling in the Shipping Note. Soon after receiving the Shipping Order from the carrier, the exporter may start to ensure the loading of the goods, supervise the loading process and get the Bill of Lading from the carrier.

Upon completion of the shipment, the exporter should give the importer a shipping advice to enable him to arrange insurance, payment and receipt of the goods. If these documents cannot be provided in time by the exporter, the exporter will shoulder the obligation for compensating for the losses of the importer.

14.2.7 | Insurance

Under CIF or CIP terms, the exporter should obtain at his own expense cargo insurance as agreed in the contract. If the importer is responsible for the insurance, the exporter should in due time send the importer all the information the latter needs to arrange the insurance coverage[8].

14.2.8 | Documentation and Payment

After shipment is made, the exporter should present to the negotiating bank the documents within the time specified by the L/C. The time should be maximum 21 days after issuing B/L and before the L/C expires. All documents must be processed in accordance with the L/C terms such as types of documents, number of originals[9] and copies, items of the documents, etc. Documentation should be completed with absolute accuracy and clarity.

It should be noted that the procedures for implementing a contract might be different according to the use of different payment terms or terms of trade. For example, if open account or documentary collection is adopted, no L/C will be used, while on CFR basis, the exporter shall not be responsible for effecting insurance with underwriter. Therefore, each individual transaction will involve a specific procedure.

New Words and Expressions

procedure	n.	程序
implement	v.	实施
precede	v.	在……之前
expressly	ad.	明确地
amendment	n.	修改
book	v.	预定
facilitate	v.	方便
negligence	n.	疏忽
schedule	v.	计划，预先安排
supervise	v.	监管，监督
original	n.	原件

underwriter	n.	保险公司
import license		进口许可证
sales contract		销售合同
shipping space		舱位
customs clearance		结关，通关
export declaration		出口申报
shipping advice		装船通知
insurance coverage		保险，保险范围

Notes

1. Therefore, it is of great importance that all the terms should be expressly agreed upon by the importer and the exporter and that the quality of goods should conform to the stipulations of the contract and the requirements of the related laws. 因此，所有的条款必须由买卖双方确定一致，货物的质量必须与合同的规定和相关的法律相符。

2. ... the cargo insurance should be effected, the importer should ask the exporter to advise the shipment in time so that the goods can be covered by insurance without delay. ……必须对货物进行投保，进口商须要求出口商及时通知装运时间，以便及时对货物投保。

3. the goods are consigned：发运货物。

4. check the L/C against the sales contract：依据合同检查信用证。

5. Only when all the terms in the L/C are consistent with the terms of the sales contract can the exporter proceed to ship the goods. 只有当信用证上所有条件与销售合同的条件相一致时，出口商才发货。

6. copy of sales contract：合同副本。

7. if the shipment can be cleared through customs：如果货物能够顺利通关。

8. insurance coverage：保险范围。

9. number of originals：原件的份数。

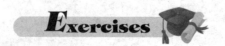

Exercises

I Review questions.

1. Please give a brief account of the import process.

2. Why is it so important for importer to conduct re-inspection?

3. What document should be submitted when the goods are cleared through the customs?

4. Why is it necessary for exporter to ask the importer to open the L/C in time?

5. What is a shipping advice, and why is it necessary for exporter to send the shipping advice to importer in time?

6. Please briefly describe the export procedure.

Ⅱ Define the following terms briefly.

1. import license

2. shipping advice

3. export declaration

4. customs clearance

Ⅲ Decide whether the following statements are True or False. Then put T for True or F for False in the brackets at the end of each statement.

1. Export licenses are adopted by all countries as an instrument to facilitate the exports. (   )

2. When requesting for an amendment to L/C, exporter should immediately notify the issuing bank in the shortest possible time. (   )

3. In most cases, a sales contract must be made in written form. (   )

4. When disputes arise during international trade, the relevant parties can resolve their disputes through consultation, arbitration or legal proceedings. (   )

5. Once sales contract is signed, all the terms should be strictly observed. (   )

6. An inspection certificate usually does not contain a validity period, for it is not so important as that in other documents. (   )

7. Contracts for export in our country are in most cases signed under CIF terms. (   )

8. If shipment fails to be made within the validity period of inspection certificate, the party concerned can ask that validity of the certificate to be extended automatically. (   )

9. As goods are cleared through customs, such documents as commercial invoice, export license, copy of sales contract and inspection certificate are usually made available to the customs officers. (   )

10. The exporter should give the importer a shipping advice to enable him to carry out his obligations stipulated in the contract in time, otherwise the exporter would likely bear the losses incurred because of his failure to that. (   )

Ⅳ Translate the following passages into Chinese.

Business enterprises have become increasingly international but most of them go international by a process of creeping "incrementalism" rather than by strategy choice. Some firms are first attracted to foreign markets by unsolicited export orders and, after discovering new opportunities, move through a series of stages to the establishment of foreign production facilities. Other firms initiate international activities in response to threats to an oligopoly position. Still others respond to specific opportunities for developing supplies of resources, acquiring foreign technology, or achieving greater production efficiency through foreign operations. And at some stage of becoming a global enterprise, many firms could be best characterized as a portfolio of diverse and separate country companies tied together by a network of ad hoc relationships.

Rarely are these early moves part of a comprehensive global strategy. But as pressures arise from competition on an international scale and from country control programs, and as firms become increasingly aware of synergistic benefits, more and more are building global strategies and adopting global planning procedures. A global strategy is a plan expressing an enterprise's strategy for maximizing its chosen objectives through geographical allocation of its limited resources, taking into account competition from whatever geographical source and the geographical opportunities and constraints.

V Translate the following passage into English.

设立海外销售办事处虽然需要一定的费用，但可以给出口商带来可观的利益。出口商在买方国家有人常驻，使买方很容易和出口商的职员当面订购货物或寻求帮助和指导。这样也能使出口商的职员扩大销售，收集市场信息，监督本公司商品的经销和负责商品的展览及储存。办事处要配备经验丰富的工程师，以便随时处理组装产品之类的技术问题。出口商要雇佣一些当地雇员，这样可以解决语言问题。

VI Read the following passages and answer questions.

Some Understanding of Counter-trade

Today an international company must include in its market pricing tool kit some understanding of counter-trading. Although cash is the preferred method of payment, more and more, counter-trades are becoming an important part of trade with Eastern Europe, China, and to a varying degree some Latin American and African nations. The key problems in successfully consummating counter-trade transactions are (1) accurately establishing the market value of the goods being offered and (2) disposing of the bartered goods once they are received. Most counter-trades judged unsuccessful are the result of one or both of the problems cited not being properly solved.

1. Types of Counter-trade

Counter-trade includes four distinct types of transactions: barter, compensation deals, counter-purchase, and buy-back.

Barter is the direct exchange of goods between two parties in a transaction. In a barter transaction, the seller must be able to dispose of the goods at a net price equal to the expected selling price in a regular, for-cash transaction. Further, during the negotiation stage of a barter deal, the seller must have some knowledge of the market and the price for the items offered in trade. But, bartered goods can range from hams to iron pellets, mineral water, furniture, or live oil — all somewhat more difficult to establish a price and market for when customers are needed. Because of the almost limitless range of goods and quality grades possible and a lack of expertise or information necessary, sellers rely on barter houses to provide information and find potential buyers for the goods received. Another possibility is the use of a switch trader, an outsider who will "switch" the traded goods to a third country where a market exists.

Compensation deals involve payment in goods and in cash. A seller delivers lathes to a buyer in Venezuela and receives 70 percent of the payment in convertible currency and 30 percent in tanned hides and wool. In an actual deal, General Motors Corporation sold $12 million worth of locomotives and diesel engineers to Yugoslavia and took cash $4 million in Yugoslavia cutting tools as payment.

An advantage of a compensation deal over barter is the immediate cash settlement of a portion of the bill; the remainder of the cash is generated after successful sale of the goods received. If the company has a use for the goods received, the process is relatively simple and uncomplicated. On the other hand, if the seller has to rely on a third party to find a buyer, the cost involved must be anticipated in the original compensation negotiation if the net proceeds to the seller are to be equal to the market price.

Counter-purchase is probably the most frequently used type of counter-trade. For this trade, two contracts are negotiated. The seller agrees to sell a product at a set price to a buyer and receives payment in cash. However, the first contract is contingent on a second contract that is an agreement by the original seller to buy goods from the buyer for the total monetary amount involved in the first contract or for a set percentage of that amount. This arrangement provides the seller with more flexibility than the compensation deal since there is generally a time period (6 to 12 months or longer) during which the second contract has to be completed. During the time that markets are sought for the goods in the second contract, the seller has received full payment for the original sale. Further, the goods to be purchased in the second contract are generally of greater variety than those offered in a compensation deal. Even greater flexibility is offered when the second contract is nonspecific, i. e., the books on sales and purchases need to be cleared only at certain intervals. The seller is obligated to generate enough purchases to keep the "books balanced" or clear between purchases and sales. For example, McDonnelle Douglas sold 22 DC-9s worth $100 million to Yugoslavia and, in turn, agreed to buy $25 million in Yugoslavian goods. Some of McDonnell Douglas's commitment to Yugoslavia was settled by buying Yugoslavian equipment for its own use, but is also sold to others such items as hams, iron castings, rubber bumper guards, and transmission towers. McDonnell Douglas held showings for department-store buyers to sell glassware and leather goods to fulfill their counter-purchase agreement. Twice a year, company officials meet to claim credits for sales and clear the books in fulfilling of their counter-purchase agreement.

Product buy-back agreement is the last of the four types of counter-trade transactions. This type of agreement is made when the sale involves goods or services that produce other goods and services, i. e., production plant, production equipment, or technology. The buy-back agreement usually involves one of two situations: the seller agrees to accept as partial payment a certain portion of the output or the seller receives full price initially but agrees to buy back a certain portion of the output.

For example, one US firm, a farm equipment manufacturer, sold a tractor plant to Poland and was paid part in hard currency and the balance in Polish-built tractors. In another situation, General Motors Corporation bought autos from Brazil in partial payment for building an automobile manufacturing plant there. Levi Strauss and Company is taking Hungarian blue jeans, which it will sell abroad, in exchange for setting up a jeans factory near Budapest. A major drawback to product buy-back agreements comes when the seller finds that the products bought back are in competition with its own similarly produced goods. On the other hand, some have found that a product buy-back agreement provided them with a supplemental source in an area of the world where there is demand but where there is no available supply.

2. US Firms Hesitant to Counter-trade

Counter-trade transactions are definitely on the increase in world trade. Some estimates of counter-trade in international trade go as high as 30 percent. More conservative estimates place the amount closer to 20 percent. Regardless, a significant amount of all international trade now involves some type of counter-trade transaction and it has been predicted that this percentage will increase substantially in the near future. Much of that increase will come in trading with Third World countries: in fact, some require counter-trades of some sort with all foreign trade. India requires all foreign companies trading with State Trading Corporations to engage in counter-trades.

Western European and Japanese firms have the longest history of counter-trade because of their trading experience with Eastern Europe. US firms have been slow to accept counter-trade, preferring to lose a sale rather than become involved in an unfamiliar situation. In fact, a recent survey of several hundred US firms involved in international trade indicated that a majority would refuse a counter-trade offer. This attitude seems to stem from inexperience and, as one respondent candidly replied, "we don't need the hassle. We have enough business without it. " Regardless of prevailing US attitudes, demands for counter-trade will increase and many firms will find they have little choice but to cope with the hassles or problems of counter-trade. It is evident that counter-trade will probably not be less important in the future.

While many US firms shun barter or counter-trade arrangements, others are profitably involved. Certainly one of the more interesting trades involves Pepsi-Cola which has barter arrangements with Russia and Romania. Pepsi-Cola sells cola concentrate to produce Pepsi-Cola and receives Vodka from Russia and bottled wines from Romania as full payment. From all indications, this has been a very profitable arrangement for Russia, Romania, and Pepsi-Cola.

Please answer the following questions.

1. What are barter and compensation deals? What are advantage and disadvantage of these two types of counter-trade?
2. What are counter-purchase and buyback? Are there any differences between them?
3. Can you illustrate the importance of counter-trade transaction by citing a case?

Chapter 15

Modes of Trade
贸易方式

The bulk of international trade is done in the general mode of buying and selling of goods and services by means of money and the market. Under specific conditions, however, special modes of transactions may be adopted to better realize one's business purposes. Among them, counter trade and its variations are perhaps the most popular modes of trade.

15.1 Counter Trade

Counter trade is a peculiar form of transaction allegedly popular in less developed countries and in centrally planned economies[1]. It has become the generic term to describe a set of cross-border contracts that link a seller's exports to imports from the buyer, and it is often associated with policy objectives of relevant economies like dealing with foreign exchange shortages and promotion of exports.

The terminology counter trade employed today can be traced to the pre-World War II years when normal trade relations were breading down. Following German hyperinflation, competitive devaluations[2] and protectionism meant a global collapse in trade and in international financial and banking markets. Unwilling to see German cut off from its traditional raw materials supplies in the Balkans, the Reichsbank agreed to the establishment of a clearing system that settled only net positions[3] — and only once a year — a measure that permitted traditional trade flows between Germany and the Balkans to continue. These arrangements were called compensation trade[4]. Another term used in the context of such bilateral clearing operations was "counter trade". During and after World War II, when financial markets[5] were in disarray, Britain used similar bilateral arrangements, as did Western Europe when setting up the European Payment Union, Subsequently the countries of centrally planned economies copied such clearing systems[6] and used them among themselves and also in trade with neighboring countries like England. Conceptually, all these arrangements are trade credit accounts between familiar trading partners exchanging unrelated goods.

In the 1970s and 1980s counter trade was different from the old practice although some similarities remained. Current counter trade partners are not necessarily familiar partners and goods exchanged are sometimes vertically related. Current counter trade can be categorized as follows:

Barter: The direct exchange of goods and services which is completed in a short period of time, e. g. , an exchange of frozen lamb from New Zealand for Iran crude oil.

Counter purchase[7]: The assumption by an exporter of a transferable obligation through separate but linked contract to accept as full or partial payment goods and services from the importer or importing country. The contract is usually stipulated to be fulfilled within a given period of time, e. g. , 5 years, and the goods or services received in return are usually pre-specified in a list and are subject to availability and changes made by the original importing country. In essence, then, counter purchase is an intertemporal direct exchange of goods and services. For example, in 1977 Volkswagen sold 10,000 cars to the former East Germany and agreed to purchase goods from a list set up by the former East Germans over the next 2 years, up to the value of the cars sold to the former East Germany.

Buyback[8]: An agreement by an exporter of plant and equipment to take back in the future part of the output produced by these goods as full or partial payment. The important difference between counter purchase and buyback is that in buyback the goods and services taken back are tied to the original goods exported whereas that is not the case in counter purchase. Another important difference is that a buyback deal usually stretches over a longer period of time (as long as 15 to 20 years) than a counter purchasing deal. For instance, the Xerox Corporation sold to China the plant and technology for the production of low-volume photocopying machines, and contractually committed to repurchase a very large portion of the photocopy machines produced in the Chinese plant.

The intriguing feature common to barter, counter purchase, and buyback is bundling: the exchanges of goods and services are bounded together (the exchanges are implemented either concurrently or intertemporally). In normal market transactions buying and selling of goods and services is unbundled, an arrangement made possible by the use of money and the market as an institution. Thus, an individual can sell goods and services to obtain monetary income and can then use the income for other desired goods and services. Such unbundling greatly facilitates transactions and allow more efficient economic exchanges.

While counter trade does not represent an extreme form of bundling, and money as a unit of account is not totally bypassed — in many counter trade deals, only a fraction of the initial purchase is paid for in goods and services — the question remains why a significant part of the buying and selling of goods and services should be bundled together.

The impression one gets is that bundled trade takes place where the market institution is imperfect. It can be said to generally take place between mature market economies and economies with less sophisticated market system. Under such circumstance there are several presumed advantages in counter trade.

(1) Counter trade is implemented because it helps a country to deal with foreign exchange shortages.

(2) Counter trade can be used to promote exports.

(3) Counter trade can be used to reduce uncertainty regarding export receipts.

(4) Counter trade is used to bypass an international price agreement like, for example, that of OPEC.

(5) Counter trade may help those nations, with serious debt problems to continue to import goods while, in effect, concealing export earnings from creditors.

However, counter trade can be very risky business. By concealing the real prices and costs of transactions it may conceal and help perpetuate economic inefficiencies in the market place. Companies may suffer losses because they could not get rid of products of poor quality. Finally, counter trade may be considered as a form of protectionism.

15.2   Futures Trading

Futures trading originated from forward contracts, which were used by producers and buyers of agricultural commodities to protect themselves against seasonal price fluctuations. They traded with each other at the current price on the terms of forward delivery before the harvest. For example, a miller reaches an agreement with a farmer on May 1 to buy 2000 bushels of corn for $2.50 per bushel. The corn will be delivered on July 1. In this way, the buyer does not need to worry about the rise of price, and the seller won't worry about the fall of the price any more.

Gradually, these forward contracts were bought and sold many times prior to the physical delivery. Some other people who were not in the grain trade, but interested in a possible gain from any change in value, also took part in the trade. They were not interested in the profits on the sales of the physical commodities themselves, therefore, not usually willing to take the actual delivery. These people were speculators, not merchants. The merchant with a contract, who did not want to absorb the risk, was willing to transfer ownership of the contract to a speculator. These people provided the need for the transformation of forward contracts into standardized futures contracts, and eventually led to the formalization of futures contracts. The market participants organized themselves into an exchange and set up the needed rules.

Futures exchanges have existed in many countries since the mid-nineteenth century. Today, many futures exchanges all over the world are active in trading futures contracts on various commodities and financial instruments, such as stock index futures, agricultural commodities futures, metals futures, energy futures, etc. The following is a list of some famous futures exchanges in the world.

Chicago Board of Trade

Chicago Mercantile Exchange

New York Mercantile Exchange

London Metal Exchange

Tokyo Stock Exchange

Singapore International Monetary Exchange

Hong Kong Commodity Exchange

15. 2. 1 | Futures Market

A futures market is basically an organized forum for the trading of futures contract under highly standardized terms. The basic elements that form this market are discussed in the following.

1. Futures Exchange

A futures exchange is usually a membership organization whose purpose is to facilitate the trading of futures contracts. It provides the physical facilities and organizational framework that make possible the execution and processing of futures transactions.

Every futures exchange may have its own unique structure. But usually, there is a board of directors, elected by exchange members. The rules, regulations and policies set by the board are implemented by an executive committee and other committee that consist of exchange members: committee on admission, arbitration committee, control committee, and new product committee, etc.

Each exchange has a fixed number of memberships. Once all the authorized membership has been sold, prospective new members must purchase a membership from a current member. Only exchange members enjoy the privileges: access to the trading area and reduced transaction costs. Nonmembers must trade by entering orders through members.

The general responsibilities of a futures exchange include providing:

(1) an adequate physical location for the trading areas in which members execute transactions;

(2) communication capabilities between the exchange floor and the outside world;

(3) procedures that ensure the swift and accurate processing of transactions that take place on the trading floor;

(4) effective margining and clearing systems to guarantee the financial integrity of the exchange's contracts;

(5) rules and regulations that meet the requirements of regulatory authorities and that ensure the fair treatment of all market participants;

(6) variable futures contracts.

2. The Clearing House

Every futures exchange has a clearing house, responsible for the operational and the financial integrity of all trades that take place on that exchange. The structure of a clearing house varies from exchange to exchange. A clearing house may be a distinct entity with their own staffs and boards that do not overlap with its related exchange. For instance, the London International Financial Futures and Options Exchange (LIFFE) uses the London Clearing House (LCH). Some clearing houses are part of the exchanges. For example, the clearing entity is a department within the CME and NYME.

Membership in a clearing house is available only to members of the related exchange and only to those who can meet strict financial requirements. These stringent financial requirements are necessary because it is the collective strength of the clearing house members that ultimately guarantees the financial integrity of all the trades carried out on the affiliated exchange.

The clearing house interposes itself between the buyer and seller: the buyer has a contract with the clearing house and not directly with the seller, and the seller has a contract with the clearing house and now with the buyer. The clearing house is not only the buyer of all the contracts, but also the seller of all the contracts. In consequence, futures traders do not need to worry about the credit risk of the other party with whom they are dealing. This greatly simplifies the administration of futures contracts, as every contract is with the clearing house. It also has the major benefit of standardizing and reducing the default risk of a futures contract.

3. Participants

According to their location, participants can be divided into those who trade on the floor of the exchange and those who do not. Floor traders can be further divided into those who trade on their own account (proprietary traders) and those who trade on behalf of others (brokers). In the United States, brokers are also called futures commission merchants, or FCMs. Some brokers may also trade for their own accounts.

According to their motive for futures trading, participants may be split into two kinds: those who use futures market to reduce his exposure to price changes (hedge) and those who attempts to profit by correctly anticipating price movements and trading accordingly (speculator). As hedging is every popularly used in international trading in our country, we will discuss the procedures of hedging in details later.

4. Margin System

Futures margin is a faith deposit regulated by the clearing house. It is intended to protect the seller against the buyer's default if prices fall and the buyer against the seller's default if prices rise.

Two kinds of margin are commonly used by clearing houses.

1) Original margin or initial margin

Original margin is the deposit that must be made when a futures position(Long or short) is initiated. It generally ranges from about 2% to 10% of the value of the future contract.

2) Variation margin or call margin

To minimize the losses from any default, changes in the price of futures contracts (as a result of price fluctuating) are settled on a daily basis. This is called marketing to the market. Each day, at the close of trading, the change in price of a futures contract during that day is calculated. If the price changes should be adverse to the trader's position, then his original margin will be reduced. All exchanges require that once a trader's original margin is reduced to a certain level, known as the Maintenance Margin, additional funds must be paid to the clearing house to keep his original margin at the normal level. This payment is called variation margin.

15. 2. 2 | Hedging

Hedging refers to the use of the futures market to reduce the risk of a cash market position. It involves entering into a futures position of a similar transaction that is opposite of the net position in the cash market. Thus, this futures market position serves to negate or minimize the risk of the cash market position.

1. Selling Hedge

A selling hedge is the use of a short position in the futures market by someone who is long in the cash market. It is often used to protect the value of anticipated production or forward purchase agreements.

For example, an elevator operator buys 100,000 bushels corn from a farmer on October 1 for $2.15 per bushel. After the grain has been brought into inventory, it is vulnerable to a price decline should the market weaken. To avoid this risk, the elevator operator can simply sell December corn futures of 100,000 bushels and maintain this short position until a buyer for the cash corn is found. Then the elevator operator would "lift" the hedge by liquidating the futures contract.

2. Buying Hedge

A buying hedge is the purchase of futures by someone who is short in the cash market. It is usually used to protect against price increases. Purchases in the futures market are made as a temporary substitute for buying the actual goods.

For example, on January 1, an exporter confirmed an order of 1,000 tons of corn oil ($360 per ton) which should be delivered three months later on April 1. To avoid the risk of price increase, the exporter may choose to buy the corn oil immediately and put it into inventory. But this will incur expenses in storage, insurance, etc. Therefore, the exporter may simply buy April corn oil futures of 1,000 tons on the futures market, and maintain this long position until a proper seller of cash corn oil is found.

Successful hedging is dependent on a close relationship between the price of the cash commodity and the price of a future contract. The closer the relationship is, the more effective the hedge is. But there is rarely perfect correlation between cash and futures. Therefore, the negative change in cash prices may not be fully offset by the change in futures prices.

New Words and Expressions

allegedly	ad.	据说
generic	a.	总称的
terminology	n.	术语
hyperinflation	n.	极度通货膨胀
Reichsbank	n.	德意志国家银行
disarray	n.	混乱

conceptually	*ad.*	概念上地
vertically	*ad.*	竖式地
pre-specify	*v.*	预先说明
intertemporal	*a.*	不同时地
intriguing	*a.*	引起兴趣的
concurrently	*ad.*	同时发生地
bypass	*v.*	避开，置……于不顾
sophisticated	*a.*	经验丰富的
expertise	*n.*	专门知识
conceal	*v.*	掩盖，隐瞒
perpetuate	*v.*	使……永久存在
futures	*n.*	期货
bushel	*n.*	蒲式耳
speculator	*n.*	投机者
instrument	*n.*	（金融）工具
facilitate	*v.*	使……方便，促进
clearing	*n.*	清算
stringent	*a.*	严格的
affiliated	*a.*	附属的，附属于……的
interpose	*v.*	干涉，介入
margin	*n.*	（期货）保证金
hedging	*n.*	套期保值
elevator	*n.*	谷仓经营着
inventory	*n.*	库存
liquidate	*v.*	偿清
correlation	*n.*	关系
offset	*v.*	抵消

net position	实际头寸
in essence	实质地
counter trade	对销贸易
arbitration committee	仲裁委员会
competitive devaluation	竞争性贬值
clearing house	清偿所

Notes

1. centrally planned economies：中央计划经济国家。西方常用此指社会主义国家。
   "economy" 在此处用作可数名词，指经济国家。

2. competitive devaluation：竞争性贬值。即一国对外贬值，其他国家也相应地采取贬值措施
   以便刺激出口和限制进口。这种竞相贬值的措施是进行贸易战的一种手段，容易引起世
   界经济的混乱。

3. net position：实际头寸。原意指经营外汇业务的银行账户上的外币余缺的数额。此处指
   通过清算协定所进行的，由于两国购销之间的差异所造成的贸易款项方面的净差额。

4. compensation trade：补偿贸易。补偿贸易是一种现代形式的、内容较为复杂的易货贸易。
   其主要特点是：以进口的设备或技术直接生产的，或与它们有关联的产品偿付进口货值。

5. financial market：金融市场。金融方面的专业市场，如货币市场、贴现市场、资本市场、
   有价证券市场或证券交易所、外汇市场及黄金市场等。

6. clearing system：清算系统，清算制度。这是指不动用外汇而通过记账相互冲销债务的方
   式来清偿两国贸易收支的政府间协定。

7. counter purchase：反向购买，互购。这是反向贸易的一种具体做法：一国对另一国出口
   的同时也从该国购买一批货物。这批货物可以由原进口公司提供，也可以由其他公司提
   供。这种方式将贸易双方的进口与出口有机地结合了起来，其优势是：① 可以不用外汇
   或少用外汇；② 有利于缺乏外汇的国家平衡收支；③ 有利于双方以进口筹码，冲破贸
   易壁垒；④ 有利于进出结合，统筹安排。

8. buyback：回购交易。这是补偿贸易的一种主要形式，出口商在出口机器和技术的同时，
   要承担购买该项设备所生产的产品。

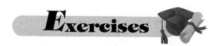

Exercises

Ⅰ Review questions.

1. What is counter trade? Why has it attracted so much attention?

2. How did counter trade originate? And what was the nature of early counter trade?

3. What are the main features of the current counter trade? Can you summarize the categories briefly
   under current counter trade?

4. What are the major differences between counter purchase and buyback?

5. What is meant by bundling? What is the opposite way of doing business?

6. What are the advantages and disadvantages of counter trade?

7. What are the basic conditions for counter-trade to exist?

8. What is the futures trade?

9. How does futures exchange function in futures trade?

10. What a role does the clearing house play in its trade?

11. What is margin system?

12. What does hedging refer to in the futures trade?

II Define the following terms briefly.

1. counter-trade

2. barter

3. buyback

4. counter purchase

5. hyperinflation

III Translate the following passages into Chinese.

Counter trade is more popular in centrally planned economies and in less developed countries. As these economies lack mature and competitive markets, the role of counter trade becomes even more important. In such an environment counter trade can be viewed as a national form of contracting to deal with transaction difficulties.

The practical advantages exist due to the peculiar environment within which counter trade usually takes place. They quite likely disappear when the environment changes — as is happening now in many countries. Restructuring and the development of markets may therefore mean that the environment within which counter trade usually takes place is changing so as to reduce its frequency. Reduced ownership restrictions are likely to shift the organizational forms towards joint ventures and wholly owned production facilities. Improved knowledge, experience, and legal enforcement of contractual obligations will likely mean increasing prevalence of longer term and more sophisticated explicit transaction contracts.

IV Translate the following passage into English.

在抵消贸易的做法中，出口商在提供资本货物的同时，需要承诺对进口方有利的某种活动。通常，主要出口货物的交易额巨大，如飞机、发电设备或对空防御系统等。为了减少此类购买活动中所需要的巨额外汇，买方一般会坚持使用抵消贸易的做法。但近年来，对于一些技术含量较低的交易，如采煤设备、机车和公共汽车等的交易，人们也越来越多地使用抵消贸易。

V Read the following passages and answer the questions.

The earliest international monetary system was known as the gold standard under which countries pledged to change their paper currencies into gold when requested to do so. The gold standard created a fixed exchange rate system as each country pegged the value of its currency to gold to establish its par value for most of the 19th century till the end of the First World War. Major trading countries followed this system and the British Pound was the most important currency in international business as a result of the economic, political and military power of the United Kingdom, hence the term sterling-based gold standard.

The pressure caused by the First World War on economy coupled with the impact of the Great Depression put an end to the fixed exchange rate system. The Bank of England was no longer able to redeem its paper currency for gold at par value and allowed its value to be determined by supply and demand. With Britain abandoning the gold standard, there appeared different areas in the world. Some countries pegged their currencies to the sterling, some countries to the US dollar and some to the French Franc, forming the "sterling area", "dollar area" and "franc area". This period witnessed the degeneration of the international monetary system as some major countries vied to devaluate their currencies to make their export goods more competitive. The benefits brought about by their devaluation were needless to say, offset by what their competitors did. International trade contracted and economic conflict finally led to the Second World War.

Towards the end of the Second World War representatives of 44 countries gathered at Bretton Woods to renew the gold standard on a greatly modified basis. One important fruit of the conference is the creation of the International Bank for Reconstruction and Development and the International Monetary Fund.

The Bretton Woods Conference established a US dollar based gold standard. Because of the dominating economic and political influence of the United Stated, the dollar replaced the sterling as the major vehicle for international settlement. Though all the Bretton Woods participants agreed to peg their currencies to gold, only the United States pledged to redeem the dollar for gold at the request of the central bank of a foreign country. Under the new fixed exchange rate system, each participant promised to maintain the par value of its currency, allowing a fluctuation of only one percent.

The country concerned had to intervene if the market value of its currency goes beyond the range. Under special circumstances, a country was allowed to adjust the par value of its currency. Thus the Bretton Woods system is said to be using an adjustable peg. The new system was also called by some people the "New Gold Standard System". This relative stability in exchange rates facilitated international business till the beginning of 1970s.

Under the Bretton Woods System, people would hold dollars so long as they trusted the convertibility of the dollar into gold. With the increase of foreign dollar holdings to finance trade expansion, the faith of dollar holders decreased in the ability of the United States to redeem the dollar for gold. To reduce the demand for the dollar as a reserve currency the special drawing right was created. Used to settle official transactions at the IMF, SDRs are sometimes called paper gold. Despite the new liquidity injected by SDRs into the international monetary system, the United States was still unable to meet the demands of foreign dollar holders for gold. On August 15, 1971 the US Administration announced severing link between the dollar and gold, signifying the collapse of the Bretton Woods system. Since then, international business has relied increasingly on the flexible exchange rate system. Most major currencies began to float in the foreign exchange market. Other currencies followed a fixed exchange rate by pegging themselves to a major currency such as the dollar, or the French Franc and float with it. From 1976 countries ceased to stipulate gold par value to their paper currencies leaving the price of their respective currency to be decided by the interaction of supply and demand

Factors influencing the exchange rate include the following.

(1) International balance of payment. It has a direct bearing on the supply and demand of foreign exchange. The value of one's own currency will go up with favorable balance of payment and drop with BOP deficit.

(2) Inflation. It is closely related to the real value of the currency and the competitiveness of the commodity. When inflation intensifies, the value of the currency will drop relative to foreign currencies and vice versa.

(3) Interest rate. Under specific conditions, high interest rate will attract short term international fund, increasing the exchange rate of one's own currency and vice versa.

The above factors may work alone or collectively. Sometimes their influences may offset each other. Generally speaking, however, international balance of payment is the most important factor in deciding the trend of exchange rate. In addition, foreign exchange policies, political events and speculation activities may also have a role to play in the fluctuations of exchange rate.

The flexible exchange rate system has never been clean float or free float. The central banks take various measures to intervene in the price of its currency. So the current practice is often called a managed float or dirty float. The common measures taken for intervention are as follows:

(1) When the price of a foreign exchange goes too high, the central bank may increase its supply by selling it out of its foreign exchange reserves. And in the opposite case, it can buy the currency in the market to increase its reserves.

(2) When the price of a foreign exchange goes too high, the government may raise the discount rate to absorb foreign fund to increase foreign exchange income of the country and vice versa.

(3) In case of acute exchange rate fluctuation, a government may have to resort to foreign exchange control or raise foreign loans to make up its balance of payment deficit and lower the demand for foreign exchange.

The two different exchange rate systems each has its own advantages. The fixed exchange rate system reduces the riskiness of international business and is also an important measure to curb inflation. However the system is vulnerable to disorderly changes in currency value. The most recent example is the Asian Financial Crisis of 1997 — 1998 when the fixed exchange rate adopted by some Southeast Asian countries like Thailand and Indonesia collapsed and dealt a heavy blow to the economy. Under the flexible exchange rate system fluctuations of the exchange rate within a definite period of time will not immediately affect domestic money circulation and is helpful to the stability of the economy. Flexible exchange rate can also protect domestic currency from the impact of foreign idle funds and helps to prevent the drain of foreign exchange reserve. But frequent wild swings of the value of currencies will increase the riskiness of trade and affect international investment.

Exchange rates are published daily in two different ways. A direct exchange rate is the price of a foreign currency in terms of the home currency. In a direct quote, an amount of foreign currency, usually one unit or one hundred units is taken as the standard and the equivalent amount of home currency is marked after it. An indirect exchange rate is the price of home currency in terms of a foreign currency. In an indirect quote one unit or one hundred units home currency is taken as the standard and the equivalent of foreign currency is given. For instance 100 USD/826. 57 RMB (or 826. 57 RMB/100 USD) is direct exchange rate from the Chinese perspective and indirect exchange rate from the American perspective. The two different quotes are used in different countries or regions mainly as a tradition or for convenience. Most countries or regions including China use the direct quote, but the United States and Britain use the indirect quote.

There are three types of foreign exchange price. The buying rate refers to the rate by which a commercial bank buys a currency. The selling rate is the rate by which a bank sells a currency. The medial rate is the average of the two. It is used in transactions between the banks and is not applicable to common customers. The difference between the buying rate and the selling rate varies from 1 per mil to 5 per mil which constitutes the profit of the bank. In the case of direct quote, the first figure after the fixed amount of foreign currency is the buying rate and the second figure is the selling rate. And in the case of indirect quote the first figure after the fixed amount of home currency is the selling rate and the second figure is the buying rate.

Please answer the following questions.

1. What is the Special Drawing Right? How was it created?
2. What are the major factors that may influence the exchange rate? Explain Briefly.
3. What is meant by clean float and dirty float? What are the common measures taken for intervention in exchange rate?
4. Illustrate the respective advantages and disadvantages of the flexible exchange rate system and the fixed exchange rate system.

References

参 考 文 献

[1] 曹菱. 外贸英语实务. 北京：外语教学与研究出版社，2008.

[2] 陈苏东. 国际贸易实务. 北京：高等教育出版社，2010.

[3] 胡英坤. 新编国际商务英语阅读教程. 大连：东北财经大学出版社，2006.

[4] 黎孝先. 国际贸易实务. 北京：对外经济贸易大学出版社，2012.

[5] 檀文菇. 国际贸易. 北京：对外经济贸易大学出版社，2009.

[6] 王学文. 国际商务英语. 北京：中国人民大学出版社，2008.

[7] 王玉章. 国际贸易英语. 天津：天津大学出版社，2002.

[8] 邬性宏. 国际商务英语教程. 上海：复旦大学出版社，2009.

[9] 吴百福. 进出口贸易实务教程. 上海：上海人民出版社，2007.

[10] 孙湘生. 国际贸易实务. 北京：北京交通大学出版社，2005.

[11] 于德社. 国际经贸英语读写教程. 北京：外文出版社，2000.

[12] 杨丽华. 贸易实务英语. 北京：首都经济贸易大学出版社，2001.

[13] 张素芬. 国际贸易理论与实务. 北京：对外经济贸易大学出版社，2003.

[14] 诸葛霖. 对外贸易实务英语读本. 北京：对外经济贸易大学出版社，2002.

[15] SHIPPEY K C. International contracts. 上海：上海外语教育出版社，2000.

[16] HINKELMAN E G. International payments. 上海：上海外语教育出版社，2000.